THERE WAS A TIME when swimming pools were a luxury enjoyed only by the rich. But all that's changed now, and in areas where the climate is favorable, homeowners have made pools as common as garages. New pool owners soon discover that there's more to a pool than just swimming in it, however, and one of the first concerns is the pool's filter. On page 996 you'll find a complete rundown on the kinds of filters available, how each type works, and its advantages and disadvantages. Keeping your water crystal clear won't be a problem after you know how to manage your filter properly

NEW FASTENERS make framing a new room or a whole house easy for an amateur. See page 1075

WHEN YOU ROOF A PATIO or make a fence, fiberglass panels offer advantages. See page 971

DON'T BUILD A GARAGE until you've read the step-by-step patio-garage story on page 1106

THERE IS RARE BEAUTY in a hardwood floor, and many kinds are available. Find out on page 1056

YOU CAN LEARN the basic technique of flycasting in just 60 minutes. Turn to page 1070

THE FISH go deep in the hot summer months, and so should your lures, according to the article on page 1032. There's some sound advice and angling wisdom from an old pro in the article

Popular Mechanics Do-It-Yourself Encyclopedia

in 16 volumes

A complete guide to

- home maintenance
- home improvement
- hand-tool skills
- craft projects
- power-tool know-how
- hobbies
- automotive upkeep
- automotive repair
- shop shortcuts
- boating
- fishing
- hunting
- model making
- outdoor living
- radio, TV and electronics

Volume 6

Book Division, Hearst Magazines, New York, N.Y. 10019

VOLUME 6

How to use your Encyclopedia

Browse. Glance through this volume, or any other volume of the Encyclopedia. Likely you will find the solution to a particular home-maintenance problem that has been bothering you, or a shop project so appealing that you will immediately head for your bench. Browsing not only is enjoyable, but is a source of ideas.

Seek specific information. Perhaps you want to find out how to cure that leak in your basement, how to keep the exterior paint from peeling, or how to tune and set the carburetor on your car.

Four reader aids, all cross-referenced, will enable you to find specific information:

1. *Alphabetical headings.* Located at the top of the page, these headings cover broad classifications of information. If you are looking for information on how to keep paint from peeling, for example, look up "Paints" alphabetically, then find the particular section dealing with peeling paint.

2. *Alphabetical cross-references.* These are shown in a box at the bottom of the page. Some material can logically be classified under more than one alphabetical heading, so if you don't find what you are seeking alphabetically (as described above), be sure to check the *alphabetical cross-references* at the bottom of the page; there you may find precisely the classification you are seeking. For example, you and your son decide to build a model airplane, and are looking for plans. You look up "Model airplanes" and find nothing under that alphabetical heading. However, if you glance at the bottom *of that same page* you will find an alphabetical cross-reference that reads: **model airplanes,** see airplane models.

3. *See also references.* These are shown at the end of many articles. They refer you to related articles which may also be of interest.

4. *Instant index.* Located at the end of Volume 16, it is thoroughly cross-referenced to help you find information under any heading.

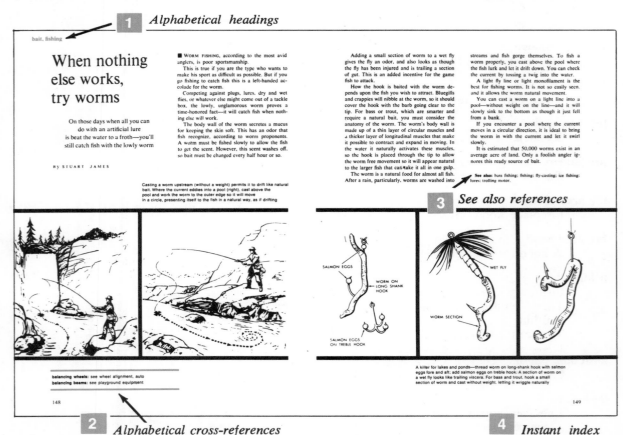

1 *Alphabetical headings*

3 *See also references*

2 *Alphabetical cross-references*

4 *Instant index*

Kid-powered "squaris" wheel

DESIGNED BY ROBERT WOOLSON

PREPARED BY W. CLYDE LAMMEY

If you'd like to start a carnival in your own yard,
here's an unusual ride
that can be fun for up to eight tots

fertilizer, lawn: see lawns

■ DUBBED A "SQUARIS WHEEL" by its designer because of its square wheel, this pint-sized back-yard version of its big brother, the ferris wheel, will bring safe carnival fun right to your own home.

Braced to make it as sturdy as possible, the wheel is designed to operate on "kid power." That is, each time around, each passenger gives the wheel a backward push with his feet. There

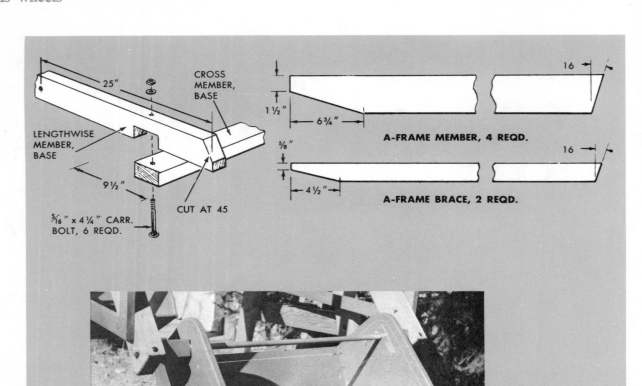

CROSS MEMBER, BASE

25"

LENGTHWISE MEMBER, BASE

9½"

CUT AT 45

⁵⁄₁₆" x 4¼" CARR. BOLT, 6 REQD.

16

1½"

6¾"

A-FRAME MEMBER, 4 REQD.

⁵⁄₈"

4½"

16

A-FRAME BRACE, 2 REQD.

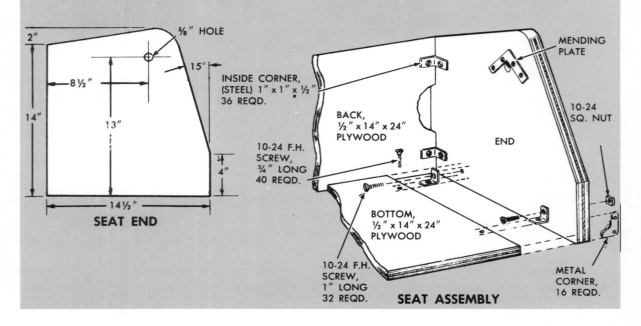

The shafts on which the balanced bucket seats pivot also serve as safety bars. The mending plates on the side panels save wear at the shaft holes

kid-powered "squaris" wheel, continued

2"

⁵⁄₈" HOLE

8½"

15°

INSIDE CORNER, (STEEL) 1" x 1" x ½" 36 REQD.

14"

13"

10-24 F.H. SCREW, ¾" LONG 40 REQD.

4"

14½"

SEAT END

MENDING PLATE

BACK, ½" x 14" x 24" PLYWOOD

END

10-24 SQ. NUT

BOTTOM, ½" x 14" x 24" PLYWOOD

10-24 F.H. SCREW, 1" LONG 32 REQD.

METAL CORNER, 16 REQD.

SEAT ASSEMBLY

966

is no danger of traveling too fast for safety, and no danger of falling out of the bucket seats, since the small riders are held in by a safety bar.

Another safety feature is a set of wheel locks, which prevent the toy from being used when mom or dad can't be around to supervise getting on and getting off.

As a first step in construction, carefully look over the pull-apart drawing on page 968. Note that many of the individual assemblies are detailed in the drawing on page 969. If you follow these details with care, the assembly will not be difficult. One word of caution: The base, the A-frames and the wheel spider are made of 2 x 4s. It is very important that you obtain clear, straight stock for these parts. There must be no knots, no weakening blemishes and no crooked pieces, as otherwise you may have trouble building and operating the wheel.

wheel must run true

The wheel must run true after assembly, and A-frames must stand plumb with the base leveled. The stand, which consists of the base and A-frame, must be set up and leveled on a solid foundation, made either by pouring a couple of narrow concrete slabs on a tamped-gravel fill or two rows of concrete blocks placed on a tamped gravel fill. Then you level the structure by shimming up the low corners. Wooden shingles are just the thing for shimming. Although standard 2 x 4s are held to quite close sectional sizes, you may occasionally find some variations in widths and thicknesses. Usually it's a good idea to check before cutting stock as any appreciable variation might affect some of the dimensions given.

no glue in assembly

After you have a proper foundation, make the base, which consists of two lengthwise members and three cross members, the latter mortised the full thickness into the lengthwise members and joined with bolts. No glue is used in the entire assembly; only bolts and lagscrews. Next, you make the A-frames, joining at the top ends first as shown in one of the pulled-apart assemblies on page 969. When cutting the top ends of the A-frame members, or legs, lay out according to the detail and saw outside the line in the waste. This permits planing the cut surface to a smooth fit against the filler.

The hole pattern on the inside and outside plywood gussets is identical except for the upper ¼-in. hole in each outside gusset. This hole takes

Pivoted wheel locks are provided as a safeguard to prevent use when no adults are present

the bent end of the pin, the lower end of which passes through a cross hole drilled near each end of the wheel shaft, preventing the latter from turning or working out of place. The shaft holes in both inside and outside gussets should be carefully located, but location of the bolt holes is not critical; just locate them uniform distances from the edges.

To assure register of all bolt and shaft holes, drill the shaft holes first through both gussets and the filler piece, then insert the shaft, clamp the parts together and drill through all three thicknesses. Remember to check beforehand the diameter of the pipe which is used as a wheel shaft.

With the top ends of the A-frames joined, bolt the legs to the base, plumb with a level and brace temporarily until you can install the permanent braces. The lower ends of the latter are joined to the center cross member of the base with lagscrews, the washered heads seating in pockets cut into the wide face of the brace with a chisel and gouge as indicated in the assembly view, A. The carriage-bolt heads at the top ends of the braces are seated in shallow counterbores, the large diameter of the latter being slightly larger than the bolt head. Tighten the bolts before releasing the temporary braces. Then check again for plumb.

Next, make the wheel spiders, noting that in the pulled-apart view on page 969 each consists

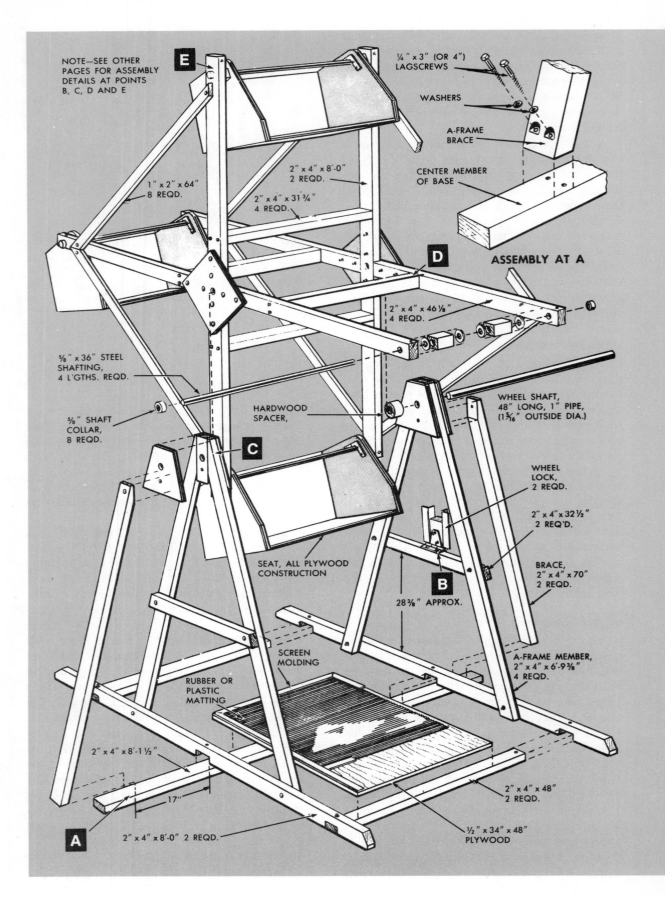

NOTE—SEE OTHER PAGES FOR ASSEMBLY DETAILS AT POINTS B, C, D AND E

E

¼" x 3" (OR 4") LAGSCREWS

WASHERS

A-FRAME BRACE

CENTER MEMBER OF BASE

1" x 2" x 64" 8 REQD.

2" x 4" x 8'-0" 2 REQD.

2" x 4" x 31¾" 4 REQD.

D

ASSEMBLY AT A

2" x 4" x 46⅛" 4 REQD.

⅝" x 36" STEEL SHAFTING, 4 L'GTHS. REQD.

⅝" SHAFT COLLAR, 8 REQD.

HARDWOOD SPACER,

WHEEL SHAFT, 48" LONG, 1" PIPE, (1 5/16" OUTSIDE DIA.)

C

WHEEL LOCK, 2 REQD.

2" x 4" x 32½" 2 REQ'D.

SEAT, ALL PLYWOOD CONSTRUCTION

B

BRACE, 2" x 4" x 70" 2 REQD.

28⅜" APPROX.

SCREEN MOLDING

A-FRAME MEMBER, 2" x 4" x 6'-9⅜" 4 REQD.

RUBBER OR PLASTIC MATTING

2" x 4" x 8'-1½"

17"

A

2" x 4" x 8'-0" 2 REQD.

2" x 4" x 48" 2 REQD.

½" x 34" x 48" PLYWOOD

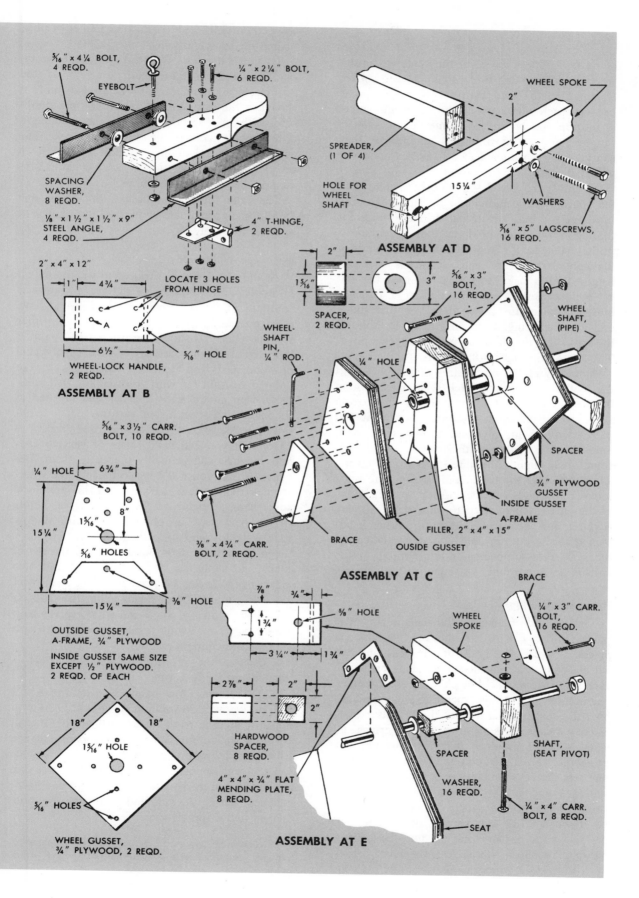

⁵⁄₁₆" x 4¼" BOLT, 4 REQD.

EYEBOLT

¼" x 2¼" BOLT, 6 REQD.

WHEEL SPOKE

2"

SPACING WASHER, 8 REQD.

⅛" x 1½" x 1½" x 9" STEEL ANGLE, 4 REQD.

SPREADER, (1 OF 4)

HOLE FOR WHEEL SHAFT

15¼"

WASHERS

⁵⁄₁₆" x 5" LAGSCREWS, 16 REQD.

4" T-HINGE, 2 REQD.

ASSEMBLY AT D

2" x 4" x 12"

1"   4¾"

LOCATE 3 HOLES FROM HINGE

A

6½"

⁵⁄₁₆" HOLE

WHEEL-LOCK HANDLE, 2 REQD.

ASSEMBLY AT B

2"

1⁵⁄₁₆"   3"

SPACER, 2 REQD.

⁵⁄₁₆" x 3" BOLT, 16 REQD.

WHEEL SHAFT, (PIPE)

WHEEL-SHAFT PIN, ¼" ROD.

¼" HOLE

⁵⁄₁₆" x 3½" CARR. BOLT, 10 REQD.

¼" HOLE   6¾"

8"

SPACER

15¼"

1⁵⁄₁₆"

⁵⁄₁₆" HOLES

¾" PLYWOOD GUSSET

15¼"

⅜" HOLE

INSIDE GUSSET

A-FRAME

⅜" x 4¾" CARR. BOLT, 2 REQD.

BRACE

FILLER, 2" x 4" x 15"

OUSIDE GUSSET

OUTSIDE GUSSET, A-FRAME, ¾" PLYWOOD

INSIDE GUSSET SAME SIZE EXCEPT ½" PLYWOOD. 2 REQD. OF EACH

ASSEMBLY AT C

⅞"   ¾"

1¾"

⅝" HOLE

BRACE

¼" x 3" CARR. BOLT, 16 REQD.

3¼"   1¾"

18"   18"

1⁵⁄₁₆" HOLE

WHEEL SPOKE

2⅞"   2"

2"

HARDWOOD SPACER, 8 REQD.

⁵⁄₁₆" HOLES

4" x 4" x ¾" FLAT MENDING PLATE, 8 REQD.

SPACER

WASHER, 16 REQD.

SHAFT, (SEAT PIVOT)

¼" x 4" CARR. BOLT, 8 REQD.

WHEEL GUSSET, ¾" PLYWOOD, 2 REQD.

SEAT

ASSEMBLY AT E

of three members joined at the center to a ply-wood gusset, making four equally spaced spokes of equal length. Note also that there is a spacer between each wheel gusset and the inside gusset at the top end of each A-frame. These spacers can be band-sawed round as detailed or they can be squares center-drilled to a free fit on the wheel shaft.

Assemble the wheel spiders on the shaft with the spacers in position, making sure that both turn freely. Then locate and drill the holes for the lagscrews which hold the four spreaders as in the detail, D. It's important to cut the ends of the spreaders square and all pieces to exact length. Drill a ¼-in. hole edgewise near the end of each spoke, insert and tighten a carriage bolt in each of the holes to prevent the spoke ends from splitting. Then drill the ⅝-in. holes in the spokes for the shafts on which the seats pivot. The 1 x 2 wheel-spider braces are installed later.

Assembly of the seats, sizes of the parts and the method of pivoting each seat are shown in detail. Cut four bottoms and four backs to the sizes given from ½-in. plywood, then eight end pieces from ¾-in. plywood to the size given. Smooth all cut edges with sandpaper and then round them slightly. Be sure there are no slivers. Then note that the backs and bottoms are butt-joined to the ends with steel inside "corner irons" as they are often referred to, nine corners being required for each seat. The ninth corner is attached to the bottom and back at the center of the seat. Precise spacing of the corners at the ends is not important; just equalize the spacing.

steel plate bearings

The method of pivoting the seats is shown in the assembly, E. Spacers and two washers are placed between the ends of the seat and the wheel spokes as indicated. The shaft on which each seat pivots is held in place by shaft collars, one at each end. A steel mending plate is placed over the shaft at each end of the seat as shown. These plates serve as metal-to-metal bearings and when screwed in place they also prevent any possibility of the plywood end piece splitting. In one seat detail metal corners of the type used on suitcases and machinist's tool boxes are suggested. These are essentially ornamental and can be attached to all four corners of each seat, to the two back corners only or may be omitted entirely if desired. At this stage the wheel braces, of 1 x 2 stock, and the platform of plywood

covered partially with corrugated rubber or plastic matting can be installed.

To finish the job you need two wheel locks, one on each A-frame and attached to the A-frame cross member. One of the two units is shown in the assembly, B. The units are duplicates with one exception which is the installation of an eyebolt in one or the other of the locks. The eyebolt permits locking one unit in the down position with a conventional bike lock, thus preventing the wheel from turning.

The hole for the eyebolt is drilled in one handle in approximately the position shown at A in the assembly, B.

use outdoor plywood

As the wheel will be exposed to weathering all plywood parts should be of the grade known as "outdoor plywood." Plywood parts should have the exposed edges filled with wood putty or other suitable filler and should be primed and painted in the color of your choice. On the original wheel plywood parts and the 1 x 2 wheel braces were painted a bright red with gold striping. All other parts were coated with a sealer and finished in the natural color with spar varnish.

When operating the wheel in your yard, it is likely that you will have riders of varying ages and weights, and probably plenty of them. Because of this, you will have to balance the wheel so that it will rotate easily. To do this, purchase some heavy weights—5-lb. lead weights, ingots of the type used by plumbers, or old window sash weights—and keep them handy.

To load the squaris wheel, release the wheel locks and hold the wheel steady. Admit two riders to the lowest car, remembering to instruct the riders to duck their heads under the shaft on which the seat is pivoted and which serves as a safety bar. Now swing the wheel a quarter turn and admit two more riders.

Continue the procedure until the wheel is loaded and ready to run.

Now remove your hands and let the wheel roll on its own for a minute. You will be able to tell which seat is the heaviest because it will swing to the bottom. When that happens, balance the wheel by putting one or more heavy weights on the seat opposite the heavy one. Fasten the weights securely so that they cannot fall from the seat during the ride and injure the tiny passenger in the opposite car.

See also: cars, sidewalk; games, children's; merry-go-round; parade floats; playground equipment; train, children's.

Fiberglass with stripes and a new angular rib shape promise all-new decorative applications

Fiberglass panels can be the answer

BY W. CLYDE LAMMEY

■ WHAT TO DO about that patio roof? A much-to-be-desired privacy fence? A room divider? Perhaps a hideaway for the garbage can? A back-drop for a flower planting or maybe an "eye-brow" awning over an exposed door?

Fiberglass panels can be the answer to the problems posed by these sample questions.

Fiberglass is a tough, colorful material, takes the weather without crumbling, peeling or flak-ing away. It lets in light, but you can't see through it; it filters infrared and lets ultra violet through. It sheds water like a duck's back, comes in rainbow colors and in big sheets that cover a lot of area in an hour or two of weekend time. You can drill the stuff, nail it, saw it, even bend it one way within reasonable limits.

The popular and perhaps the most useful pat-tern is a corrugated panel similar to metal cor-rugated roofing. This and other configurations such as flat sheets in plain colors or with em-bedded fibers in various designs in outline are available almost anywhere you might ask. Any of these can be framed into colorful fencings, room dividers, indoor planters, door panels and, well, you'll think of other uses, indoors and out.

Handling and working fiberglass panels calls for only a few minor precautions. You don't have to baby the stuff in the handling; you just avoid throwing it about or hitting it hard with a ham-mer. You don't drive nails through it without first drilling a nail-size hole. You stay at least ⅜ in. away from any edge of the panel with a drilled nail hole; better ½ in. or more if there's space. And you always use the approved nails and neoprene washers when attaching the panels to any framing. Of course, you can always use screws or even wood clips or other improvised fastenings, also the ready-cut moldings in struc-tures where there is no undue stress on the panel. Otherwise you handle and work the material much as you would plywood.

Your materials dealer will have work sheets and other data that will help you plan and install any form of fiberglass panel in any project in which the use of such panels is suitable.

continued next page

See also: boats, used; fiberglass construction; patio roofs; remodeling; remodeling ideas; swimming pools.

---

fiberglass boats: see boats, used

Always paint, stain (and rotproof) any lumber that is to be used out of doors with fiberglass paneling. This makes for a neater job, avoids drips and spatters

Use a line, level and spacer when placing vertical supports for fiberglass paneling. Accuracy is important, prevents trouble later on

Photos courtesy Filon Division, Vistron Corp.
Precutting grooves in posts and rails of framing aids in assembling the whole structure. Rails can be toenailed or, better, notched into the posts

If you do toenail the rails, set the nail heads below the surface and fill with putty. Corrugated panels can span greater distances without support

Corrugated roof and sidewall panels, also those used as fencing, should be held in place with matching molding available wherever panels are sold

This fence shares light and color yet offers complete privacy to both sides of the property line. Such a structure also affords a good windbreak

When you nail through into end grain be sure to start your nail dead center for maximum holding power. Notice zigzag spacing of these center supports

Always follow manufacturer's specs for panel lap on roofs and always drill holes for the nails. Use the approved nails and neoprene washers

Careful with that hammer! Fiberglass will withstand almost anything but hammer blows, which may cause it to "craze" and eventually break up about the nail

Photos courtesy Filon Division, Vistron Corp.

Specs usually call for weatherstripping the lap joints of roofings. It's easy to apply and prevents any tendency to leaks during driving rains

If your patio roof joins siding you'll need to install flashing of the kind that comes to you preformed, ready to install, for complete waterproofing

After all that work—which wasn't much after all—this is what you get, a sheltered place in the sun, colorful and showerproof. How'd you do without it?

Plyfoam: new workshop wonder

BY ARTHUR MIKESELL

With this new miracle material you can produce fiberglass projects in your own workshop without the usual complicated forms. Just form it under a heat lamp

■ A THOUSAND SHAPES to suit any project, plus featherweight construction with incredible strength—it's all possible with Plyfoam, a revolutionary new material that makes fiberglass construction practical in your home workshop.

A true thermoplast, Plyfoam is a rigid foam sheet that becomes as pliable as felt when heated to about 200 deg. You can form it into compound curves, bend it with almost complete freedom of shape. Once it cools, however, it becomes rigid in the new shape and can be covered with fiberglass to produce an ultralight, strong sandwich construction.

Available in 46 x 56-in. sheets of ¼-in. and ½-in. thicknesses, Plyfoam is a special type of unicellular polyvinyl chloride plastic from Ply-foam, Inc., E. Bethpage Rd., Plainview, N.Y. You can cut it with a razor blade or pocket knife, sand and shape it more easily than balsa wood. It costs about 46 cents per sq. ft. for the ¼-in. thickness, 80 cents for ½-in. And considering what you can do with the material, these are reasonable prices.

Everyone is familiar with the virtues of fiberglass-reinforced plastic: tough, waterproof, durable and almost completely maintenance-free. In normal fiberglass construction, however, you have to start with a complicated mold, and making this mold usually turns out to be at least as much work as building the project itself.

With Plyfoam, all you need is a simple form to hold the material to shape as it cools. Once shaped, the foam becomes a mold over which you apply the resin and fiberglass to produce a strong sandwich construction.

In addition to eliminating the need for a mold, Plyfoam makes a vital structural contribution to the finished project.

Make a simple form for bending the foam into compound curves, with support at 2-in. intervals

Fiberglass cloth should be precut to size and then pressed into the resin. Brush resin on any dry spots

A single layer of fiberglass-reinforced plastic is flexible. To prevent unwanted flexing or "oil-canning," the standard practice is to build up layers of glass until the required stiffness has been achieved. This is not only a lot of extra work, but it also makes the project much heavier and more expensive.

When used as the filling, or core, for a fiberglass sandwich, Plyfoam works like the struts of a steel bridge and produces an enormous improvement in the strength-to-weight ratio. A sandwich panel of ½-in. Plyfoam between ⅛-in. layers of fiberglass increases the stiffness of the fiberglass by about 20 times. Such a panel will be stronger than high-grade plywood of the same thickness, yet weigh only about half as much.

Building a project with Plyfoam is simplicity itself. Normally, it involves three steps: making a simple dimension control frame or shaping form; assembling the project in Plyfoam; covering the structure with fiberglass bedded in resin.

Forms and frames. Many simple projects can be built without any frame or form, since the Plyfoam sheets are quite rigid. For larger projects involving "cold forming" (bending the unheated Plyfoam to form simple curves), a simple wood frame is required. If no bending is necessary, this frame need only supply support points at 2 or 3-ft. intervals. If the Plyfoam must be curved, the support points will usually be spaced closer together.

A simple way to determine the proper spacing in such cases is to draw the curve full-size on a piece of lumber or plywood, then bend the Plyfoam sheet along this curve and tap small nails into the board to hold the sheet in place. This will quickly fix the minimum number of constraining points necessary and the proper spacing between them.

Any old pieces of lumber will do for the frame, so long as they provide the proper support.

If the project involves compound curves, the Plyfoam will probably have to be heated, and this means that you must provide additional support

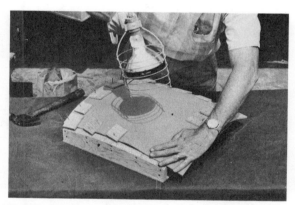

Heat the foam one area at a time, working it down to conform to the curve and then anchoring the edges

Use a wide paintbrush to spread the resin evenly over the curved surface before adding the fiberglass

Use a squeegee to press the cloth into the resin for thorough saturation, then remove excess resin

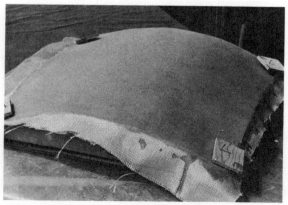

The completed job should show the texture of the fiberglass cloth evenly. Trim the excess cloth off later

Plyfoam, continued

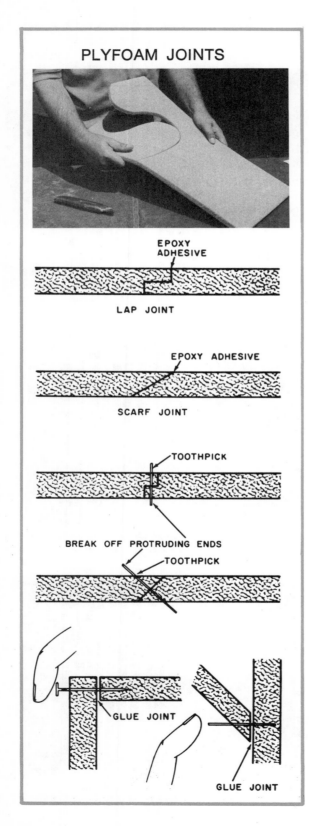

PLYFOAM JOINTS

EPOXY ADHESIVE

LAP JOINT

EPOXY ADHESIVE

SCARF JOINT

TOOTHPICK

BREAK OFF PROTRUDING ENDS

TOOTHPICK

GLUE JOINT

GLUE JOINT

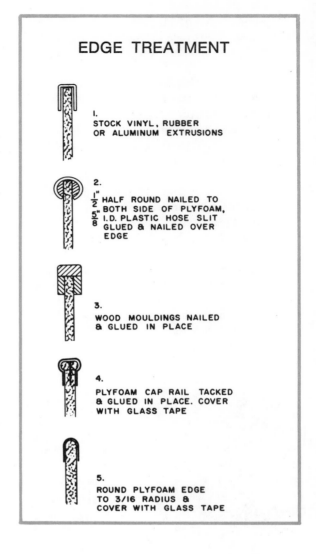

EDGE TREATMENT

1. STOCK VINYL, RUBBER OR ALUMINUM EXTRUSIONS

2. HALF ROUND NAILED TO BOTH SIDE OF PLYFOAM, I.D. PLASTIC HOSE SLIT GLUED & NAILED OVER EDGE

3. WOOD MOULDINGS NAILED & GLUED IN PLACE

4. PLYFOAM CAP RAIL TACKED & GLUED IN PLACE. COVER WITH GLASS TAPE

5. ROUND PLYFOAM EDGE TO 3/16 RADIUS & COVER WITH GLASS TAPE

to define the curve. Lath or 1-in. strips of ¼-in. plywood, spaced about 2 in. apart and nailed over the frame where necessary, will prove sufficient.

The heated sheet will resemble a piece of heavy felt in consistency—carpet padding, for instance—and must be held firmly in position as it cools. Keep this in mind when determining the degree of support needed. Remember, however, that the frame can be very rough carpentry. The important thing is to provide the dimensions of the shape you wish to achieve, plus minimal temporary support for the foam sheet.

Working with Plyfoam. Almost any kind of knife may be used to cut the Plyfoam to the shape desired, though the ideal choice would probably be a shop knife with changeable blade. Just mark the outline on the foam sheet and run the knife along the line. You don't have to cut completely through the foam, since it will break cleanly in any direction once cut about halfway through.

Shaping is best handled with a Stanley "Surform" file, though any coarse file, rasp or even sandpaper will work. A portable saber saw can also be used. It's especially handy for cutting duplicate parts by making one pass through several stacked sheets.

Plyfoam joinery is such a simple operation that you find it difficult to believe until you've done it. Basically, each joint is held with a two-part epoxy glue. Ordinary toothpicks or annular-ring nails are used to hold the joint temporarily while the adhesive sets. You simply push these in with your finger. Once the glue sets, any protruding toothpick ends can be broken off flush with the surface. Nails should be countersunk and left in the work. The joint thus produced is stronger than the foam itself, and a fiberglass sandwich incorporating such joints is as strong as if there were a continuous core.

A simple butt joint is usually sufficient for edge-joining two sheets, though somewhat more elaborate joints are sometimes desirable when making up a large sheet from several small pieces.

Right-angle joints are made in the same way as flat butt joints, applying the adhesive first and pinning the two pieces together by pushing nails or toothpicks through the joint.

Another way of holding a butt joint while the adhesive dries is useful when fitting successive sheets to a frame. It involves looping a wire across the joint, pulling it flush to the foam surface and twisting the two ends together around a frame member under the joint. When the adhesive has set, the wire can be cut.

Where more strength is required, add a fillet of foam. This will impart extra rigidity to a right-angle joint. It's also a good idea when mounting load-bearing panels, such as shelves or boat seats.

Heat-forming Plyfoam can be accomplished in a number of ways. Sometimes it's possible to

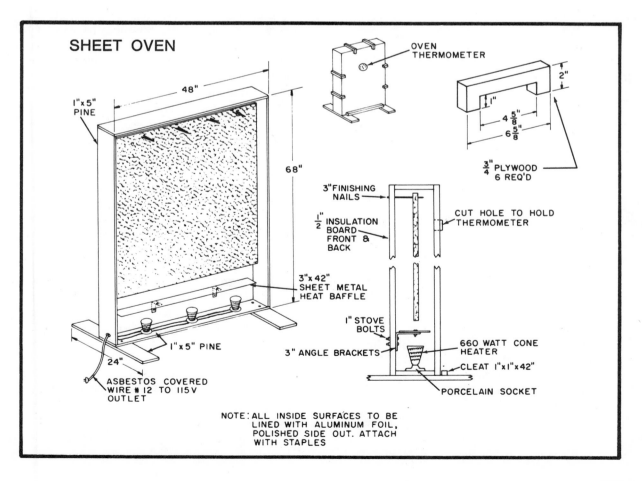

SHEET OVEN

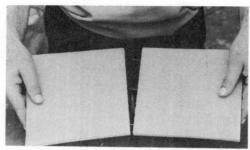

A flat butt joint that is fastened with adhesive and reinforced with toothpick pins is even stronger than the foam itself

An alternate method of securing a butt joint while the adhesive cures is to wire it to a building frame member temporarily

A fillet of foam used to reinforce a butt joint should be taped with glass so the load is transmitted from one panel to the other

Plyfoam, continued

form the desired curve by using a heat lamp, shaping one small area at a time. Hold the heat lamp a couple of inches away from the foam. Depending on the shape you want, this technique may even be used with large panels.

If the project is a small one, you can heat the sheet in a kitchen oven. And don't forget that almost anything can serve as a form—a box for a good 90-deg. bend, for instance, or a can for a radius.

A "planking" technique is sometimes the

easiest way to produce a large compound curve. By fitting strips together, one at a time, beveling the butting edges as required, you can produce extremely complex shapes using a heat lamp. Use glue and toothpicks to assemble the strips.

To produce a large compound curve from a single sheet, however, you'll probably have to heat the whole sheet at one time. Where Plyfoam is used in manufacturing operations, a large industrial heating blanket takes care of this. Since such blankets are too expensive for general use, a simple, low-cost oven has been designed which accomplishes the same thing. It's detailed on page 977.

Once the sheet becomes pliable, it must be quickly transferred to the form and anchored in position. A heat lamp used as a supplementary local heat source will help to prevent too-rapid cooling and allow more time for manipulation. It will also come in handy for spot-heating when putting the finishing touches on the shape.

trim off the surplus

When producing a deep, domed shape from a single sheet of Plyfoam, some surplus material undoubtedly will wrinkle around the edges, just as would a thick piece of felt. Trim off this surplus with a sharp knife. As with any other Plyfoam joint or surface, a few inaccuracies won't matter since the whole thing will be hidden under fiberglass. Cut filler pieces to plug any gaps left by your trimming and glue them in place.

The result of patching up in this way is exactly the same as a continuous sheet in the finished project, so don't worry. And as this implies, every scrap of material can be used up by piecing small projects together, trimming as you go.

When assembling a Plyfoam structure, keep in mind that it will be necessary to have access to *both* sides of the material in order to apply the fiberglass reinforcing layers. Thus, it's often desirable to plan your project as two or more subassemblies which can be joined together after each has been fiberglassed.

Fiberglassing Plyfoam. Be sure to follow all the standard safety precautions when covering your Plyfoam project with fiberglass. Work in a well-ventilated area maintained at a comfortably warm temperature (about 75-deg. F.).

Wear rubber or plastic gloves when handling the wet resin. Avoid prolonged contact between wet resin and skin. Wash thoroughly and frequently.

The first step is to spread the fiberglass cloth flat over the shaped Plyfoam and mark it for cutting. For most projects, 10-oz. cloth is recommended. During this preliminary fitting, make sure that joints in the cloth won't coincide with joints in the foam.

Cut all the cloth required at one time so as to avoid delays once the resin has been mixed. Leave between 2 and 4 in. excess at joint edges and about an inch for final trimming to size.

It's extremely important that you follow the manufacturer's instructions when mixing the resin. Measure quantities carefully and *mix well*. Don't prepare the resin until you're ready to go to work, however, for once mixed it will remain in a liquid state for only a limited time. Just how long depends on the type of resin, but an hour is the common period of time. Mix only as much resin as you can conveniently use during this period.

Instead of painting your project, you may wish to add coloring to the resin itself. Special color pastes for use with epoxy are available from most dealers handling resins.

Epoxy is the recommended resin for use with Plyfoam; polyester may be used after a prime coat of polyurethane varnish.

With a wide paintbrush, spread the resin evenly over the exterior surfaces of the project. Then lay the glass in the resin and smooth it out. Use a rubber or plastic squeegee to work trapped air to the edges of the glass cloth.

Put enough pressure on the squeegee to work the resin through the fabric, thoroughly saturating the cloth. Remove any excess resin. The finished appearance should show fibers of cloth evenly wetted with resin over the whole surface. If "dry" spots persist, work a little resin into them with the brush and squeegee.

add reinforcing strips

Finish off the outside of the project in this manner, adding reinforcing strips of cloth along all angle joints. The joints between pieces of cloth may either butt squarely or overlap slightly.

As soon as possible, remove the project from the frame and cover all inside surfaces. This will eliminate the possibility of warping which might arise due to one layer curing without the stiffening effect of the second layer. With a layer of glass on both sides no warping will occur.

On larger structures requiring even greater rigidity, apply two layers of glass to each side. Such a sandwich will be strong enough for practically any project; 40-ft. sailboats have been built from ½-in. Plyfoam with just two layers of 10-oz. glass on each side.

While the glass-cloth texture makes a satisfactory and pleasing finish, you may wish to have a smooth surface. If so, fill the surface with epoxy or polyester filler and sand it down; paint with an epoxy or polyester paint and polish when dry.

On projects involving flat surfaces or simple curves, unusual effects can be achieved by substituting other rigid sheet materials for glass on one side of the Plyfoam.

Embossed aluminum and Formica are two obvious choices.

Again, with flat surfaces or simple curves it's possible to produce custom decorative panels by borrowing some of the standard techniques of fiberglass molding.

A Formica surface can serve as the mold. Apply a layer of wax "parting coat" (you can buy this from any fiberglass supply house) and spray or brush a layer of clear resin over the wax. Lay a patterned fabric on the resin, pattern down, and over this lay a layer of glass fabric saturated with resin. Apply another layer of resin, then the Plyfoam, and finish with a final layer of resin and glass fabric.

Once everything has dried, remove the Formica mold and you'll find a high-gloss clear finish protecting the patterned fabric.

Alternatively, this process may be used to produce a high-gloss colored surface by using colored resin.

how to attach fittings

To attach fittings, handles and hinges to a Plyfoam project you may either add wood inserts in the Plyfoam core before fiberglassing or drill holes in the finished laminate and install fiber or plastic screw anchors with adhesive.

Load-bearing attachments can be glassed into position and reinforced by applying successive strips of fiberglass at different angles.

A wide variety of edge treatments is possible. For a square edge, cut back the Plyfoam and fill the edge with epoxy or polyester filling compound of putty consistency. Sand the edge smooth and paint it. For a rounded edge, just file the edge round and cover it with fiberglass tape.

Capping strips can be mounted with epoxy adhesive, or you can make up Plyfoam "nosing" and fiberglass over it.

Don't be afraid to let yourself go when working with Plyfoam. It has tremendous potential and the main need for taking full advantage of its possibilities is a generous helping of imagination.

Hooded chaise

Now you know how Plyfoam works—how its moldability banishes many of the restrictions that may have cramped your workshop style. And yet *because* it's so new and so unlike material you're familiar with, we asked noted designer Franklyn Jacoby to sketch up a few projects that would test Plyfoam's design potential.

One of his projects—the hooded chaise you see here—was actually dimensioned and built as a practical demonstration. Other of Mr. Jacoby's ideas appear on this and the next pages, reproduced directly from his sketch pad to springboard your own imagination toward the creation of projects that weren't possible before.

5 wild and wonderful toys

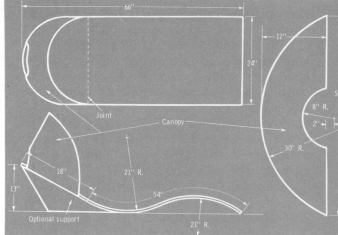

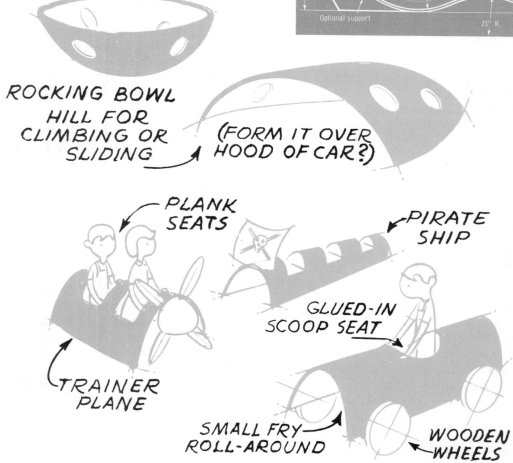

ROCKING BOWL
HILL FOR
CLIMBING OR
SLIDING

(FORM IT OVER
HOOD OF CAR?)

PLANK
SEATS

PIRATE
SHIP

GLUED-IN
SCOOP SEAT

TRAINER
PLANE

SMALL FRY
ROLL-AROUND

WOODEN
WHEELS

Easy chair

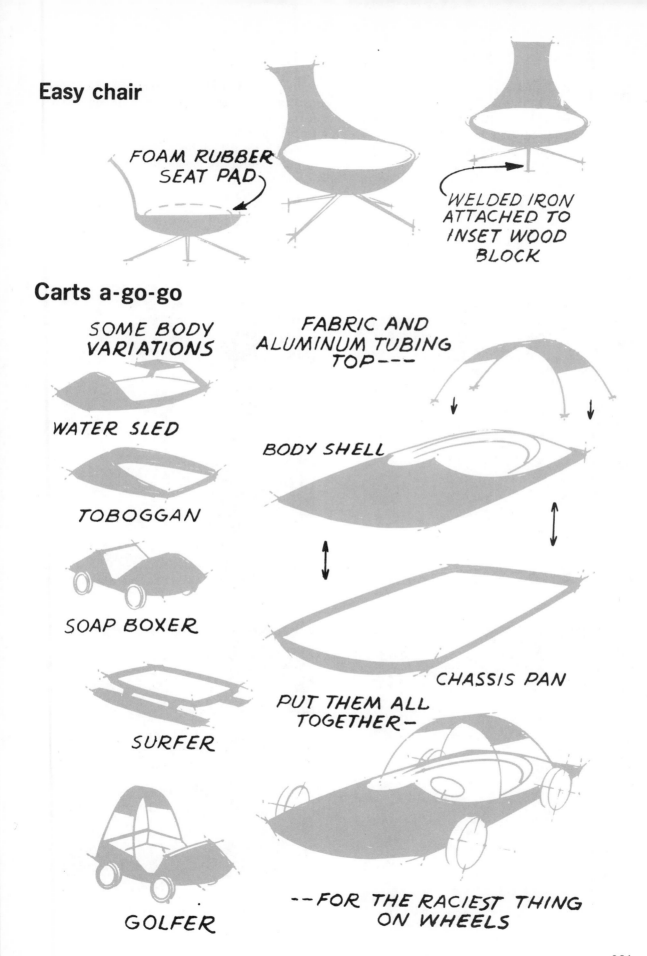

FOAM RUBBER SEAT PAD

WELDED IRON ATTACHED TO INSET WOOD BLOCK

Carts a-go-go

SOME BODY VARIATIONS

WATER SLED

TOBOGGAN

SOAP BOXER

SURFER

GOLFER

FABRIC AND ALUMINUM TUBING TOP---

BODY SHELL

CHASSIS PAN

PUT THEM ALL TOGETHER-

--FOR THE RACIEST THING ON WHEELS

Boat building

Plyfoam is an ideal material for building boats, not only because of the general construction advantages mentioned earlier, but because it provides built-in flotation, like wood.

As a matter of fact, the material was originally developed for use in boat construction. John T. Potter, president of Potter Instrument Co., Inc., and an enthusiastic yachtsman, heard about PVC foam in Europe. Upon further checking, he learned that B. F. Goodrich had a strong background in the field of foam plastics.

Potter went to Goodrich with his requirements—a PVC foam with thermoplastic characteristics, density and strength suitable for

Plyfoam, continued

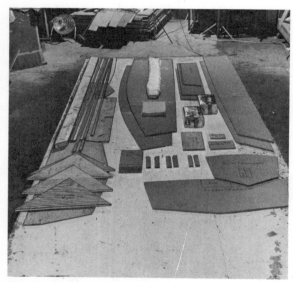

The Sea Shell pram kit includes all the necessary parts for the boat, precut to the proper size

The building frame is assembled on a single 2 x 4 and rests on two sawhorses. The floor should be level

When applying resin and cloth, work quickly. Use a squeegee to remove wrinkles and trapped air

After the resin cures, lift the hull from the frame and place it in a cradle to glass the interior

marine construction—and a jointly operated development program resulted in Plyfoam. Plyfoam, Inc., is the company founded by Potter to market the new material, manufactured by B. F. Goodrich exclusively for this company.

Touche III, the first boat built from Plyfoam, is a 37-ft. trimaran with a beam of 20 ft. Designed for Potter by Britton Chance Jr., it weighs only 5000 lbs. and carries a 1200-lb. keel. Under ideal conditions, it can beat any America's Cup 12-meter.

While many boat companies expressed immediate interest in Plyfoam for production boats and are now engaged in design research work with it, the first Plyfoam boats to be made available to the public are two kits from McNair

Polyethylene sheeting stapled on the frame acts as a separation membrane to simplify hull removal

After assembling the hull with push pins and glue, the edges are rounded so the fiberglass will adhere

Seat supports and transom inserts are added before you begin fiberglassing the hull interior

The completed pram has all the virtues of fiberglass construction, but weighs less than a stock glass pram

This lightweight pram is a Plyfoam prototype undergoing tests. A number of designs have been built and kits may be offered to the public

Boat Works, Inc., 27 Munson St., Port Washington, N.Y.

The largest is a 15-ft. 6-in. runabout OBC rated for 95 hp and weighing about 400 lbs.

The other is an 8-ft. Sea Shell pram, construction of which is illustrated here. A 40-lb. lightweight, it's the kind of small utility craft that you can toss on top of your car or into the back of your station wagon. The $116.50 kit includes all the necessary Plyfoam parts, precut to size, plus fiberglass cloth, epoxy resin and fittings. In addition, it contains all materials required for the simple building frame.

The Sea Shell pram can be put together without heating the Plyfoam. You simply pin the pieces together around the frame with annular-ring nails (which are included) and cover the hull with fiberglass. Complete plans and building instructions are included with the kit. In general, however, the construction procedure follows that outlined earlier for making any Plyfoam project.

See also: building; fiberglass; framing; measurements.

Plyfoam, continued

This is the Touche III, John Potter's big trimaran, which was the first boat built of Plyfoam. It has a 51-ft. mast and carries 650 sq. ft. of sail

This 15½-ft. runabout from the McNair Boat Works sells for about $750 in kit form. Except for a wooden deck and transom, it's entirely Plyfoam

This 10-ft. tunnel hull is another research prototype from Plyfoam, Inc. It is unsinkable and carries enough flotation to keep five people afloat

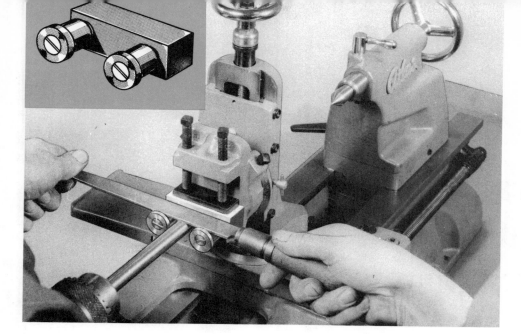

EXAMPLES OF SHAPES WHICH CAN
BE FILED WITH THE ROLLER GUIDE

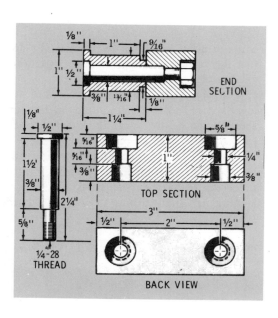

END SECTION

TOP SECTION

BACK VIEW

¼-28 THREAD

File true flats with a roller guide

■ OLD-TIME MACHINISTS did much of their work with a hand filing guide like the one shown here. Clamped in the milling attachment, the guide makes it easy to file octagons, hexagons, squares and many other shapes, as well as sharpen the teeth of end mills, rod drills and spot facers.

The base of the guide is made from 1-in.-square cold-rolled steel, drilled and counterbored as detailed. The pivots which support the rollers are of drill rod, whereas the rollers are made from tool steel. Each roller should be drilled a bit undersize and reamed to its final fit. The shouldered pivots are turned to size, filed smooth and polished for a close running fit in the holders.

To use the guide, lock the headstock spindle with the back gear lever; then select a flat file having parallel edges. Hold the file's safe edge against the guide flanges. As the work nears final size, keep the file bearing on the rollers.

See also: band grinder; bandsaws, blades; grinding; hand grinders; honing; rasps, power.

Accurate contour filing with templates

BY WALTER E. BURTON

Shaped openings can be made in steel plate, but an insert arrangement may be easier. Here a section from a socket wrench is sliced on a lathe after a shoulder is machined in it

■ YOUR MOST USEFUL TOOLS can include templates you make yourself. They can guide files in making neat corners, notches, half-rounds, vees, dovetails, ovals, special washers, numerals and letters and many other shapes in sheet metal, plate, plastic, fiber, hardboard and wood. Templates can help duplicate blanks for brooches, trays and models; make chassis openings for electronic equipment and rounded corners to specified radii.

The secrets to making templates for accurate contour filing are your own ingenuity and the fact that a file will cut soft metal but not hardened steel.

You can start with hardenable tool steel or low-carbon (soft) steel, usually in the form of sheet stock $\frac{1}{32}$ to $\frac{1}{8}$ in. thick. Sometimes discarded tools or tool parts can be shaped into templates. In this case, with the steel already file-hard, it can be shaped by grinding, with care taken not to overheat the parts.

Annealed high-carbon steel can be hardened

A wide variety of shapes can be rendered in template form from diverse materials. Below is a variety of templates and a sample of the work produced from them

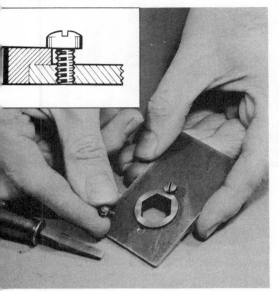

Tap holes in a ⅜₂-in. sheet of mild steel for 8-32 retaining screws on both sides of a ring opening. Case harden the ring. The ring was cut from a socket wrench section. See opposite page

A radius template can be ground by swinging sheet steel on a pivot. The inside curve is drilled and cut

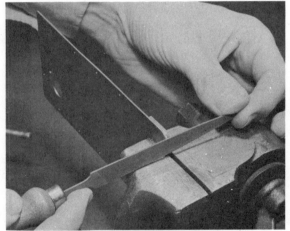

Draw the file toward the template so the work is pressed against it on the cutting stroke

Making washers is easy. Use standard washers with oversized blanks sandwiched between them. Drill the center holes and bolt through

An oval or large round insert is machined from cold-rolled steel bar. Use a fine-toothed file. The oval is squeezed in a vise before hardening

by heating and quenching. Low-carbon steel templates are case-hardened with a commercial hardening compound. When quenching the high-carbon steel, the portion of the template that the file will touch should hit the water first. Thin, flat pieces are generally dunked edge first.

Hold the file at right angles to both work and template and draw the file across the work and toward the template. A fine-tooth file is best.

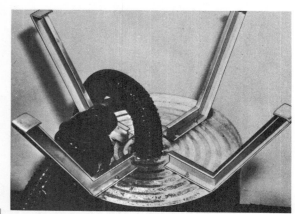

3 A fiberglass filter is placed over the holes drilled in the garbage-can cover to trap dust

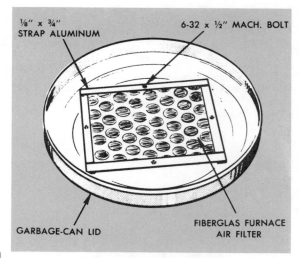

1/8" x 3/4" STRAP ALUMINUM   6-32 x 1/2" MACH. BOLT

GARBAGE-CAN LID   FIBERGLAS FURNACE AIR FILTER

4 The filter is held in place by means of four aluminum straps. The filter should be cleaned occasionally

1 The dryer handles twenty-four 4 x 5 cut-film negatives or several film strips on upper and lower hangers

Ten-minute film dryer

BY MANLY BANISTER

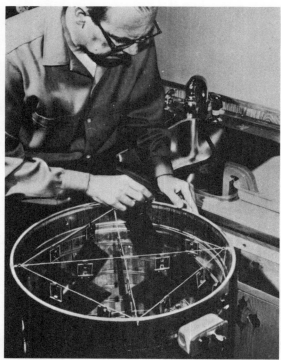

2 Legs can be made by notching and bending aluminum T-shapes. Note how suction hose slips over the outlet

■ BUY A 32-gal. galvanized garbage can and you have the main part of this efficient controlled-heat film dryer. It will accommodate up to twenty-four 4 x 5 cut films or several lengths of roll film, and the novel heating element, plus the filtered air flow, together provide a constant circulation of warm air.

Assembled, the whole affair consists of the can, 60 ft. of 300-watt heat tape, a small motorized blower with flexible hose, an electric-iron thermostat, four pieces of T-shaped aluminum extrusion for legs plus the necessary cord, plug and pilot-light switch.

The first step is to clean the inside of the can thoroughly to remove all traces of the residues remaining from the galvanizing process. Then sweat spots of acid-core solder in vertically spaced rows to the inside of the can as in the righthand view, Fig. 11. There should be about 6 rows of spots equally spaced around the inside of the can, the spots being spaced 2 in. on centers and the first one being located about 2¼ in. below the rim of the can. The first spot in the

988

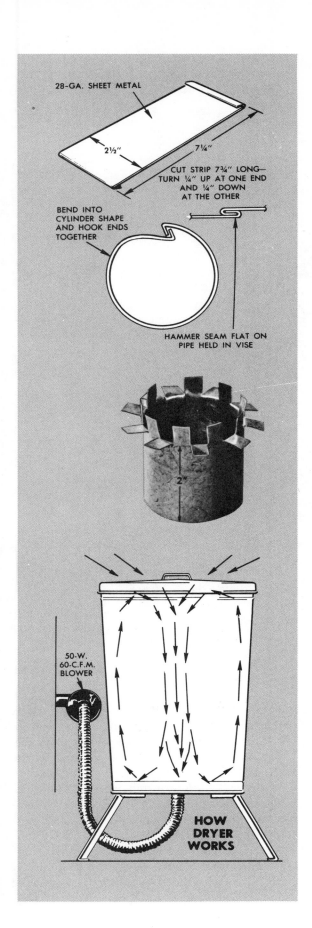

28-GA. SHEET METAL

2½"

7¼"

CUT STRIP 7¾" LONG—
TURN ¼" UP AT ONE END
AND ¼" DOWN
AT THE OTHER

BEND INTO
CYLINDER SHAPE
AND HOOK ENDS
TOGETHER

HAMMER SEAM FLAT ON
PIPE HELD IN VISE

2"

50-W.
60-C.F.M.
BLOWER

HOW
DRYER
WORKS

5 The drawings on the left show how the air outlet is
constructed. Above is the finished film dryer

second row is located about ⅜ in. lower to give
a spiral progression from top to bottom of the
can. These solder spots serve to anchor clips
made from 1¼-in. lengths of 16-ga. wire. Bend
a slight offset, about ⅛ in., near one end of
each length of wire, hold the end nearest the
offset on a solder spot and sweat in place. These
clips support the heat tape which is placed inside the can in a continuous spiral. Figs. 11
and 12.

Next, make the air outlet connector as shown
in the detail, Fig. 5, and cut ⅜-in.-wide tabs all
around one end, bending every other one outward. Cut a 2⅛-in. hole in the bottom of the
garbage can, insert the tabbed end of the connector and bend the straight tabs over inside the
can to form a flange. Then solder them to the
bottom of the can, Fig. 8. Cement ₁/₁₆-in. felt
around the outside of the outlet for a nice force-
fit of the air hose, Fig. 2. Drill holes in the can
cover as in Figs. 6 and 7 and to trap dust, install a filter on the underside of the can cover
as in Figs. 3 and 4. The filter is made by strip-

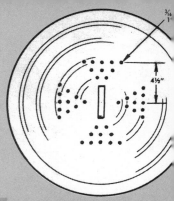

7 Drill 10 holes in each group, keeping the holes 1 in. apart an spacing the groups as shown

6 Holes in a V-shaped pattern are drilled through the can cover. Deburr them with a reamer to prevent hand injury

9 Film racks are made by stringing picture wire inside the can

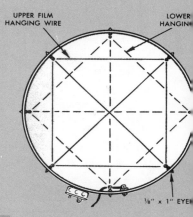

UPPER FILM HANGING WIRE   LOWER HANGIN

⅛" x 1" EYE

8 The air outlet is soldered into a hole cut in the bottom of the can. The outlet is covered with ¹⁄₁₆-in. felt

10 Two picture-wire racks are placed the can, the second rack about 12 in. below the upper one

ping off the cardboard frame from a standard 12 x 16-in. furnace filter and cutting it square. Strips of ⅛ x ¾-in. flat aluminum are used at the edges to hold it in place, the ends being lapped.

Legs can be made from aluminum Tees or anything else that's handy. Fasten them to the can with ³⁄₁₆ x ½-in. stove bolts with heads inside the can. Next locate the hole for the female plug, Fig. 11, by placing the surface box so that it clears the lid. The hole for the thermostat wires should be large enough to accommodate a protective grommet. Drill three holes a few inches from the grommet hole for mounting the thermostat, Fig. 11. Prepare the surface box by removing the center knockout and enlarge the hole to fit the wafer-type female plug, Fig. 12. Install the plug and mount the unit on the side of the can. The switch is a combination single-pole and 6-watt red pilot-light unit installed as in photo, Fig. 5. The electric-iron thermostat should be grounded either through a 3-pronged plug or directly from the dryer to a water pipe. Plug the heat tape into the wafer-type plug inside the can and as you unreel insert it behind each clip in a uniformly descending spiral. Finally, install the upper and lower film-

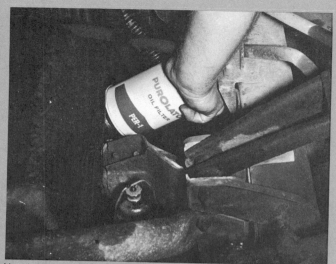

Hand-tightening is all oil filters need. Using a wrench or other tightening tool can crush the canister or ruin gaskets

Air cleaner elements need replacing, too. While the surface dirt can be washed away, the embedded particles usually remain

tool when putting on a new spin-on filter; install the filter *hand-tight* only.

- Before putting the filter on, dip your finger in oil and run it around the gasket. This will prevent the gasket from abrading as it's run up on the base plate. Wipe the base-plate seat clean before installation.

- When the filter's in place, run the engine for a minute. Wipe the filter off with a dry cloth and check for leaks. Leaks can occur if the filter is defective (a rare occurrence), if dirt on the seat prevents the filter from seating properly or if the filter wasn't screwed on tight enough.

How often should you replace an oil filter? Well, some car manufacturers recommend that you replace the filter once every second oil change. The point is that there is no way to tell when an oil filter is plugged, so the new-filter-every-other-oil-change rule is as good as any. But, frankly, I don't see the sense of filling the crankcase with clean oil and leaving a dirty filter to contaminate it. So I change my filter every time I change my oil.

Air-intake filters. These air-cleaning units prevent airborne dirt from getting into the carburetor and thence to the engine. The consequences of a clogged-up air filter can be serious. It can lead to an over-choked condition, resulting in the burning of too much fuel.

Even more important, an air filter prevents dirt and dust from getting to the cylinder walls where it would act like sandpaper on walls and rings.

The material used in a good-quality air filter is a micronic paper that must fulfill the same requirements as that used in oil filters—with one important addition: It must be fireproof so that it will not burn under backflash.

Can air filters be cleaned?

"Not really," according to Al Taylor, technical director at Purolator. "That paper is hit by very high-velocity dirt that embeds itself deeply into the material. When a filter is 'cleaned,' you're really only getting rid of surface dust and dirt."

How often should you replace an air filter? Most manufacturers say every 12,000 miles, more frequently under dusty conditions.

Air filters are easy to inspect because you can see the dirt. Take a filter, tap it on a table and you'll see the (surface) dirt falling off. If there's an appreciable accumulation that filter should be replaced.

Filters are among the easiest parts of a car for the mechanic-owner to check, replace and generally keep up to snuff. And remember, the cleaner they're kept, the cleaner will be your engine and the better it will perform.

See also: auto repair; carburetors, auto; cooling system, auto; fuel consumption, auto; idling, auto.

All about swimming-pool filters

BY ERNEST E. HICKMAN

Whether you have a built-in pool
or a small above-ground splasher,
the whole family will enjoy it more
if the water is kept clean and clear.
That's what filtering is all about

1 FILTERING

Diatomite is mixed with water to form a slurry which can be circulated through the filter and deposited on the cloth septum

If the septum were used without diatomite, filtration would be much less efficient and the surface would then soon become plugged

The precoat slows down the formation of a seal. By periodically adding small amounts of diatomite, filter runs can be extended

■ THERE IS NOTHING quite as delightful and inviting as crystal-clear water in a swimming pool on a warm day—and the invitation holds whether you have a big installed pool or the smaller variety for children. But clean, clear water is more than a matter of invitation; a polluted pool is not a healthy place to swim.

Without proper filtration, that inviting crystal-clear water in the pool quickly turns into liquid smog. Airborne dirt, bacteria and the salts left by water-treatment chemicals are always working to cloud the water, and the only way to maintain clarity is to "turn over" the whole pool once every 24 hours.

While efficient filters will remove a certain amount of bacteria from the water, the primary purpose of pool filtration is to restore clarity. A good pool filter can do no more than eliminate most of the causes of pollution. Purification is a job for chemicals, and a number of good chemicals that are prepackaged for quick use can be bought at swimming-pool supply houses —and even in some supermarkets.

A pool filter simply strains the water through a very fine sievelike material which traps the particles that would otherwise cause clouding. Sand filters are too coarse to catch extremely small particles, so a floc is usually used to coat the grains so that they can snag particles.

Keeping a pool in top swimming condition involves more than filtering, of course. The pool should be "vacuumed" regularly, using a vacuum attachment to a hose or a self-contained vacuum unit. The vacuum nozzle should have a brush built in for scraping the sides and bottom of the pool to remove the algae that forms there and can't be removed by filtering. The algae is formed through the action of sunlight on the water, and can be controlled by chemicals added to the water, but an occasional vacuuming is still necessary.

Dry leaves, bits of grass and insects land on the surface of the water and must be removed. Most built-in pools have skimmers as a part of the original equipment. The smaller pools set above ground seldom do. Small, electrically-operated skimmers can be bought for these pools, or they can be skimmed by hand, using a long-handled net. If they are not skimmed, this top debris soon becomes soggy, begins to deteriorate, and becomes a part of pool pollution.

Diatomite filters. Diatomaceous earth, also called diatomite or filter aid, is a powdery material made up of the intricate fossillike skeletons of microscopic water plants. When used in a pool filter, a thin layer of this material is deposited on a cloth septum (Fig. 1), forming a screen with 2,500,000 openings per sq. in. The largest particles which can slip through this screen measure 1½ microns (a micron is only

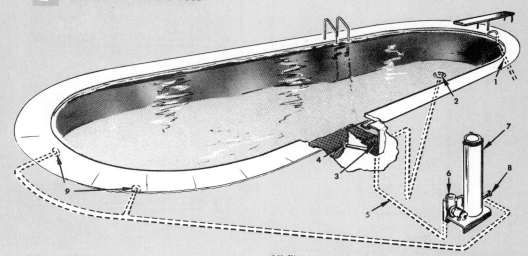

1. FILLING SPOUT
2. MAIN DRAIN (LOWEST POINT IN POOL)
3. SKIMMER
4. VACUUM-CLEANER FITTING
5. MAIN SUCTION LINE
6. STRAINER AND PUMP
7. DIATOMITE FILTER, PRESSURE TYPE
8. DRAIN FOR BACKWASHING FILTER
9. POOL INLETS

All filters must be served by the proper size of pipe, and water velocity through the pipe shouldn't exceed 10 ft. per sec. While steel pipe is sometimes permissible above ground, copper or polyethylene is preferred. Pipe shutoffs should be fullway valves

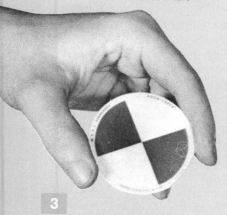

3

If you can see this 2-in. disk through 8 ft. of water, the pool meets NSPI standards for clarity

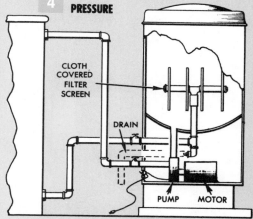

4 PRESSURE

When the pump is located ahead of the filter so that it pushes water through, it is a pressure-type filter

You can recognize a suction, or vacuum, filter by the location of the pump on the return line to the pool

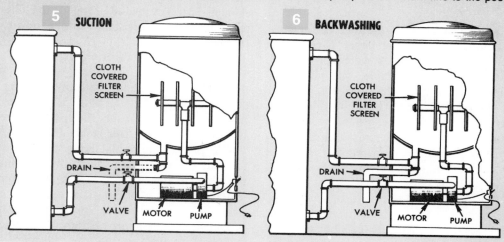

5 SUCTION

6 BACKWASHING

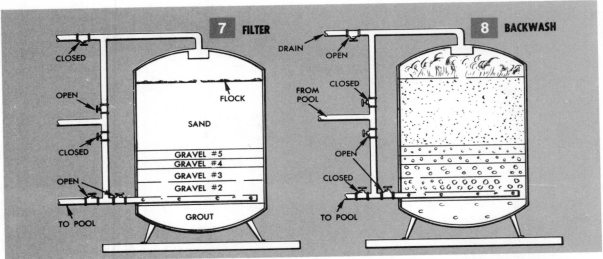

The filter area of a sand filter is always much smaller than a diatomite filter in the same tank

Sand filters, like diatomite filters, are backwashed by reversing the direction of the water flow

swimming-pool filters, continued

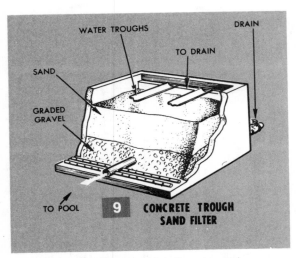

Gravity-type sand filters are hardly ever used today. Pressure type filters are much more common

39/1,000,000 in.), and such filtration is fine enough to remove most of the larger bacteria.

Diatomite filtration produces water of unbelievable clarity. As an example, one movie studio installed a diatomite filter for use with underwater photography tanks, but immediately ran into trouble. The diatomite proved so efficient that underwater color pictures looked as though they had been faked on a regular sound stage. (The problem was finally solved by adding blue dye to the water.)

Since diatomite will cling to a vertical surface or even the underside of a horizontal surface, the septum (supporting element) can be made in almost any shape. This makes it possible to

cram a lot of filter area into a small space, Fig. 4.

The septum probably has been the subject of more experimentation than any other part of the filter. Many materials and designs have been employed with varying degrees of success, but synthetic fiber fabric seems to be the most promising for residential pool filters. Such elements are too thin to collect deeply embedded dirt, can't fissure and pass unfiltered water, aren't affected by pool chemicals and are flexible enough for easy cleaning.

Unfortunately, a few manufacturers have gone overboard in trying to make diatomite filters compact, and have failed to allow enough space for unrestricted water flow between surfaces or the formation of a good filter cake. Others have exaggerated the filter area by basing it on the size of the cloth before folding or lapping and disregarding impermeable supports. If the filter element is too frequently lapped, the filter will present too much resistance to flow and require frequent cleaning.

There are two types of diatomite filters available. In a pressure filter, Fig. 4, water is pumped into the filter tank before filtration. In a vacuum or suction filter, Fig. 5, water is pumped away from the tank after being filtered. The pressure type is more popular for residential pools.

The precoat, or initial layer of diatomite, is formed by circulating a slurry of diatomite into the filter. Water, always seeking the course of least resistance, distributes the diatomite evenly over the elements. About 1.6 oz. per sq. ft. will provide a coating approximately 1/16 in. thick. At frequent intervals during the filtration cycle, small amounts of diatomite are added to prevent the precoat layer from becoming plugged.

Normally, a filter run (cycle) ends when accumulated dirt clogs the element enough so that the pressure drop across the filter reaches a predetermined point. (This varies with different filters.) A good filter of the right capacity will operate for about 7 days before this point is reached.

A diatomite filter is cleaned by reversing the flow of water, or backwashing, Fig. 6. This breaks up the filter cake which is drained off.

Sand filters. Since the passages in a sand filter are much larger than many of the particles to be trapped, a floc is usually used to catch the smaller particles. This floc is a gelatinous coagulation formed by the action of aluminum sulphate (alum) and the slightly alkaline pool water. It permeates the upper layer of a bed of sand, turning each grain into a sticky trap for passing particles and holding them by a combination of mechanical and electrochemical attraction. A proper floc requires from 1 to 3 lbs. of alum for every 10 sq. ft. of fiter area. This is usually injected into the filter intake by means of a venturi tube.

two types of sand filters

There are two principal types of sand filters: pressure, Fig. 7, and gravity, Fig. 9. The only difference is that in one case water flows by gravity through a bed of sand, then through graded gravel, while in the other a pump is used to push it through these same materials. Most pool filters are of the pressure type.

A sand filter should be backwashed at least once every 7 days to prevent packing, Fig. 8, and this takes a lot of water. A flow of 10 gal. per min. for each sq. ft. of filter must be maintained until the water leaving the filter is clear. This usually takes from 5 to 15 min. The high flow rate required for backwashing (twice the flow rate for filtering) is often arranged by using a multiple tank setup, with the same pump supplying all tanks during filtering but backwashing only one at a time.

The sand and gravel bed should be checked periodically, since dirt penetrates deeply into the sand bed during filtration and cannot always be removed by backwashing. This dirt combines with sand and chemicals to cause the formation of agglomerates (called mudballs), cracking of the filtering surface and shrinkage of the filter bed from the sidewalls of the tank. Such conditions not only hamper effective filtering, but permit the filter to become a breeding ground for organisms which may contaminate the water. If you discover mudballs in your filter, it's time to remove the old sand bed and replace it.

Filter capacity. Two factors determine the capacity of a pool filter: Rate of flow and filter area. The maximum recommended flow rate for a pressure-type diatomite filter is 3 gal. per min. for every sq. ft. of filter area, and for a vacuum type, 2¼ gal. For a sand filter, the maximum rate is 5 gal. per min. per sq. ft. At these flow rates, there should be enough filter area and matching pump capacity to run the whole poolful of water through the filter in 18 hrs. or less. Remember that these are minimum specifications, and a filter that meets them but still needs cleaning more often than once every four days is too small.

Choosing a filter. The filtration system and plumbing, Fig. 2, will account for at least 25 percent of the cost of a conventional concrete pool, so be sure to take this into consideration when deciding what size pool you wish to build. Both sand and diatomite filters have good points. A sand filter will cost 4 to 5 times as much as a diatomite filter per sq. ft. of filtering area. However, it will also be cheaper to operate and its higher flow rate will enable you to turn over the whole pool in about half the time required by a diatomite filter.

diatomite more efficient

A diatomite filter will provide more efficient filtration, removing particles measuring 1½ microns vs. a sand filter's 12 microns. Some people feel that such high efficiency is unnecessary, since a particle must measure 80 microns to be visible with the naked eye at 10 in.

There is one big advantage in diatomite filters. They are smaller, lighter and can be installed almost anywhere. Since sand filters of comparable capacity are much larger and heavier, they often present installation problems. A quality filter may cost twice as much as its economy counterpart but will last much longer.

A growing number of communities have enacted swimming-pool ordinances which include filter specifications. Instead of specifying particle size or distribution, most use the National Swimming Pool Institute's visual test which stipulates that a 2-in. disk with alternate red and white quadrants, Fig. 3, must be visible through 8 ft. of water.

See also: cabanas; floats and docks; grotto; patios; swimming pools.

999

Children find that the water in their back-yard pool is remarkably clear after being run through this small but efficient diatomite filter. It's easy to make and can be operated by a child

Back-yard plastic pools don't require large filters. This compact unit, only 18 in. high, is perfectly adequate for the small children's pool shown here

The water in your plastic "swimmin' hole"
can be crystal clear
with the help of an inexpensive,
compact filtering unit
you can make yourself

Skimmer filter for above-ground pool

BY WALTER E. RUNKEL

finishes, antique: see antique finishes

■ FOR VERY LITTLE MONEY you can add a filter, vacuum cleaner and skimmer to any small, above-ground children's pool. The diatomite unit described here has a filter area of 3 sq. ft., which is adequate for most of the shallower 10 to 20-ft. plastic pools.

The filter tank is an old popcorn-oil can 11 in. in diameter and 17 in. high. Any fractional-horsepower motor can be used to drive the small centrifugal pump. First, cut a circular piece of ¾-in. plywood about 2 in. larger than the diameter of the can and attach it to the top of the can lid. Next, using ¾-in. hanger iron, mount three eyebolts equidistant and near the top of the can so that they extend through registering holes drilled in the plywood disk. Replace the regular seal of the can lid with a ⁵⁄₁₆ x ⅜-in. strip of sponge rubber and use wing nuts on the bolts to pull the lid down tight.

The intake fittings are detailed, right. A ¾-in. standard metal fitting for coupling plastic pipe to metal pipe is used to connect hoses to both inlet and outlet. Input to the pump is a 1-in. hose and all others are ¾-in.

The filter bag is 8½ in. in diameter and 14 in. high, but can be made larger if you use a larger container for a tank. Make the bag of ticking, sewing the seams with nylon thread and adding a zipper across the top. This bag sits on a false bottom of screen wire supported by a strip of sheet metal 1 in. wide, bent zigzag fashion and placed on edge in the bottom of the can. Before using the filter, give it a couple coats of enamel to prevent corrosion and seal any leaks around fittings with roofing compound.

Make the skimmer from a No. 2 soup can, cutting a hole in the bottom for a short piece of 1¼-in.-dia. pipe. After soldering the pipe in the hole, cut a ½-in.-wide slot in the side of

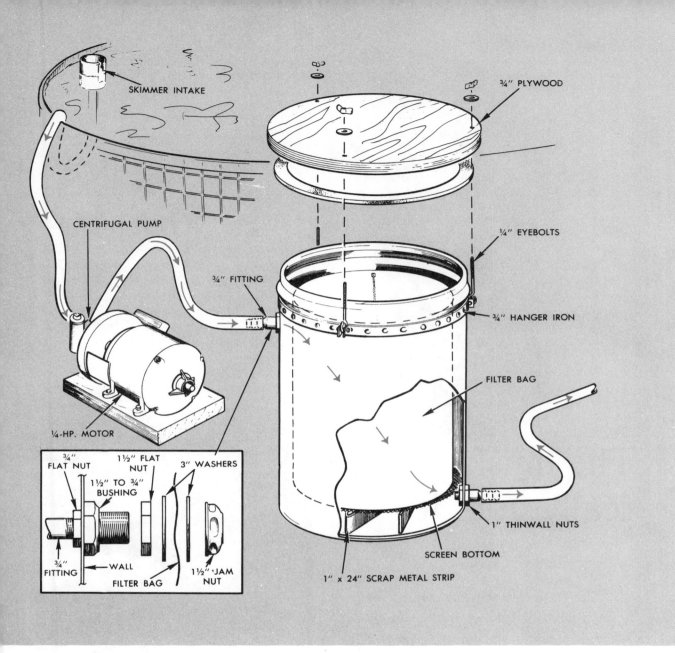

SKIMMER INTAKE

¾" PLYWOOD

CENTRIFUGAL PUMP

¾" FITTING

¼" EYEBOLTS

¾" HANGER IRON

FILTER BAG

¼-HP. MOTOR

¾" FLAT NUT

1½" FLAT NUT

3" WASHERS

1½" TO ¾" BUSHING

¾" FITTING

WALL

FILTER BAG

1½" JAM NUT

1" THINWALL NUTS

SCREEN BOTTOM

1" x 24" SCRAP METAL STRIP

the can for about three quarters of its length, paint the unit and couple it to the inlet hose with a piece of radiator hose. Bend the hose so that the skimmer remains in an upright position when hanging in the water on the side of the pool. Mount the skimmer so that the water level is about the middle of the slot. With this arrangement, the water level can vary slightly without the pump losing its prime.

To clean the bottom of the pool, remove the skimmer and attach a long-handled vacuum-cleaner nozzle to the input hose with a section of flexible vacuum-cleaner hose. (Be sure that the nozzle is equipped with a brush; otherwise it will stick to the bottom of the pool.) Keep the nozzle and hoses under water while connecting the cleaner so as not to lose pump prime.

Before using the filter, prime the pump by filling the input hose and then turn on the motor. Next, connect the skimmer to the input hose, being careful not to lose prime, and feed about 4½ oz. of diatomite into the skimmer. At first, the pump should push about 600 gal. per hr. through the filter. Flow rate can be checked by letting the outlet hose run into a bucket of known size and counting the number of seconds it takes to fill it. When the flow rate decreases to about 200 gal. per hr., it's time to take the filter apart and clean it. Normally, you can clean the bag by rinsing it in cold water, but occasionally it should be given a good washing in hot soapy water. The small centrifugal pump described here can be obtained from the Labawco Pump Co., Belle Mead, N.J.

The finish really does it

BY W. CLYDE LAMMEY

Slap-dash finishing has ruined many a good piece of cabinet work. Here's how to schedule sanding and finishing procedures to produce a "factory" job

Many craftsmen like the finishes that come in spray cans, especially opaque finishing materials, but others stick by the conventional equipment for spray application. Both are fast and economical

■ THAT'S RIGHT! THE FINISH really does it. But the finish can be no better than the surface over which it is applied.

You've spent hours of fun dreaming up a shop project of your very own, selected the best woods the market affords, lavished weeks, maybe months of spare time on joinery that matches that of the professionals.

Now all that's left to do is the finishing, and time is wasting.

It's at this point that one must guard against any tendency to hurry the job—skimp a little here and there, yield to that pressing urge to slap on a finish so you can see at last what the job is going to look like.

If you examine your project closely you may see a few sanding marks here and there, planer marks still showing, sharp edges and corners, a roughness in places.

These defects will show under any transparent finishing materials, even under some opaque finishes. You can't finish a sharp corner; the finish won't stay on it. You can't conceal those ripply planer marks with half a dozen top coats, and visible sanding scratches left by coarser grades of abrasives are not the mark of a master craftsman.

Photo courtesy W. P. Fuller & Co.

Every good finishing job begins with thorough sanding. Start with a coarse abrasive and finish with
extra fine when you're sanding by hand

On open-grain woods, such as oak or walnut, sand
with the grain or at a slight angle to it. All marks
of previous sandings must be removed as you go

Photo courtesy Black & Decker

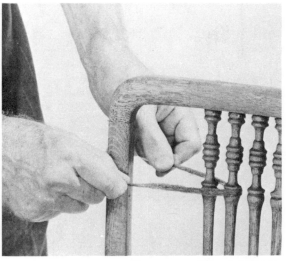

Photo courtesy Wilson-Imperial Co.

Power-driven pad sanders work nicely for finish sanding with fine abrasives. On open-grain woods sand
at a slight angle to the grain; others with the grain

When you can't sand use a "ribbon" of steel wool to
smooth turnings and other irregular surfaces. Use
wool from coarse to fine

Usually it takes only a few minutes more.
You'll be secretly if not openly admiring your
own special project and you'll be looking at it
for a long time to come, so instead of putting
up with those little irritating defects let's take
a few minutes more and produce surfaces that
will take a top-rate finish.

Usually this means sanding and more sanding,
a little more here, a touch or two there, a
delicate rounding of exposed edges—until both
surface and edge feels really s-m-o-o-t-h to the
tip of your finger.

If you're working with a wood having oblique
graining—that is, grain that meets the surface
at an angle—brush off the dust frequently and
examine the surface closely in good light. The
mill planer will often chip such surfaces slightly
here and there leaving tiny, wedge-shaped holes
that are difficult to see even after a careful dust-

ing. But you must catch them if the surface is
to take that perfect finish.

You also have to be especially careful not to
"sand in" ridges and valleys. The best check
for these defects is the sensitive tip of your
finger rubbed lightly across the surface at nearly
right angles to the direction of sanding. Just
keep a running check with that fingertip while
sanding any large, flat surface.

If you're using a portable belt sander be
watchful to prevent the machine from tilting
even slightly; and don't permit it to stop on the
surface for more than the instant it takes to
reverse its direction at the end of a stroke. Keep
it moving uniformly with the grain or, on some
open-grained woods, at a slight angle.

Don't bear down on a belt sander; as a rule
the weight of the unit is sufficient to keep the
abrasive cutting at maximum.

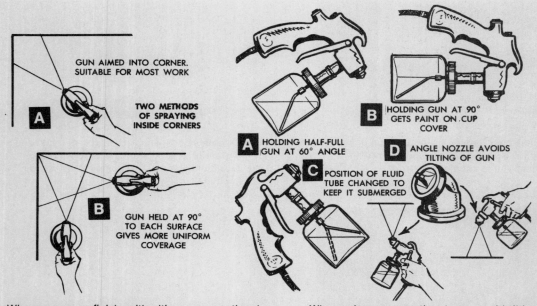

GUN AIMED INTO CORNER. SUITABLE FOR MOST WORK

A TWO METHODS OF SPRAYING INSIDE CORNERS

B GUN HELD AT 90° TO EACH SURFACE GIVES MORE UNIFORM COVERAGE

B HOLDING GUN AT 90° GETS PAINT ON CUP COVER

A HOLDING HALF-FULL GUN AT 60° ANGLE

D ANGLE NOZZLE AVOIDS TILTING OF GUN

C POSITION OF FLUID TUBE CHANGED TO KEEP IT SUBMERGED

When you spray-finish, with either a conventional gun or spray can, hit the inside corners first, using all three positions for uniform application

When using a conventional gun, avoid tilting more than 50–60 deg. Or change angle of the nozzle for horizontal or overhead surfaces

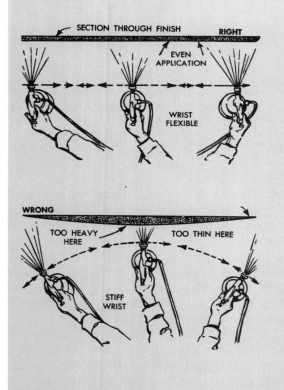

SECTION THROUGH FINISH | RIGHT

EVEN APPLICATION

WRIST FLEXIBLE

WRONG

TOO HEAVY HERE | TOO THIN HERE

STIFF WRIST

The "right" and "wrong" of spray-finishing a surface. Hold gun always at a uniform distance from the surface. If the stroke is curved (without flexing wrist) finish will "pile up" at center

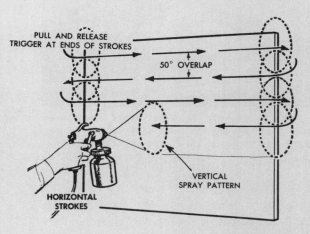

PULL AND RELEASE TRIGGER AT ENDS OF STROKES

50° OVERLAP

VERTICAL SPRAY PATTERN

HORIZONTAL STROKES

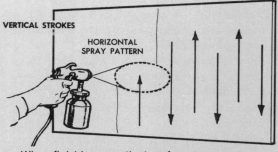

VERTICAL STROKES

HORIZONTAL SPRAY PATTERN

When finishing a vertical surface you can use an up-and-down stroke, but usually the horizontal stroke is best. Keep the distance uniform, pull and release the trigger at ends of the strokes

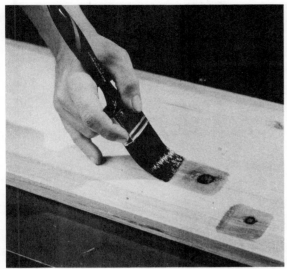

When finishing knotty pine or other knotty woods it's best to seal knots with a thin coat of white shellac to prevent undue absorption or "bleeding"

If the brush sheds bristles (and all brushes do), be sure to flick off the loose bristles that otherwise will adhere to the finished surface

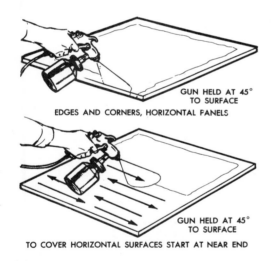

GUN HELD AT 45°
TO SURFACE

EDGES AND CORNERS, HORIZONTAL PANELS

GUN HELD AT 45°
TO SURFACE

TO COVER HORIZONTAL SURFACES START AT NEAR END

When spray-finishing a horizontal surface hit the edges and corners first. Finish with horizontal strokes, triggering the gun at each edge

When sanding by hand or power you downgrade the abrasive (the numbers go up from coarse to fine) as you go. Sanding by hand you'll likely find it best to start with the coarse (No. 1 or No. 2) grade to remove any surface irregularities quickly. Then you go to, say 4–0, then 6–0 and finally to the 8–0 grade. After each sanding, dust and examine the surface to see that all marks of the coarser abrasive have been removed. The 8–0 grade leaves a glass-smooth surface.

If you're sanding with a portable power unit and the wood is in fairly good condition to begin with, you generally can start with a medium-grade abrasive. No need to use the coarse grade unless it is necessary to reduce marked irregularities of the surface. But when you change from a coarser abrasive to a finer grade, always dust the surface and examine it to see that all sanding marks of the preceding grade have been entirely removed.

Now that you have a satisfactory surface for finishing, keep in mind that any clear finishing material will darken the wood somewhat by changing its light-reflecting properties. By dampening the smoothed surface of a piece of scrap from the project you can get a good idea how the wood will look when finished in its natural color.

apply sealer

Although some of the new finishing materials act as a sealer and top coat, it's often advisable to apply a sealer as the initial coat if the wood is of a soft, absorptive texture. Some finishing materials are supplied as a separate sealer, or base coating, and a recommended top coating. Some are compounded to "build" on the surface, such as the natural varnishes and various synthetic clear finishes. Others are combinations of special oils designed to penetrate deep into the wood. These are applied to bare wood with no top coating.

Before you set up a finishing schedule determine whether or not you will use stain or finish

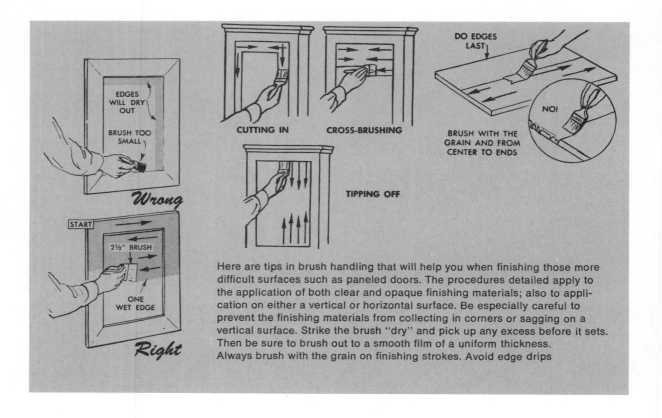

CUTTING IN   CROSS-BRUSHING

DO EDGES LAST

BRUSH WITH THE GRAIN AND FROM CENTER TO ENDS

NO!

TIPPING OFF

EDGES WILL DRY OUT

BRUSH TOO SMALL

Wrong

START

2½" BRUSH

ONE WET EDGE

Right

Here are tips in brush handling that will help you when finishing those more difficult surfaces such as paneled doors. The procedures detailed apply to the application of both clear and opaque finishing materials; also to application on either a vertical or horizontal surface. Be especially careful to prevent the finishing materials from collecting in corners or sagging on a vertical surface. Strike the brush "dry" and pick up any excess before it sets. Then be sure to brush out to a smooth film of a uniform thickness. Always brush with the grain on finishing strokes. Avoid edge drips

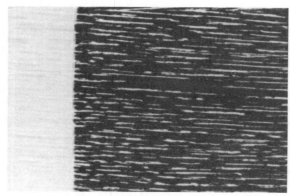

One novel way of finishing an open-grain wood is to coat sanded surfaces with a black opaque finish, then fill the grain with a white filler

Some craftsmen use a coarse, lintless fabric for applying wiping stains. In many instances this method gives better control of the color depth

in the natural color. If staining seems desirable, run several test panels of stain colors to check color range and tonal depth, using smoothed scrap from the project. Allow the stained panels to dry so you see the true colors.

Artist's color will mix with most sealers, and combining the two usually makes a good stain-sealer combination. The sealer serves as the penetrating vehicle to carry the stain into the wood. Or, use the prepared non-grain-raising stains if you prefer and follow with a sealer as a base coat.

On open-grained woods such as oak and walnut you can use the top coats as the filler, thus eliminating a separate filler entirely. The process is commonly used in hand-finishing gun-stocks but can be applied to other small projects as well, especially where the wood is to be finished in the natural color or by light staining. It's done by repeat applications of top coat and a sanding between coats across the grain. The procedure is calculated to remove nearly all the coating each time, leaving only the pores of the wood filled. After the finish "builds" to a

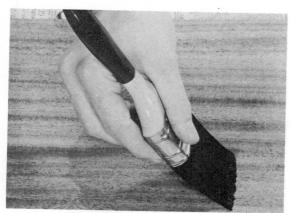

Photo courtesy Grand Rapids Varnish Corp.

Hold your finishing brush like this and don't bear down on it unduly. Held in this way, a brush releases its load in a smooth, uniform film

Load your brush uniformly when applying an opaque finish. Lay the stuff on with a sweeping, one-way stroke, then come back over it lightly

smooth surface it is rubbed down with either very fine steel wool or a prepared rubbing compound.

Exploiting the beauty of the grain is one of the main reasons for finishing finer cabinet woods in their natural colors or with light staining. So, assuming that you are to finish a close-grained wood such as birch, maple or cherry, you might set up a finishing schedule something like this:

● Brush or spray a non-grain-raising (commercially prepared) stain of desired color and wipe lightly if necessary to attain desired tone. Allow to dry at least 30 min.

● Brush or spray a sealer. (Lacquer or white shellac can also be used if thinned to proper consistency). Allow ample drying time.

● Smooth lightly with 6 or 8–0 abrasive; dust off.

● If sealer shows any uneven absorption, apply a second coat, sand and dust as before.

● Spray or brush two top coats, sanding lightly between the first and second applications. Allow to dry thoroughly.

● Rub to a satiny finish with fine steel wool (3–0 or finer), pumice-stone paste or a rubbing compound.

This is a simple, basic finishing schedule which may be altered for any special condition. For example, you can substitute what is known as a "sanding sealer" for regular sealer, lacquer or white shellac. This dries within an hour or so to a sanding surface. Also as a finishing top coat you can substitute a rubbed-effect varnish or lacquer. This product dries to a soft, satiny sheen and requires no rub-down if protected from dust while drying.

For an open-grain wood such as walnut, oak or mahogany a basic schedule might be set up as follows:

● Brush or spray a stain of desired color and allow to dry.

● Brush or spray a thinned "wash" coat of white shellac or lacquer.

● Sand very lightly with fine abrasive. Dust.

● Tint a prepared filler slightly darker than the stain, thin to brushing consistency and lay onto the surface with one-way strokes of the brush. Allow to dry flat (about 15 min.) then rub off across the grain with a coarse fabric.

● Sand lightly and dust.

● Brush or spray sanding sealer (you can use regular sealer but wipe off any excess after 10 to 15 min.).

● Sand the sealer satin-smooth to remove any dust flecks and any tiny air bubbles. Dust off.

● Brush or spray two coats of finish of your choice—lacquer, synthetic or natural varnish.

● Sand very lightly, then rub satin-smooth with a rubbing compound or 4–0 steel wool.

Always make sure the preceding coat of any finishing material is thoroughly dry before applying a succeeding coat.

You'll get a better job by spraying any of the materials except filler. Usually a suitable sprayer can be rented from your paint dealer. Where possible tip the piece so that the wet material is applied on a horizontal surface. Where you must apply on a vertical surface take special care to prevent sags and drips at the edges.

See also: abrasives; antique finishes; finishes, non-skid; finishes, removing; finishes, urethane; finishes, wood; floor finishing; refinishing; staining, wood.

Clean the floor thoroughly, using sandpaper where necessary. Then catalyze the polyester resin and pour it evenly over the floor. A pint of resin will cover most small-boat floors

Spread resin carefully with a piece of cardboard, filling all cracks and covering corners. Work quickly, since resin will begin to set and become more difficult to distribute

Non-slip floor for your boat

BY V. LEE OERTLE

Why take a chance on a tumble? This low-cost safety finish is slip-proof, even when wet

When resin becomes tacky, scatter sand evenly on floor. You can make either a shaker-type dispenser from a tin can or punch holes in a plastic bag. Brush out excess sand when dry

■ ANY FISHERMAN or duck hunter realizes the impossibility of keeping a small boat floor dry. And a slippery boat floor is like an accident waiting to happen.

Commercial non-skid finishes do a fine job of taking the slip out of a wet floor, but few sportsmen would want to use these relatively expensive products on a knock-around fishing boat which may double as a duck blind. However, here's a low-cost non-skid finish that you shouldn't hesitate to use anywhere, even on small floats or docks.

Made by sprinkling screened sand over tacky polyester resin, it provides a rough surface texture that won't become slippery when wet. And in addition, it protects the floor from wear.

For the best surface use No. 30 crystal sand, which may be obtained at any building supply house. If this isn't available, any common fine-screened sand may be substituted. Before applying it, make sure that the resin is tacky, otherwise the sand will simply settle down into the resin instead of remaining on the surface.

See also: abrasives; boat repair; deck, boat; finishes, furniture; finishes, removing; finishes, urethane; finishes, wood; floor finishing; refinishing; staining, wood.

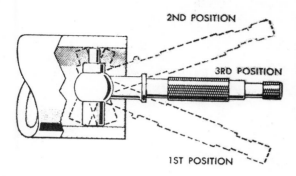

Measuring inside diameters to thousandths of an inch can be tricky with a telescoping gauge—especially if the compression spring is weakened through long use. For greater precision, place the gauge in the tube or hole with its handle at an angle to the axis (1st position, above). After the gauge expands, snug the knurled ring, rock the handle upward past the axis and bring it back down.

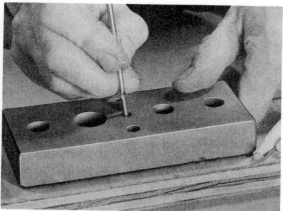

A ball-point pen cartridge is handy for marking holes of small diameter in thick blocks where a pencil won't fit. The cartridge is slender enough to make nearly a full-size tracing of a hole as small as ¼-in. dia. The cartridge may be fitted with a dowel handle to make it more comfortable to hold.

A 12-compartment muffin tin serves both as a sorting and storage tray for nuts, bolts and small parts. A lid of ⅛-in. hardboard is hinged to one long edge; light chain holds it upright. For quicker selection or sorting, a sample from each corresponding bin can be glued to a label stuck to the underside of the lid. Or, if it's a bolt, turn it through to protrude slightly and trim it flush on top.

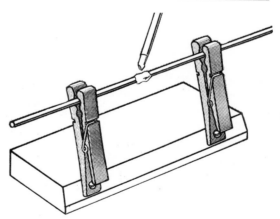

Trying to keep two pieces of wire or light rod in perfect alignment while manipulating solder and a soldering iron can be pretty frustrating. Fortunately, there's an easy way to handle this tricky job. A simple jig can be made by screwing two spring-type clothespins to the beveled edge of a block of scrap wood. The jig holds the work firmly in the desired position and lets you concentrate on applying the solder.

Strip away the old finish

BY W. CLYDE LAMMEY

It looks like a lot of work
but when you get into it
stripping an antique or
any old piece can be fun

Photo courtesy Stanley Electric Tools
When preserving the age color of old wood is of no importance
grab a belt sander and sand through the old finish to the bare wood

■ So YOU'RE GOING to refinish that old, beat-up chest of drawers. The wood in it is as good as ever, with a fascinatingly beautiful grain, but the finish looks terrible.

Now that you've made up your mind let there be no turning back. First step is to remove the hardware and save every jot of it. Authentic replacement copies of old brasses are expensive, so save everything that's polishable and reuseable.

What you do from here on depends largely on what you've visualized as the desired result. If you're thinking of a complete renewal job, using a transparent or opaque finish, that's one thing. But if the piece is very old and it's desirable to preserve the age color (patina to purists) that fine woods acquire only by natural aging, that's something else.

In either case the first step in actual stripping is a thorough scrubbing with mild soapsuds. This will get rid of most, if not all, the accumulated grime and permit a remover to "cut" faster, or a sander to work more efficiently.

Assuming that the piece stands fairly solid on

Often a disc sander can be used to advantage but be careful not to cut all the way through and leave deep swirl marks on the bare wood

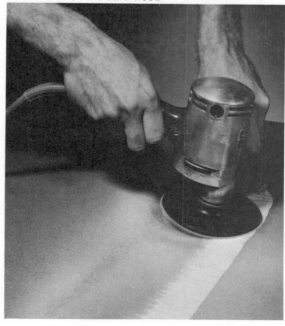

Use a "pick" stick, made by pointing the ends of a short length of dowel, to scrape residue from beads, flutes and other shapes a brush won't reach

A square cut from burlap often proves to be just the thing for cleaning softened finish from turnings. Use the fabric dry. Notice the rubber gloves

Medium steel wool glued to a strip of heavy fabric is especially helpful when cleaning softened-finish residues from small-diameter rounds

A wrapping of steel wool on one end of your pick stick will clean those parts of carvings a scrubbing brush won't reach handily

its legs without any unusually rickety joints and that you want to remove the old finish but not the patina, you flow on a chemical remover of the wash-off type, using a one-way stroke of the brush. Lay the stuff on quickly and as uniformly as possible and don't brush back over it. Cover only a small area at a time, say about 2 sq. ft., or perhaps a medium sized drawer front.

Caution: Fumes from chemical removers are toxic and also irritating to the bare skin. If possible do the work out of doors or place a fan to exhaust the fumes from a closed room. Wear rubber gloves and *protect your eyes from spatters.*

Have clean, cold water and a clean cloth at hand. Wait only a few minutes, then wipe the remover off a small area with the wetted cloth and note the "cut" of the chemical closely. If the finish has been softened all the way down to the wood, wash it off the whole treated area quickly and wipe the surface dry. If not, wait only a minute or so longer and check again.

The purpose of this repeat check is to make sure the remover cuts the finish only through to the wood, no farther, as continued action of the chemical may tend to lighten the age color of some woods. After one or more repeat checks you'll know the time it takes the remover to cut through that particular finish, whether it be varnish or paint, or both.

Then you proceed in a more or less regular fashion, applying remover, waiting a given interval and then washing off. Keep the wash-off

Before stripping drawer fronts remove the hardware and if it's old save every useable piece. Authentic replacement brasses are expensive

Raise a shallow dent by wetting a square of fabric, folding to several thicknesses and heating with an electric household iron set at low heat

Spills that cause discolorations don't always yield to a solvent. You may have to go to a bleach and then refinish the "new" wood to match the old

Photo courtesy Behr-Manning Company

Some refinishers prefer to remove old finishes with an abrasive "floated" in a linseed oil-turpentine mixture. Use coarse steel wool or sandpaper

Want to see how it will look finished natural color? Spray a small area with clear finish. Wipe off with solvent after the finish has served the purpose

cloth rinsed well and wet the softened finish only sufficiently to make removal easy. Avoid wetting the wood more than necessary and always wipe it dry after each wetting to remove softened finish.

If there are carvings or other detailed construction use a wetted scrub brush to remove the softened finish. In corners that the brush won't reach use a "pick" stick, made by sharpening a length of ¼-in. dowel to a point.

Once all the old finish has been removed you may notice a few small areas where the chemical has not cut entirely through to the wood. Touch these lightly with the chemical and wash off.

Now, after the piece is thoroughly dry, comes

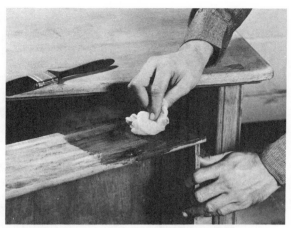

To check the color of a stain on old wood you can sometimes use the side of a drawer as a test panel. Brush on, then wipe off to desired tone

Photo courtesy Behr-Manning Company

To get remover quickly onto a large, flat surface pour it directly from the can onto the surface and then spread to a uniform film with a brush

Photo courtesy Grand Rapids Varnish Corp.

Sanding out imperfections may destroy age color. By mixing a wiping stain with artist's color you can usually blend "new" into old nicely

the tricky step. All surfaces must be sanded *very lightly* with a fine abrasive to smooth any roughness (raised grain) that may have resulted from wetting. In some instances, fine steel wool (3-0 or finer) will best serve this purpose. Also the new product known as Scotch-brite is very good for such light abrading.

Carvings and other detail can be smoothed with a brush having fine metal bristles. A suede shoe brush usually is just the thing.

Ordinarily the piece is now ready for the new finish. If the old wood turns out to be a fairly uniform color and all surfaces seem smooth to the touch, you may not need a sealer at all. As a

rule you can use one of the newer two-part transparent finishes consisting of a base coat and a following top coat. Sand the base coat very lightly and smooth the top coat with fine steel wool (3-0 or finer) to dull the semi-gloss and make the finish appear "old." For a refinish job in the natural color this simple treatment usually does it, especially on such close-grained native woods as birch, maple and black cherry, also on the figured mahoganies where it is particularly desirable to preserve the aged straw color.

On some old pieces you may turn up an age color that varies quite noticeably. Of course, if this variation in tone is pleasing to your eye

When preparing an old piece for refinishing it's the little things that count. Here touch-up sanding is being done on an old piece

then let it ride as is. But if you feel the color needs uniforming then mix artist's oil color with a sealer such as that known as Firzite Deep Finish and thin according to instructions on the container. Match the color of this sealer-stain combination to the darker areas of the wood and try on a small area. If the stain brings the color to the desired tone, then stain all those surfaces showing a marked variation. If not, add color, or thin the mixture and test again. Once the color suits your eye allow the sealer-stain to set until the surface dulls; then wipe off the excess and allow to dry 24 hrs. or more.

raising dents

Generally you can raise shallow dents—before any finish is applied—by folding a dampened cloth to several thicknesses, placing over the dent and heating with a household iron. Deeper dents can be filled with colored stick shellac or you can just leave 'em as an age mark.

A scratch is something else. If the scratch is in the old finish only it will, of course, be no problem. But if the "scratcher" cut into the wood you do one of three things: leave it as is, fill with stick shellac or sand out entirely. If you choose the latter step you'll have to stain the "new" wood in the sanded area to match the old.

If the sanding must cut rather deeply then it may be best to sand off the whole panel, or top, or whatever surface is involved and refinish the whole. This is a bit tricky but it can be done by using artist's colors, thinning with pure turpentine and adding a few drops of dryer.

Old stains don't always yield readily to common solvents. Usually such stains are on tops and you either sand them out or try bleaching the wood with a chemical bleach. Using either method you generally have to go all the way and then refinish the entire top or whatever part may be involved.

Removing old finish by sanding (when preservation of the age color is of no importance) is quite simple. Just grab your portable belt sander (or rent one from your paint dealer) put on a coarse abrasive belt with spaced grains and go right down through the old finish to the bare wood. Then sand with belts from medium through the fine grades until you get a smooth surface with no abrasive marks showing from previous sandings.

stripping carvings

Where there are carvings or other structural detail you resort to the remover followed by a vigorous brushing to get down to bare wood. A medium wire wheel fitted with an adapter and driven by a portable electric drill usually makes short work of removing residues of old finish and smoothing the carvings and other detail preparatory to refinishing. On some work you can use a sanding disc to advantage but you have to be careful to prevent the disc from leaving deep swirl marks on the bared wood.

Intricately molded edges of tops, stiles and some other parts often present a problem; here refinishers often resort to scraping to bare the wood after removing the old finish with a chemical remover.

Turnings are usually easier to strip than carvings or moldings. After using the chemical remover follow with a thorough brushing with either a stiff-bristle scrub brush or a medium wire wheel. This treatment usually cleans the average turning ready for refinishing. Fill any dents, scratches or gouges with stick shellac and sand smooth.

Do any necessary repairing or replacing of parts after stripping the old finish and before applying the new.

See also: abrasives; antique finishes; finishes, furniture; finishes, non-skid; finishes, urethane; finishes, wood; refinishing; staining, wood.

A portable leaf burner that offers the ultimate in lawn protection is a wire trash burner placed in a wheelbarrow. The wheelbarrow catches all of the ashes and does away with those ugly burned areas.

Here's a labor saver to pass along to your wife that really saves time when she is whipping cream. A pinch of salt added to the cream before whipping will strengthen the fat cells and make them more elastic. This makes the cream stiffen much more quickly.

Folding money—or a check—shouldn't be mailed if it will show when the envelope is held to the light. Always fold it in carbon paper placed face down on lightweight backing paper.

Build this simple lazy susan for your wife's spice cans. It's just a tin plate with a nail through the center and two washers underneath for easy spinning.

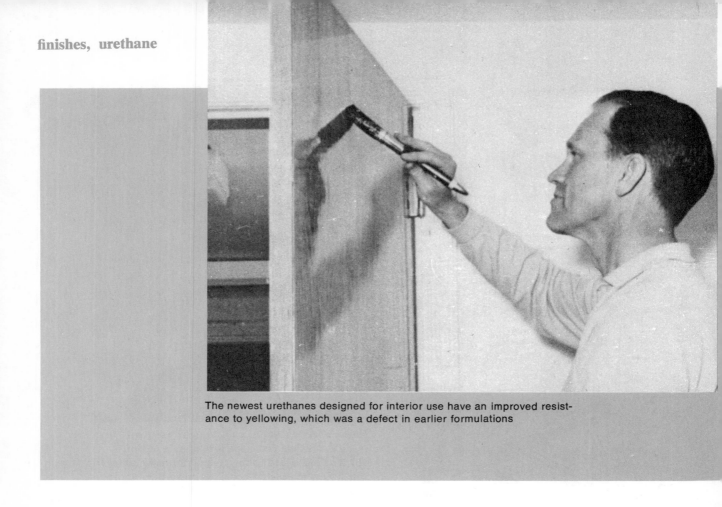

The newest urethanes designed for interior use have an improved resistance to yellowing, which was a defect in earlier formulations

Those magic urethanes

BY MERLE E. DOWD

They'll give you better than double wear and cut your maintenance in half

■ MODERN CHEMISTRY has made another giant step forward in the "do it once and forget it" school of maintenance.

Lumped under the name "urethanes," this versatile family of finishes, coatings and sealants seems almost too good to be true. They wear longer on floors, resist sun and weather on your boat, and resist chemical attack (even rust and corrosion) far better than most other coatings. Urethane finishes can be hard enough to roller skate on, or flexible enough to stretch like rubber. But these specialty finishes aren't all alike.

Some urethanes come in two parts and must be mixed before application. Others come in a single can and look like regular varnish or a high-grade enamel. Two-part urethane sealants outperform both putty and caulking and can be gunned into place.

Here's just one example of urethane "magic" from my own personal experience. A cork floor in our kitchen was driving my wife wild. She loved the cork because it was easy on the feet, and glasses didn't break nearly as often when dropped on it. But keeping the floor clean and preventing wear at high traffic spots were taking too much time. The best paste wax lasted about four weeks in winter and two in summer.

A three-coat application of PRC 470 polyurethane cured this maintenance headache. It's a two-part coating that's tough enough to stand up under constant wear, yet flexible enough to bond to the resilient cork tile in our kitchen.

Before application most of the old wax was washed off with a remover. A floor sander then smoothed the wear spots and removed the last remnants of wax.

For first and second coats, a 1:1 mixture of Parts A and B was thinned with 50 percent special thinner (PRC Solvent No. 6)—that is, two parts 470 mixed to one part solvent. The first

After checking to make sure that the old finish won't lift, roughen it before applying the urethane

Flow the urethane on smoothly over the roughened surface. Apply at least two coats, preferably three

coat was brushed on with a full, flowing action; half an hour later, the second coat was applied.

About 4 hrs. later, a third full coat of PRC 470, cut with about 25 percent solvent, was brushed on evenly. For a glossy finish, the third coat could be applied full strength.

The solvent may be irritating to breathe, particularly if applied with a spray gun. Therefore, a brush or lambswool applicator is recommended. Where spraying is desirable, it's best to wear a mask.

During any application provide ventilation with a fan to prevent a build-up of solvent vapor. To avoid skin contact, wear gloves during application. Clean the brush or spray gun in methyl-ethyl ketone (MEK) or PRC Solvent No. 5.

PRC 470 cures in two ways, by chemical reaction between the two parts and by absorption of water from the air. Once applied, the coating cures tack-free in four hours at 75 deg. and 50 percent humidity, but it requires 72 hrs. for full curing under the same conditions; drier and cooler air will extend the curing time. However, the surface can be walked on as soon as it is tack-free.

Cork is only one floor covering for which

urethane finishes are adapted. Since PRC 470 is clear, two coats (mixed with 25 percent solvent) will seal an unglazed ceramic tile surface. Similar seal coats can be applied to slate, porous mica or other slab-stone floors. Once such floors are sealed, regular waxing can be stopped.

One-part wood floor finishes are simpler to use, yet still keep floors new looking longer than ordinary varnishes, lacquers or penetrating finishes. Gym floors, for example, are usually hard maple and have to be refinished at least once a year. However, with two coats of urethane floor varnish, refinishing is required only once every two years.

One-part wood floor finishes for home use are no more difficult to use than ordinary floor finishes. Since urethane finishes are oil-thinned, mineral spirits can be used to clean brushes. As might be expected, however, simple one-part finishes will not perform as well as two-part catalyzed finishes where abrasion resistance must be combined with flexibility, as on the cork floor. One-part floor finishes can also be used on concrete or stone interior floors.

Abrasion resistance tests indicate that urethane floor finishes have at least double the life of the

The clear marine urethane finish will last up to six times as long as most of the common spar varnishes now in use

Special urethane floor finishes have extra abrasion resistance and last twice as long as standard floor varnishes

best tung or phenolic-base varnish. A number of paint manufacturers market pigmented urethane floor finishes, as well as clear. The addition of a slight amount of pigment makes a varnish stain that both colors and protects the floor at the same time. You can either buy—or mix yourself —simulated mahogany, oak, cherry and light walnut stains.

For best results on your floor, always select a urethane finish specifically designed for floors. While many all-purpose urethane varnishes can be used for floors, added abrasion resistance is usually built into floor varnishes or porch and deck paints.

Urethane finishes generally adhere to new surfaces without trouble, though previously coated surfaces may require special attention. Shellac, lacquer and some paints may prevent a good bond. Some urethane finishes will lift lacquer sealers, while others won't affect existing finishes. Waxes, particularly those containing any proportion of silicone resins, will prevent urethane finishes from bonding.

When in doubt about a previously coated surface, try a patch test in an inconspicuous corner. If the undersurface doesn't wrinkle or soften, the urethane finish will adhere. If there is any question, however, remove the old finish completely.

Any surface to be coated should be dry and free of dust. Roughen glossy undercoats by sanding before applying the first coat of urethane, then sand each coat lightly to provide "teeth" for the next coat.

Concrete floors should be etched with full-strength vinegar or a 5-percent solution of muriatic acid before applying urethane finish. Rinse the floor down well and allow it to dry before you begin applying the urethane.

Urethane finishes sometimes fail by "sheeting" or peeling. This usually results from a lack of bonding to a previously coated surface. Peeling can be prevented by preparing the surface.

Natural-finish wood sidings of cedar, redwood, mahogany and cypress have required annual finishing because weather causes rapid deterioration of ordinary varnishes and sealers. Weathering is hastened by the naturally oily character of some woods, and the wood itself turns black or darkens with age.

The difficulty and expense of maintaining natural wood sidings have discouraged many owners from enjoying the warm beauty of natural wood siding. Urethane varnishes, however, withstand two to four years of exposure to the elements between coatings. Slightly pigmented varnish stains resist ultraviolet radiation from the sun even more than clear finishes, and at least one clear exterior finish includes an ultraviolet shield that extends the recoating interval.

One of the primary reasons for the excellent weathering characteristics of urethane finishes is their extremely low water-vapor permeability. Since urethane finishes do not "breathe," extra care should be taken to keep water from seeping back of finished surfaces or from condensing inside walls. When interior walls are not completely protected by a built-in vapor barrier, two coats of a urethane finish will reduce water-vapor penetration through the wall. For maximum adhesion on exterior walls, roughen any glossy surfaces and sand lightly between coats. For porous new wood, use three coats. Two coats will ordinarily protect dense woods and prevent "sheeting."

Urethane finishes are practically made to order for boats. The combination of humidity, sun and saltwater provides the utmost test of a finish's durability. Many spar varnishes, for example, begin to turn white and chip after only six months' exposure. Ordinary marine paints need to be freshened about once a year, and every few years the accumulated coats must be stripped off down to the bare wood.

Urethane clear finishes have remained in good condition and retained their bright gloss for up to three years. Pigmented urethane marine finishes, however, have not yet proved quite so successful. Urethane paints tend to lose their gloss after about six months' exposure to the weather. However, the slight chalk or haze that reduces the gloss has little effect on the durability of the finish coat.

no-mix urethanes

Most of the readily available urethane marine finishes are packaged as one-can materials. Both clear and pigmented marine finishes are available in two-part formulations for added durability, but the added cost and more difficult application of the two-part materials do not usually warrant their use on pleasure boats. These are designed primarily for industrial marine application, where extremely heavy-duty service is important.

Industrial applications have demonstrated the durability of urethane paints under other extreme conditions. In one test, urethane and alkyd finishes were applied side by side on a blast furnace. After several months the alkyd coatings were completely gone. The urethane paints were still tight though they had lost much of their gloss. Highly corrosive hot fumes of hydrogen sulfide and hydrochloric acid have failed to penetrate urethane coatings in chemical plants. Urethane coatings' resistance to abrasion and corrosion was proved on steel roll-up doors where metal rubs metal as the door moves up or down. Where ordinary finishes were rubbed off in a month, urethane paint was still preventing rust after six months.

Metal surfaces subject to corrosion can be protected by cleaning the surface and applying a wash primer of zinc chromate of red-lead rust sealers. This slows down any corrosion under the top coats. Apply a polyurethane primer for additional corrosion protection and aid in bonding the final coats of polyurethane. Two top coats of a polyurethane pigmented paint will keep out weather and corrosive gases. Steel, aluminum or other metals can be protected with this build-up of primer and top coats. Where a natural appearance is desired, use a clear urethane finish to keep metal bright. For applications where corrosion is less severe, pigmented urethane finishes can be used without primers.

the sealant story

Flexible sealants made from polyurethane rubber are available for marine caulking and bedding, and for sealing joints between dissimilar materials like wood and brick or concrete around your home. These sealants perform much like synthetic polysulfide sealants, but are more difficult to use since they are two-part mixtures with a limited pot life.

Once cured, polyurethane sealants are highly resistant to oils and grease. The U.S. Navy uses them for caulking the joints between teak planks on aircraft carrier decks. At least two brands are available—PRC Rubber Caulk 3000 and Pro-Seal 962. Both are two-part mixtures and require a primer for best performance as caulk in wood or porous masonry joints. Detailed instructions for surface preparation, priming and application may be obtained with the materials. Polyurethane rubber caulk generally costs less than the one-part polysulfide rubber sealants.

Whenever shopping for urethane finishes, *check the label.* Some materials advertised as "urethane" or "plastic" finishes actually contain only a small percentage of a urethane, polyurethane or diisocyanate resin. If you want the best urethane finish, compare the quantity of urethane resin in one product with another—the more urethane the better.

See also: abrasives; antique finishes; finishes, furniture; finishes, non-skid; finishes, removing; finishes, wood; floor finishing; refinishing; staining, wood.

Schedule those finishing jobs

BY ARTHUR M. MIKESELL

Lacking a schedule, you may skip one important step and spoil what might have been a good finish on that pet project

■ SCHEDULING A FINISHING procedure pays off. You checkmark each step as it's carried out; you keep track of drying time; you know at any point in the procedure what is on the wood and what is yet to be applied. Here are sample schedules for the common woods:

BASIC SCHEDULES

Open-Grain Woods, darker tones—brush or spray application, single-stain system:

1. Brush or spray NGR (non-grain-raising) stain of desired color. Dry 20 to 30 min.
2. Brush or spray wash coat of lacquer or white shellac. Dry 10 min.
3. Sand with 6–0 garnet abrasive; dry and dust.
4. Fill with paste wood filler of desired color. Dry according to instructions on container.
5. Brush or spray wet coat of sanding sealer. Dry 1 hr.
6. Sand with 6–0 garnet; dry and dust.

7. Apply second sealer coat, sand as before.
8. Spray two coats clear lacquer or brush one coat of varnish. Lacquer should dry overnight; varnish 24 to 48 hrs. before rubbing.
9. Rub to satin-smooth surface with rubbing compound applied with burlap or thick felt pad. Note: Step No. 9 can be eliminated by using final coat of rubbed-effect varnish or lacquer. Step No. 2 also can be omitted. Where the term "varnish" is used it applies to both natural and synthetic clear finishes. Follow application instructions on container.

Open-Grain Woods, double-stain system:

1. Brush or spray NGR stain. Dry 20–30 min.
2. Fill with paste wood filler. Dry 24 hrs.
3. Apply sanding sealer. Dry 1 hr.
4. Sand with 6–0 garnet. Dust.
5. Apply second coat of sealer. Dry and sand.
6. Brush wet coat of pigmented wiping stain, the color a shade darker than NGR used. Wipe with soft, lintless cloth after 2 to 10 min. Continue wiping until desired color shows.
7. Apply top coats of varnish or lacquer.
Note: Double-staining is often used on off-color woods, also for shading and antiqued effects. Such toning also can be done by spraying a special shading stain. Use wiping stain for brush application.

Close-Grain Woods, lacquer system:

1. Apply NGR stain (brush or spray).
2. Spray sanding sealer. Dry 1 hr.
3. Sand with 6–0 garnet. Dry and dust.
4. Apply (spray or brush) two to three coats of clear-gloss lacquer, sanding between coats with 6–0 garnet. Dry overnight or longer.
5. Rub to satin surface. See rubbing schedules.

Close-Grain Woods, double-stain system:

1. Brush NGR stain. Dry 30 min. to 1 hr. Sand lightly with 6–0 garnet.
2. Brush pigmented wiping stain of same or slightly darker color. Dry 1 hr. or longer.
3. Brush (or spray) sanding sealer. Dry 1 hr.
4. Sand with 6–0 garnet. Dry and dust.
5. Spray (or brush) two coats of lacquer or one coat of varnish.
6. Rub down.
Note: For high quality work 3–4 coats of top material may be used to "build" a heavier finish film for more thorough rubbing to a high-luster.

Close-Grain Woods, spray only, double-stain:

1. Spray a pigmented wiping stain, wipe off

and dry 30 min.

2. Thin same stain, 1 part to 3 parts naphtha. Spray-shade but do not wipe. Dry 30 min.

3. Finish with sealer and top coats.

Note: Although this 3-step procedure is similar to those preceding, notice change in stain and application.

Close-Grain Woods, double-stain system:

1. Brush (or spray) pigmented wiping stain of a desired color. Let dry until it begins to "flat," then wipe to desired tone. Dry 30 min.

2. Brush or spray sanding sealer. Dry 1 hr.

3. Sand with 6-0 garnet. Use 3–0 steel wool, or finer, for any moldings or carvings.

4. A second coat of sealer is optional. If applied, sand as before.

5. Repeat Step No. 1.

6. Apply varnish or lacquer top coats.

Note: This schedule turns out an attractive finish on a variety of close-grained woods such as maple, poplar, birch and pine.

UNIFORMING PROCEDURES

Schedule A, for finishing open and close-grain wood in same piece:

1. Spray or brush NGR stain in desired color. Dry 30 min.

2. Apply paste wood filler to all open-grain wood and to end grain of the close-grain wood. Wipe and allow to dry.

3. Brush (or spray) pigmented wiping stain of a matching color on the close-grain wood only. Dry 30 min.

4. Brush or spray sanding sealer. Dry 1 hr.

5. Sand with 6-0 garnet.

6. Repeat No. 4 and 5.

7. Spray (or brush) pigmented wiping stain over entire piece, wiping and blending (while still wet) until uniformity of color is achieved. Dry 30 min. (An alternate procedure is to spray with diluted wiping stain, or better, with a shading stain to uniform the color. Do not wipe. Dry at least 30 min.

8. Apply finish coats of varnish or lacquer. Note: On some woods in combination as above it is possible to do a quickie job of uniforming with two or more coats of varnish stain, spray-applied, and rubbed to a satin surface.

Schedule B

1. Apply NGR stain to the lighter sapwood only. Wipe with cloth dampened with alcohol to uniform the color. Dry 10 min. or more.

2. Apply NGR stain lightly on darker wood, but heavier on light wood. Dry 30 min. or more.

3. Spray lacquer wash coat over all.

4. Sand lightly with 6-0 garnet. Dust off.

5. Fill open-grain wood with paste wood filler.

6. Reduce same filler, 1 part filler to 2 parts naphtha. Apply to close-grain wood only. Wipe off and allow to dry.

7. Spray (or brush) sanding sealer. Dry 1 hr.

8. Should further color toning seem necessary, spray a shading stain or thinned wiping stain.

9. Apply finishing coats, after preceding stain coats are thoroughly dry.

LIGHT TONES

Coloring System, spray application on selected "white" woods such as birch, poplar, basswood:

1. Spray uniform coat of blond lacquer.

2. Spray two coats of water-white lacquer.

Note: Other colors also can be applied, such as gray, cream, or various shades of green. Deep tans and grays may be used on dark woods.

Coloring System, brush application:

1. Brush blond, platinum or wheat-colored pigmented wiping stain and allow to dry until slightly tacky. Then wipe off with lintless cloth. Dry at least 4 hrs. or overnight.

2. Top-coat with varnish.

Note: As an alternate apply 1 coat of 2-lb. (2-lb. cut) white shellac, sand lightly and follow with paste wax rubbed to a satin sheen. After wood has been colored, almost any top finish can be used. The water-white top coatings are preferable as these retain more nearly the pure tones of the stain.

Stain System, light tones in pastel shades on selected white woods:

1. Spray (or brush) diluted NGR stain in your color choice. Various shades of yellow, orange, and green are attractive. Dry 30 min.

2. Finish as in any of the basic schedules with a sealer and top coats.

Bleach System, open grain woods (attractive light finishes on the darker woods):

1. Mix one part (solution No. 1) of a two-solution commercial bleach with two parts of the No. 2 solution. Apply with a rubber sponge (or a piece cut from sponge rubber). Bleaching action takes about 1 hr. but work should dry at least 12 hrs.

2. Sand lightly with 6-0 garnet and dust.

3. Apply paste wood filler. Wipe and allow to dry overnight.

4. Sand lightly, apply a sealer; dust and dry, then finish with two or more top coats.

Note: Color in this procedure is obtained entirely from the filler. Use a filler designated as "natural" for the lightest tone. Tint natural filler with oil colors for other shades.

Bleach System, alternate method (open-grain wood):

1. Bleach the wood as above.

2. Brush (or spray) NGR stain in pink, light yellow, or light green.

3. Apply wash coat of white shellac. Dry 30 min.

4. Apply filler. Use natural filler or tint to approximate color of stain. Sand lightly.

5. Finish with top coats.

Note: Color in this system is obtained from the stain rather than the filler. Always use a wash coat in this method to prevent darkening due to absorption of oils in the filler.

Bleach System, close-grain woods:

1. Bleach the wood and allow to dry 12 hrs.

2. Sand lightly with 6-0 garnet. Dust.

3. Brush (or spray) wiping stain in wheat, suntan, platinum, etc. Allow to stand until stain begins to flat then wipe clean to the desired tone.

4. Brush (or spray) sanding sealer. Dry 1 hr.

5. Sand with 6-0 garnet and dust.

6. Spray two coats water-white lacquer or brush one or two coats of varnish.

7. Rub to satin finish.

Note: After bleaching, the wood can be finished by following any schedule for close-grain wood.

VARIOUS FINISHING MATERIALS

White Shellac:

1. Brush or spray one coat of 1-lb.-cut shellac. Dry 30 min. and sand with 6-0 garnet.

2. Apply second shellac coat, 2-lb. cut. Dry 3 hrs. and sand lightly.

3. Apply final coat of shellac, 3-lb. cut. Dry 3 hrs. and smooth-sand with 8-0 abrasive, or 3-0 (or finer) steel wool.

Orange Shellac, on open-grain wood:

1. Apply one coat, 3-lb. cut. Dry 1-2 hrs. and sand down to bare wood at slight angle with grain.

2. Apply second coat and sand to bare wood, allowing 3-4 hrs. to dry.

3. Apply final coat, 3-lb. cut. If color is that desired, sand with 8-0 abrasive and finish with paste wax rubbed to a satin sheen. Or, omit wax and spray one coat of rubbed-effect varnish.

Note: This is a coloring finish. By applying successive coats and sanding down to bare wood the materials are used as a filler on open-grain woods. The last coat colors, or "stains," the wood, the depth of color depending on the number of coats applied. The procedure makes a very attractive finish on maple, or produces a maple finish on any similar woods such as poplar or basswood. Should be sprayed.

Urea-Alkyd (*catalyst finish*), an extremely hard and durable finish for table and bar tops:

1. Stain with NGR stain to desired color. Do not use pigmented wiping stains.

2. Mix urea-alkyd base with required amount of catalyst (see instructions on containers) and apply with brush or spray. Dry 1 hr., or as directed.

3. Sand with 6-0 garnet and dust.

4. Apply second coat and dry overnight.

5. Rub down with fine steel wool, 3-0 or finer.

Note: The above scheduling is for the air-dry type of finish. The mixed solution must be used within 4 hrs.

Salad-Bowl Finish, a wax-resin finish for salad bowl and other woodenware:

1. Spray impregnating salad-bowl sealer on wood. Dry 1 hr.

2. Sand with 6-0 or 8-0 garnet. Dust.

3. Spray 1-2 coats of salad-bowl lacquer.

Note: The above is a lacquer system and the materials must be sprayed. A brushing top coat also is available. It makes a satisfactory finish without the impregnating sealer.

NOVELTY FINISHES

Limed Oak, a popular finish for oak, ash or chestnut; white on gray ground:

1. Bleach wood (on white oak of uniform color, bleaching can be omitted) and stain with NGR silver-gray stain. Alternate procedure is to spray with reduced gray lacquer.

2. If wood has been stained apply wash coat of clear lacquer.

3. Sand very lightly and fill with white paste wood filler. Wipe off any excess across grain and dry 48 hrs. Sand lightly with 6-0 garnet.

4. Spray (or brush) top coats of water-white

lacquer.

5. Waxing is optional.

Note: It is essential that the wood be sanded glass-smooth as otherwise the finest scratches will pick up the white filler.

Ebonized Oak:

1. Spray reduced black lacquer on bare wood to obtain desired black color.

2. Fill with a white filler. Allow 48-hrs. drying time and sand lightly with 6-0 garnet.

3. Top-coat with clear lacquer.

Note: Numerous other color combinations are possible.

Ebony on Maple or Birch:

1. Apply heated black NGR stain. Warm by placing container in pan of hot water. Allow to dry and repeat at least once.

2. Sand lightly with 6 or 8-0 garnet. Dust.

3. Apply one or two top coats of any clear finishing material.

3. Alternate: Finish with black polishing wax (see shellac and wax schedule).

Beechwood Fir, a subdued-grain finish for Douglas fir, white or yellow pine, and similar woods:

1. Brush or spray clear plywood sealer. Let dry 4 hrs.

2. Sand with 6/0 garnet. Dust.

3. Apply brush coat of beechwood (light gray-green) stain, pigmented type. Let stain dry 5-10 minutes. Wipe clean with cheesecloth. Allow it to dry overnight.

4. Apply top coats of varnish or lacquer.

Note: Both the sealer and pigmented stain help to subdue the grain. After coat of plywood sealer, the wood can be finished with any schedule for close-grain woods. If NGR stain is to be used, reduce the priming sealer coat with 25 percent turpentine.

Old-World Walnut, an open-pore finish suitable for walnut, mahogany, or oak:

1. Stain the wood medium to dark brown, using pigmented oil stain. Let stain dry 5 min. and then "dry-brush," wiping brush occasionally on cheesecloth to remove excess stain. Then, with clean cheesecloth pad, wipe centers of panels clean, blending stain to darken at edges. Let dry overnight. Do not sand.

2. Brush or spray sanding sealer. Dry one hour.

3. Sand with 6/0 garnet. Dust.

4. Apply top coat of lacquer or varnish.

5. Rub with 3-0 steel wool.

6. Wax with dark mineral wax.

Note: Feature of the above schedule is that all shading and color is obtained by dry-brushing and wiping the single coat of pigmented stain. A wash coat of shellac or plywood sealer can be used as a primer if desired and will facilitate smooth blending of stain coat.

Pickled Pine:

1. Stain with NGR gray stain for pine.

2. Brush or spray sanding sealer or 2-lb.-cut white shellac.

3. Brush overall coat of white pigmented wiping stain. This can be wiped clean or streak-glazed with a dry brush. Another treatment is to wipe the stain across the grain, producing a smoked effect.

4. Brush or spray 2-lb.-cut white shellac or clear synthetic.

5. Optional: Rub down with 3-0 steel wool and apply coat of liquid wax.

Note: The true pickled finish is a gray finish with an overcast of white, like the tone acquired by pickle vats. The finest work is done by first bleaching the wood. Gray stain for pine then produces an even color.

ENAMEL FINISHES

Lacquer or Synthetic Enamel:

1. Spray mist-coat lacquer enamel.

2. Sand back to bare wood with 6-0 garnet. Dust.

3. Apply two or more coats of enamel, sanding lightly between coats with 6-0 garnet.

Enamel with Undercoat:

1. Wash coat of shellac. Dry 20 min.

1. Alternate: Mop, brush or spray plywood sealer thinned 1 part turpentine to 3 parts sealer. Dry 1 hr.

2. Sand with 6-0 garnet. Dust.

3. Brush or spray undercoater. Spray lightly or brush out well. Dry as required.

4. Apply full wet coat of undercoater.

5. Patch. Use water putty, lacquer putty, thickened undercoater or other suitable patching material.

6. Brush or spray first enamel coat. Sand with 6-0 garnet when dry. Dust.

7. Apply second enamel coat.

8. Optional: Spray only. Apply finish coat of water-white clear lacquer or regular clear lacquer

with a small amount of enamel added.

9. Optional: Rub down with 8-0 (280) silicon carbide abrasive with water, followed by rubbing compound for high-gloss finish.

Note: This schedule applies generally to lacquer, synthetic, or oil enamel. Undercoater in Step 4 may be tinted with the enamel color if desired, using 25 to 50 percent enamel. One coat of white undercoater and one coat of enamel will usually make a satisfactory finish.

Ebony Black, a combined stain-and-enamel schedule for a permanent gloss black:

1. Stain with black NGR stain.
2. Fill with black paste wood filler. The filler used for red mahogany is suitable.
3. Apply two coats of black lacquer.
4. Apply two coats of water-white lacquer.
5. Rub and polish to high gloss.

Note: On close-grain woods, the filling operation is not required.

RUBBING SCHEDULES

Dull Satin:

1. Rub with 3-0 steel wool.
2. Polish with dry cloth.

Note: This rub will cut gloss quickly but will not level the surface.

Satin:

1. Rub with FF pumice and water, using felt pad. Flush with water.
2. Rub with rottenstone and water or rottenstone and rubbing oil.
3. Use wax or furniture polish, if desired.

Note: When finish consists of a sealer, a first varnish coat and a second varnish coat, the second coat can be rubbed with 320-grit wet-or-dry paper with water lubricant. The purpose is to build a level surface before the top coat is applied.

Satin, alternate method:

1. Rub with 280 or 320-grit wet-or-dry paper with soapy-water lubricant. Soap can also be applied to paper to prevent gumming. Use hard-felt backing block to make sure of level surface.
2. Wipe surface with cloth and continue rubbing with 3-0 or 4-0 steel wool.
3. Apply coat of liquid wax and rub dry.

Note: This schedule is especially good for lacquer rubbing, either clear or pigmented.

Satin-to-Polish:

1. Rub with ready-mixed rubbing compound. Use burlap pad.
2. Clean up and wax.

Note: A satin-to-polish finish is produced depending on the grade of rubbing compound used. This is as fast as a steel-wool rub and has somewhat higher gloss. About 10 strokes bring up a satin polish.

High Polish:

1. Follow any satin schedule. Let dry 12 to 24 hrs.
2. Rub with polishing oil.
3. Remove excess oil with cloth dampened with alcohol. Polish with dry cloth.

High Polish, Alternate Method:

1. Follow any satin schedule.
2. Rub with a polishing compound or automobile polish.

Note: Numerous rubbing and polishing compounds are available.

French Polish (high gloss):

1. Apply any finish with lacquer, shellac, enamel or varnish.
2. Sand with 6-0 garnet. Dust.
3. Dilute ready-mixed French polish with about 25 percent of special solvent provided. Apply mixture to cloth pad and flatten pad on palm of hand. Pad the work with circular strokes and then finish with the grain.

Note: Use only improved French polish such as Qualasole, which requires no lubricant.

These are basic schedules using common procedures and finishing materials readily available at the time of publication. New finishing materials and new procedures will be developed from time to time and put into common use. Always check the manufacturer's instructions printed on the container when using any finishing material.

See also: abrasives; antique finishes; finishes, furniture; finishes, non-skid; finishes, removing; finishes, urethane; floor finishing; refinishing; staining, wood

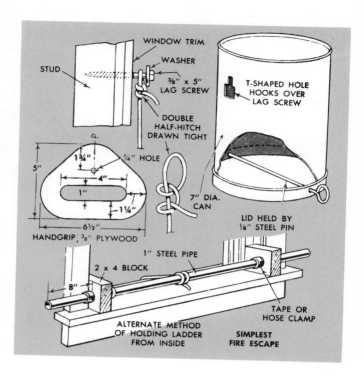

Emergency ladders for a fire

These easy-to-build escape units
may save your life

BY E. R. HAAN

FIRE THAT STARTS at night in your home
may burn for hours without being discovered by
passersby, or giving you a warning by the smoke
seeping under a door or down a hallway. Any
smoldering fire in the basement, walls, or else-
where can flare suddenly into a conflagration
that spreads rapidly throughout the house. By
the time you, or some one of your family, are
awake to the danger you may be trapped up-
stairs with only seconds to get out. It's a long
way down from even a second-story window,
even though you may hang from fingertips and
then drop to the ground. Don't risk it. Always
have an escape ladder ready.

One of the simplest and most reliable escape
ladders is the single-rope unit detailed. It's installed on the outside of the window casing and
drops full length ready for use when you pull

1025

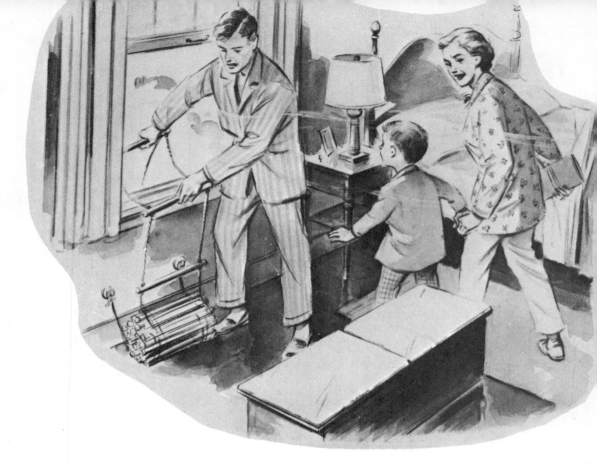

A rope ladder is always ready. It takes only a few seconds to push the seat aside and drop the ladder outside to serve as a pathway to safety

emergency fire ladders, continued

the pin that holds the cover of the can in which it is stored. The ¼-in. nylon rope has a tensile strength of 1500 lbs. On a frame building the rope is tied to a lagscrew turned securely into a hole drilled through the window casing and into a stud behind it. For attachment to a brick wall the lagscrew is turned into an expanding screw anchor seated in a hole drilled in the mortar between two courses of brick. A large washer under the screw head prevents the rope from slipping off when in use. Be sure to mount the can containing the ladder in the proper position so that the ladder is easy to mount for someone coming out of the window in a hurry.

Handgrips are safer to grasp and hold than are knots tied in the rope. The grips are made of ⅜-in. waterproof-bonded plywood and are spaced about 15 in. apart. Knots tied in the ¼-in. rope on either side of the handgrips hold them in place. The grips also serve as foot or knee holds, enabling the user to obtain additional holding power when letting himself down hand over hand.

The press-lid can in which the ladder is stored is inverted when in use and is held on the lag-

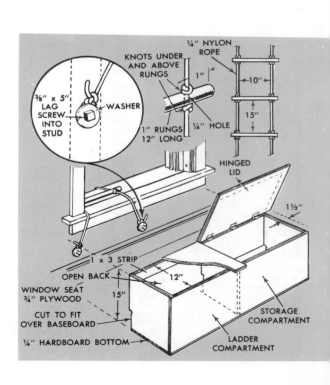

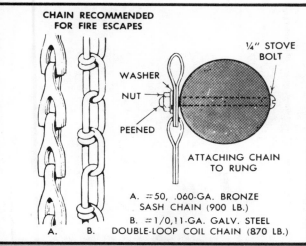

CHAIN RECOMMENDED
FOR FIRE ESCAPES

WASHER
NUT
PEENED

¼" STOVE
BOLT

ATTACHING CHAIN
TO RUNG

A. ≠50, .060-GA. BRONZE
SASH CHAIN (900 LB.)
B. ≠1/0,11-GA. GALV. STEEL
DOUBLE-LOOP COIL CHAIN (870 LB.)

A.   B.

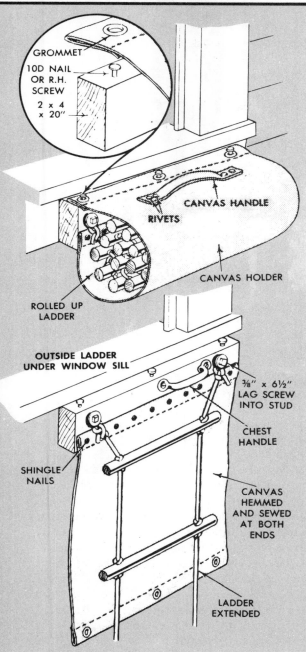

GROMMET
10D NAIL
OR R.H.
SCREW
2 x 4
x 20"

CANVAS HANDLE
RIVETS
ROLLED UP
LADDER
CANVAS HOLDER

OUTSIDE LADDER
UNDER WINDOW SILL

⅜" x 6½"
LAG SCREW
INTO STUD

CHEST
HANDLE

SHINGLE
NAILS

CANVAS
HEMMED
AND SEWED
AT BOTH
ENDS

LADDER
EXTENDED

screw by means of a T-slot cut in the side as in the details. The pin that holds the lid from slipping off under the weight of the ladder stored inside goes through both lid and can as indicated. A large eye is bent at one end so that the rod can be pulled out with minimum effort.

For a portable arrangement, the rope can be held on a length of 1½-in. steel pipe that spans the window as shown. Two blocks, bored to slide on the pipe, are spaced to fit just inside the trim pieces. They are then fixed in position on the pipe with tape or hose clamps.

The double-rope ladder fitted with hardwood rungs is easier to use than a single rope fitted with handgrips, especially for older members of a family. It is similarly attached to lagscrews driven into studs and can be located either inside or outside a window as suggested in the details. The ropes pass through holes in the rungs which are held in place by knots. For small children it may be advisable to space the rungs closer than the 15 in. indicated. Where the ladder is anchored and stored inside, a window seat may be used to conceal it. Part of the seat can be fitted with a hinged cover and utilized as a storage compartment.

can be installed under sill

While the inside location of the double-rope ladder provides greater protection against the elements, it can be installed outside just under a window sill as detailed. The rolled-up ladder is held by a piece of canvas, which when loosened by simply pulling up on the handle allows the ladder to drop instantly.

The piece of canvas is doubled at the ends and sewed for extra strength. One end is nailed to the cross piece and three grommets are fitted in the hem at the other end. The latter slip over 8d nails or roundhead screws driven into the top edge of the cross piece. As the nails extend only slightly and are close to the sill they cannot catch in clothing. A heavy chest handle screwed to the cross piece at the location indicated provides a firm handhold on the way out the window. Note that the double-rope ladder is located at the right side of the window (viewed from outside) as is the single-rope ladder.

Where chain is preferred to rope use the types and sizes given in the upper detail at the left. The chains listed provide more than ample strength for the purpose. The obvious advantage of chain is that it is fireproof. Attachment of rungs to chain is shown in the detail.

See also: ladders; lifesaving.

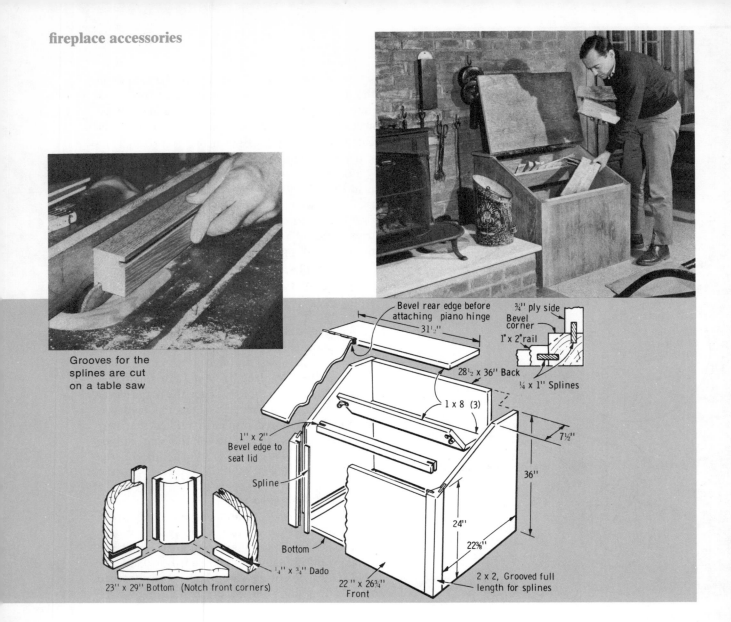

Grooves for the splines are cut on a table saw

Bevel rear edge before attaching piano hinge

¾" ply side

Bevel corner

1" x 2" rail

31½"

28½ x 36" Back

¼ x 1" Splines

1 x 8 (3)

7½"

1" x 2"
Bevel edge to seat lid

Spline

36"

24"

Bottom

22⅜"

¼" x ¾" Dado

23" x 29" Bottom (Notch front corners)

22" x 26¾" Front

2 x 2, Grooved full length for splines

Fireplace wood box

■ ON THE LONG WINTER nights, a roaring fire can eat up a lot of logs, sending you out into the cold to replenish your supply. But if you fill this big-capacity wood box before the sun goes down, you won't have to stray from the hearth.

Its simple, straightforward design makes it particularly appropriate for an Early American setting—especially if you make it from pine plywood and lumber, and finish it with a warm colonial-pine stain.

It'll take cordwood more than 2 ft. long if built to the dimensions shown, and it features a top bin (supported by cleats and steel angles) for kindling and old newspapers. The slanted lid folds against the wall for easy access to the contents.

Construction is easy, except for the splined joints at the front corner posts. The splines are 1-in. strips ripped from ¼-in. plywood and glued into dadoes cut in both plywood and posts. This feature greatly increases the sturdiness of the unit and adds to its appearance—as does the solid-stock rail across the top of the front panel. Such an edge will withstand the impact and scrape of the logs without showing wear. This solid stock also solves the edge-treatment problem. You use veneer tape only on the front and sides of the lid.

See also: fireplace hood; storage buildings.

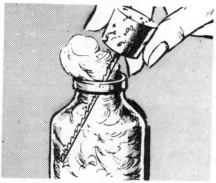

To keep it clean and dry, many people remove cotton from the box in which it is sold, and store it in a bottle. You can make a simple tool for removing cotton from a bottle by gluing a broken jigsaw blade in a slit cut in the cork stopper.

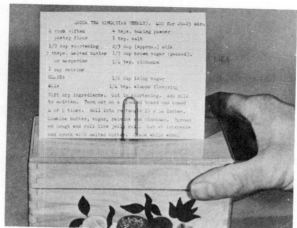

Add a handy card holder to the top of your wife's recipe file box. Just bend a large paper clip slightly more than 90 deg. and mount it on top of the box with a thumbtack.

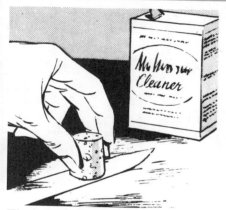

The best method of scouring a knife blade is with a dampened cork. It allows you to apply a firm pressure over a fairly large area.

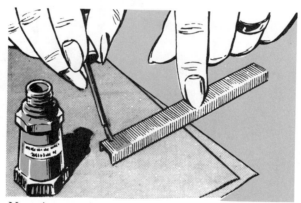

Next time you buy a box of staples, take time out to dab the last few staples in each row with red nail polish. These red staples flag your attention when it's about time to refill the gun.

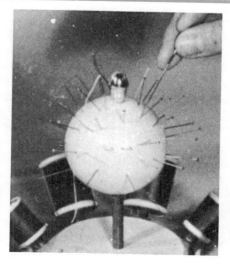

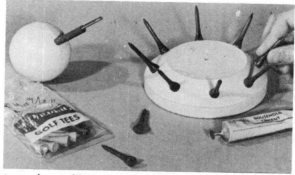

This sporty sewing caddy is made by gluing golf-tee spool holders to a bevelled base, then pushing a threaded rod through a rubber-ball pin cushion and slipping plastic tubing over the rod. Finally, screw a drawer pull on top.

A hood for your fireplace

BY ROBERT E. RUSSELL

■ MODERN FIREPLACE walls often pose problems for home decorators, especially when the wall expanse is relatively large. For such walls a fireplace hood of a simple design usually proves to be the answer. Not only does it introduce certain decorative values in both line and proportion, but a hood can serve a functional purpose as well in helping to offset any tendency of the fireplace to smoke when draft conditions and temperatures vary.

Instead of metal, this hood is made of ¼-in. asbestos-cement board, a tough, durable, fire-safe material available from any building materials dealer. You will require about 6 sq. ft. for the average fireplace. The board can be cut with an ordinary hand saw or with an abrasive wheel on a power saw. After you have cut the six pieces to size, square and smooth all the edges with a file, then drill two ¼-in. holes in each of the asbestos-board mounting plates, Figs. 1 and 3. Clamp the end pieces to the front panel and make sure the assembly is square. Then join by building up a fillet of epoxy cement at each joint, using your finger to get a good spread on both surfaces, Fig. 2. Don't apply the cement to the area of contact as you do with other adhesives.

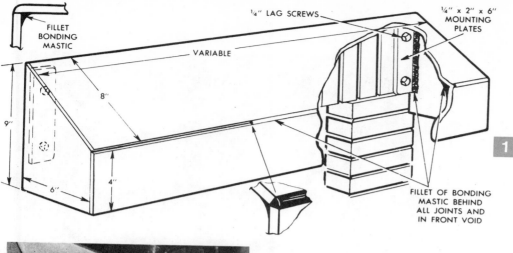

FILLET BONDING MASTIC

VARIABLE

¼" LAG SCREWS

¼" x 2" x 6" MOUNTING PLATES

9"

8"

6"

4"

FILLET OF BONDING MASTIC BEHIND ALL JOINTS AND IN FRONT VOID

1

2

3

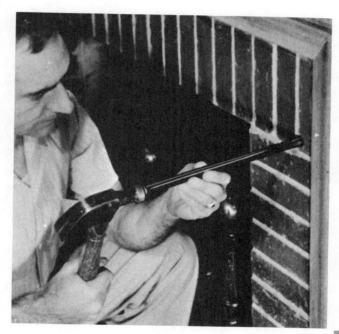

4

It's the built-up fillet that makes the bond. Hold the top panel in place with strips of transparent tape and fill the V-shaped gap where it meets the front panel with epoxy to finish it off, Fig. 1. Turn the hood upside down and form fillets of mastic along the other joints. Now put it aside until the epoxy sets which usually takes about five hours. No heat or pressure are necessary and when dry, the pieces are permanently bonded

together. Round the front edges with a file and go over the hood with fine sandpaper.

You will have your own ideas about matching finish and trim. The hood pictured was given two coats of dull-black lacquer, the type available in a pressure can, and decorated with wood-fiber trimmings attached with epoxy and painted gold color. With a star drill make two holes in the masonry on each side of the fireplace opening, Fig. 4, insert expansion plugs or lead anchors and fasten the hood in place with four lagscrews.

In working with epoxy cements mix only the amount needed since once the hardener is added to the mastic, any left over cannot be reused.

See also: fireplace accessories; storage buildings; vacation homes.

Smart fisherman's reward: A tremendous string of bass on a hot summer day

Fish deep
in summer heat

BY DICK KIRKPATRICK

Living is easy, but the fishing
    is tough in summertime . . . unless
you know how to find and take
    fish in their favorite
hot-weather hideouts

■ IN SPRING AND FALL, when fishing is at its best, the average fisherman is busy hanging screens, storm windows and what not. Then, in midsummer, with house chores pretty well under control, he takes his fishing vacation—at a time when it's difficult to catch anything.

Fishermen, guides and resort owners have a lot of explanations for the slow fishing in hot weather. They range from the familiar comment that they simply aren't biting to the unsubstantiated theory that northern pike shed their teeth during the heat of summer.

True, the fish aren't feeding as ravenously as they did in the spring when they came out of their winter dormancy, and they aren't as active as they were during the spawning season. But they're still eating. Most fish biologists agree that a big fish must feed almost constantly simply to stay alive. The trouble isn't based on their feeding habits; it's that the fish have moved out of the shallow feeding grounds.

As the days grow longer and the sun climbs

higher, surface water, especially in the shallows, warms until neither game species nor bait fish are comfortable in it. They move into deeper, cooler water. Smart fishermen go after them—and catch fish. The rest use the same methods in the same places that took fish in April—and very often get skunked.

When fishing becomes hunting, it pays to understand your quarry's habitat. As the summer sun warms the surface waters, the water in a deep lake forms itself into three layers. A light, warm water stays on top; the colder, denser water stays deep; and the boundary area between them becomes a thin belt, roughly 6 to 20 ft. deep, with a very rapid temperature drop from top-water temperature on one side to bottom-water temperature on the other. This area of rapid temperature drop, called the thermocline, has the two things the fish are looking for—cool water and enough oxygen for comfort. The warm water above the thermocline isn't comfortable, though game fish will make occasional forays upwards after bait fish, and, except in deep, cold, sterile lake-trout-type lakes, the cold water beneath the thermocline hasn't enough oxygen for them.

Species with a good tolerance for warm water, like largemouth bass, will move up into the shallows at dusk and feed through the night until dawn. But during the day, when the fishermen are out, they're lying in more hospitable waters.

Your heat-shy fish will also find cool, oxygen-heavy water around mouths of streams and underwater springs. You can usually spot a cool area by watching a lake while the morning mist is burning off in the sun. The cool spots will be the last to clear. They're also the first to mist up when it turns cool.

thermocline's bottom

Best spot to look for them, then, is that area where the thermocline layer meets the bottom. There you'll find all three of the things your quarry looks for—cool water, oxygen, and the bottom cover where his own quarry, the bait fish, hang out. Finding that area becomes the big challenge. To keep in touch with that payoff layer of water, you'll need some tools. Something—anything—to tell you the depth at a given spot and the water temperature at a given depth.

The equipment can be pretty simple. A weighted length of heavy line, marked with knots or bits of thread every few feet, will read the bottom depth for you within limitations, and you can pick up a sampling thermometer for as little as $2.50. You lower it to the depth you think you're looking for, leave it there for at least a minute, then haul it back up and read the thermometer. After a few samples, you'll get the picture.

Much better, though more expensive, is the electronic equipment made to do the same jobs almost automatically. A sonic depth indicator (photo, page 1034) gives you a constant reading of the depth under your boat. A good one will also show a different signal for different types of bottom—rocky, weedy, flat or sloping—and will register a "blip" when a fish swims through its cone of sound. That can be a real help when you're after schooling fish, but it's of secondary value. You're more interested in keeping track of the bottom.

Ideal way to find the temperature at any depth is with a good electronic depth thermometer (page 1034, right). They work with a small thermocouple on the end of a light wire marked for depth. You lower the weighted end, reading the depth on the wire and the temperature on a dial. That way you get a constant, running report from the thermocouple as it sinks, and can pinpoint the water temperatures precisely.

A third electronic tool is side-looking sonar (page 1034, left). It locates moving objects anywhere in the water and translates the find—usually a fish—into audible signals through a set of earphones. While it's primarily intended for use on fish in the more familiar shallow waters, it'll also work straight down if necessary, and the deluxe models include a built-in conventional depth indicator.

too expensive?

Just how expensive these three tools are will depend on the value you place on your fishing time—and success. If an electronic tool keeps you from coming home empty-handed on a $50 fishing weekend, you'd have to admit it was worth it.

Expensive? Not to me. My fishing time is valuable and in short supply. I own all three of the electronic helpers shown, and wouldn't part with any of them. They pay their way in fish.

Another good tool is a map that shows depths and underwater contours. Especially on a strange lake, it'll show the deep holes, submerged islands, watercourses and dropoffs you're looking for. Most state conservation departments either supply such maps or can give you a source for them.

So you've found your fish—or at least you've found the area they should be in. Now the odds

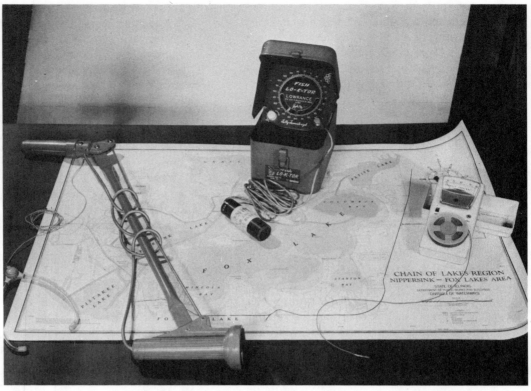

Four good "assistants": From left, fish finder, depth indicator, depth thermometer, and a good map

summer fishing, continued

have switched to *your* side; all you need to do is catch them.

Few fishermen understand how really hard it is to fish at even medium depths, because they almost invariably overestimate the depth they're fishing. You can prove that for yourself easily. Find a spot where you know the water is, say, 25 ft. deep. Now put on your deepest diving lure and try to hit bottom. It's harder than you think.

Few standard lures will go beyond 12 or 15 ft. down on a normal cast. Almost none of the wobbling spoons, retrieved fast enough to bring out their action, will run even that deep. Spinners are even worse, since most fishermen retrieve them too fast anyway, and they tend to rise on the retrieve.

The obvious answer for fishing that tricky 20- to 40-ft. depth is to stay with lures designed to go deep and to fish them carefully to get down as far as possible. Big-lipped diving plugs get down fairly well, but need help. Cast them as far as you possibly can, and retrieve at the lowest speed that will bring out their action. Spoons of maximum weight for their size, stamped or forged from thick metal, will sink fast, and can

be kept deep by using a pumping, pull-and-slack retrieve, allowing them to sink between pumps. Some, like the two spoons shown on page 1036, are made specifically for a deep, jigging retrieve.

Jigs and jig-and-plastic-worm lures do a fine job of scratching the bottom. They sink better than stones, which is the big reason for their sudden popularity. You can't help but fish them deep, and fishermen who never fished below 15 ft. before are taking fish at 40 ft. simply because the leadheads get there before they can finish their retrieve. But even the leadheads will only give a 30 to 50-ft. working retrieve from a 100-ft. cast over 50-ft.-deep water.

You can increase that distance by giving the lure all the slack line it'll take while sinking, retrieving it as slowly as your patience and its action will allow, and working it as close to the boat as possible before lifting it off the bottom. Even then you're spending a lot of time and effort to cover only a few feet of productive water.

To extend the working area of a lure in the middle depths, and to get a lure 'way down when your quarry is in really deep water, you have to change your style. Casting won't do it one third as effectively as drifting or trolling. Some casters, especially shoreline bass fishermen, regard the troller with scorn, and insist that trolling is dull. It is—if you drag a lure or bait around all day behind a throttled-down outboard. But it needn't be; trolling or drifting can be every bit as sporty as casting. Properly done, it can be as interesting as a long retrieve.

Basic trolling is pretty simple. You put a lure or bait over the side, pay out line until you're fishing the desired depth, then keep it going until you either catch something or decide to try another depth. Rod and reel aren't too important— you can use the same gear you'd use for any other kind of fishing, though it helps if it's a little heavier. The three most important factors for success are your terminal tackle, line, and the way you handle your boat. If you combine the right ones, you'll double your catch over anyone using "conventional" methods. Here's how:

The three-way rig shown in foreshortened form, page 1037, is my favorite. Your main line from the reel is attached to one eye of a three-way swivel. Your lure drops back from another eye on a monofilament or solid wire leader at least 3 ft. long, preferably six or eight. (I usually make the lure leader the length of the rod I'm using to simplify landing fish and handling the rig ashore.)

in case it breaks

The pound test of the main line and the lure leader should be about equal, with the lure leader a couple of pounds lighter. That way, if something breaks, you're only out one lure instead of a couple of hundred feet of line. The third eye takes a much lighter line to hold your sinker, since it can hang up pretty easily, and it's the most expendable piece of tackle down there. The sinker leader should be from a foot long to half the length of the lure leader. With experience, you'll learn to adjust the sinker leader until your lure is working the desired distance above bottom when the sinker is touching occasionally.

For this kind of fishing, your lure should be as light as possible, and should give a good action at the lowest possible speed. The low-speed floating plug and ultra light, thin spoon, page 1036, are ideal. With bait, a minimum of weight is usually best; some fishermen even install a small float just ahead of the bait to make sure it stays off the bottom. A lip-hooked or harnessed minnow works best as bait.

Shown with the rig are four weight systems. For trolling at fairly high speeds, especially in salt water, a trolling plane is ideal, since it'll plane your lure to a maximum depth with a minimum of dead weight on your line and strain on your rod.

For ordinary slow trolling or drifting, the long, thin "pencil sinker" works very well, and is nearly snagproof. The break-away rig is even more snagproof—the sinker is held onto the leader by a pinched split shot; no knots at all. If it hangs up, the line will slide through the shot, dropping the sinker but saving the rest of the rig. The jig sinker makes a deadly combination in states where two lures on a line are legal— it works as a sinker, but catches fish, too. Sometimes more than the lure.

The line you use will make a big difference in your success. Surprisingly, lines that cast well troll badly, and vice versa. The soft, light, braided line on your casting reel is worst of all. Its high water resistance and light weight will make a big "belly" between rod and lure. It'll be tough to get down very deep without a lot of weight ahead of your lure, and even then the belly in your line will make it hard to feel bottom or strikes, and harder to strike back at a fish.

best line

Best line for drifting or trolling at depths over 50 ft. is light solid wire. It's very heavy for its diameter, and has a smooth surface for low water resistance. In many cases, you can get to reasonable depths with no weight at all; the wire supplies the weight. Braided wires are second best; their added diameter per pound creates somewhat more water resistance than solid wires.

Unfortunately, the unchallenged superiority of wire for fishing deep is balanced by its handling difficulty. It's springy, kinky, and tough on reels and guides. With a little experience, you can learn to handle it, but it looks formidable to the beginner.

Best compromise between unweighted lines and solid wires are the lead-cored lines, which are a braided line around a core of dead-soft lead wire. The wire supplies plenty of weight; only trouble is that its diameter is many times that of solid wire, so it offers more water resistance. Saving grace is that it's as easy to handle as braided line. A new lead-core is plastic-finished like a fly line to reduce friction, which helps.

One other advantage to lead-core is that it comes in metered spools—the braided outer layer changes color at intervals, usually thirty feet, so you can tell at a glance how much line is out. You can get metered monofilament the same way. Either one saves a lot of trouble measuring or

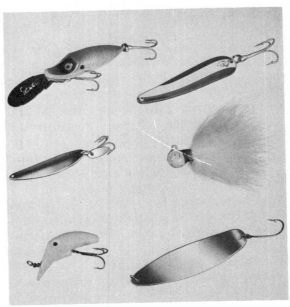

Lures for deep fishermen: Top four are caster's deep lures; bottom two are light lures for drifters

Special gear helps. From left, light wire-line outfit, big wire-line reel, lead-core line trolling rig

summer fishing, continued

Line performance comparison (not to scale) for a fisherman on a slow drift. Equal lengths of line don't reach equal depths; on faster drift, or troll, the difference is greater. For light-tackle fans, un-weighted solid-wire line goes deep easily

Boat handling methods for deep drifting or trolling: The sea anchor controls drift speed and also can be mounted to produce "tacking" drift across the wind

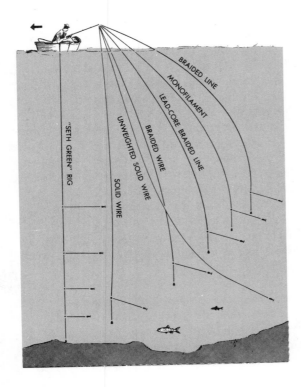

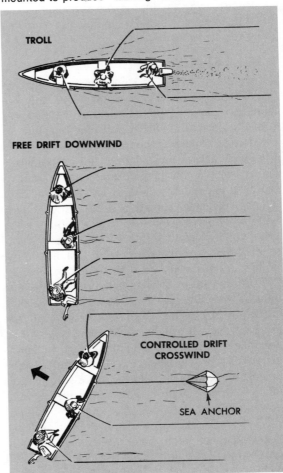

TROLL

FREE DRIFT DOWNWIND

CONTROLLED DRIFT CROSSWIND

SEA ANCHOR

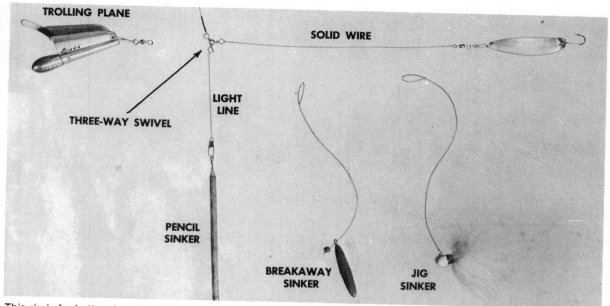

TROLLING PLANE

SOLID WIRE

THREE-WAY SWIVEL

LIGHT LINE

PENCIL SINKER

BREAKAWAY SINKER

JIG SINKER

This rig is for bottom bumping. It has been foreshortened here. The jig sinker provides weight and also takes fish

estimating the amount of line out—an important factor if you aren't bumping bottom at a known depth.

You can add wire line to your regular casting outfit easily by simply adding 50 or 100 ft. of light wire on top of your regular line. Light wire —8 to 15-lb. test—is very thin, and doesn't take up much room on the spool, and will work nearly as well that way as with the special tackle. When you aren't using the add-on wire, keep it handy on a large-diameter storage spool.

It boils down to this: The smallest, smoothest line works best. A smart fisherman will use the heaviest, least resistant line he can handle for best results.

One way to beat the line problem is to use a Seth Green rig, an old deep-fishing dropline developed in New York's Finger Lake country. Usually fished on a handline, the rig is almost a vertical trotline with a heavy weight on the bottom and lure or bait leaders spaced above it. Some states only allow one or two lures; others permit more. The idea is that you'll probably have a lure working at the right level, wherever it is. With no rod, you can use a couple of pounds of weight if necessary, and hit bottom almost anywhere. Only problem is that smaller fish don't have much chance to fight against the heavy rig, and really big fish are tough on hands. A good compromise is to use a very long rod and rig a light Seth Green outfit with two or more short droppers and as much weight as possible.

The way you handle your boat to control your

trolling or drifting speed will make a big difference. For really thorough bottom-bumping, a slow downwind drift is best. You let the boat drift free, broadside to the wind, then at the end of your drift, start your small outboard (the smaller the better) and troll as slowly as possible back to your starting point.

If a brisk wind drifts your boat too fast, a sea anchor or other dragging device will cut it down. You can pick up a 2-ft., parachute-type surplus sea anchor for two dollars, or make your own from canvas and light rope.

To control the direction of a drift, you can slant the boat against the wind by moving your fishermen toward either end of the boat; their bodies will act like sails, and your boat will angle toward the downwind end. The angle of the boat can also be controlled by leaving the outboard in the water for drag, or, best of all, by attaching a sea anchor off center. On a slow drift, an occasional stroke with the oars will also keep you in position over the bottom area you want to fish.

Easing along, adjusting your line to touch bottom occasionally or to change depths, your drift or troll becomes every bit as interesting as the retrieve from a long cast. And more effective.

That's all there is to it—find your quarry's daytime summer hangouts, then rig to get your bait or lure down and keep it there. They'll hit it.

See also: anchors, boat; bait, fishing; bass fishing; boats, buying; flycasting; ice fishing; lures; pram; riverboat; trolling motor.

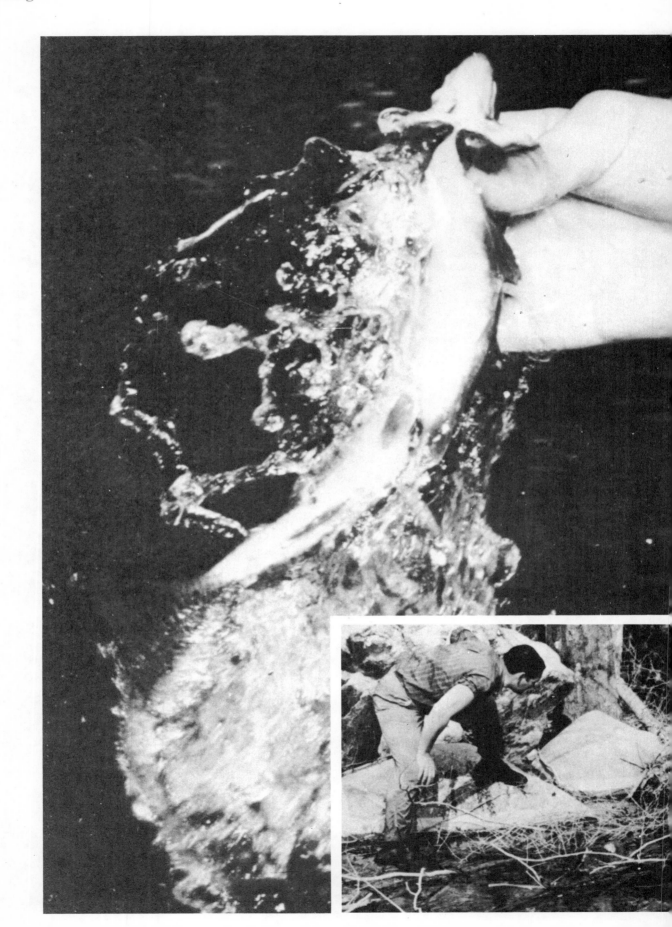

Fly casters can be artists, but the best take
a back seat when "noodlers" are on the scene

There's a one-handed catch to fishing

BY JAMES JOSEPH

■ "YOU GOT TO HAVE THE FEEL," the grizzled
old Arkansas backwater hand said.

"Maybe they're born with it. I don't know.
But when one of them boys snakes his hand down
under a rock and freezes like he's dead, it's just
a matter of time afore he's gonna whip up a fish.
Now some places they're called ticklers, and I've

Whipping a fish out by hand (left) is the art of the noodler who scorns rod
and reel. Stalking the banks of a stream (below left), the noodler looks for
holes under rocks, logs or the stream bank where the fish will hide out when
the sun is high, seeking the cool shade. Spread out on a rock (center), he
braces with the left hand and slips the right hand slowly into the pool. Fif-
teen minutes later, from sensing the fish to finding the gills, he snaps his arm
back (right) and brings in a pan-sized brook trout

After the tedious period of holding the hand motionless until he "feels" the fish, the noodler goes in for the catch, moving his hand about one inch per minute. With fingers fanned out he starts at the tail (1) with thumb and forefinger poised over the fish's back. He inches the hand forward until thumb and forefinger are poised near the gills (2) and he can feel them opening and closing (3). He carefully judges the rhythm of the breathing (4), and as the gills open he plunges thumb and forefinger in (5) to catch the fish

one-handed fishing, continued

heard 'em called guddlers, but down here they're noodlers."

And when a noodler goes fishing, the only equipment he packs are his bare hands—and an uncanny "feel" for fish.

With infinite patience the noodler slips his hand into a deep pool near the bank of a stream where, during the day's heat, fish are likely to lurk. He holds it there motionless, getting used to the cold water, his eyes closed so he can "think" into the pool. His surgeon-sensitive fingers can actually feel the backwash of an imperceptibly moving tail. The hand moves slowly in toward the quarry, then holds and waits, the hand still motionless, fanned fingers sensing every eddy and ripple. Perhaps the current will drift the fish against his fingers and he'll be able to tell the species and how it lies in the water. The tail moves again and he feels the ripple.

Ever so slowly, now, the hand moves in. There is the slightest contact of a fingertip, and the noodler knows he's after a trout. The hand is curved over the top of the fish, thumb and forefinger ready to pinch. It moves slowly along the flank of the motionless fish until thumb and forefinger can sense the opening and closing movement of the gills. By now he knows pretty well the size of the fish, and he waits with the fingers poised. The gills open, then close. Open. Close. He times the rhythm. The gills open and the thumb and forefinger plunge in and clamp together. With the fingers in the gills the fish is hooked. In a single, lunging movement the arm whips out of the water and the trout is flung to the bank to be served that night.

This is noodling, a fishing sport that goes back in history to the ancient Macedonians, was a way of life for many tribes of American Indians and is still practiced by the Lengua Indians of South and Central America.

In the U.S., noodlers are most active in Arkansas and Indiana, the Pacific Northwest, and throughout the South. It's not often, however, that you catch a noodler in the act. This is an art that is handed down through families, and is as closely guarded by its practitioners as a missile secret. And in some states catching fish by noodling is illegal.

hypnotize the fish

One of America's legendary angling authorities, Edward Ringwood Hewitt, was a skilled tickler, and his method is still unique. Feeling a fat trout lurking beneath a log or rock, he'd gently massage its flanks, being careful never to touch a fin, which invariably "woke" the fish from its tickled trance. When the trout was perfectly quiet, Hewitt cupped one hand over its snout, the other around the tail, and gently lifted it from the water—all but unconscious.

Although the terms are interchangeable in many places, the true tickler differs from the noodler in that he goes in toward the gills from the bottom of the fish and gently strokes the underbelly until the fish is literally put to sleep before he makes his lunge for the gills and whips the entranced fish out of the water.

Noodling is not an easy sport to learn, but if the novice has great patience and is willing to spend several years dipping his hand under rocks in cold water, he can learn to catch fish.

Forty-one-year-old Kenneth J. McCredie, who learned the sport from his father in Michigan, says that once an angler learns to noodle he'll never go back to a rod and reel. "A hand-angler will always take more and bigger fish," McCredie says. "And he can take his pick. Brush a fish with your fingertips and you can tell whether it's trout, bass or catfish."

When McCredie stalks the stream bank he keeps to the sunny side where the fish will be more likely to be seeking the shade of a recessed hole, and where his shadow will not be cast to frighten fish. The best times for noodling are at the heat of the day, roughly an hour before and after noon, when fish are holed up. This is the opposite of the best conditions for rod and reel, where fishing is usually best early in the morning, late in the day or at night.

the noodler's light touch

One question the skeptics ask about noodling is: "Why don't the fish dart away at the first contact?" Sometimes they do, but if the contact is deft enough and the fish is not too skittish, the touch must seem like a bit of floating debris, and the fish holds.

"You won't get them all," McCredie explains. "It takes about 10 minutes to get your hand from the tail to the gills, and a lot of things can happen. Or the fish can just decide to take off on its own."

Really adventurous noodlers go after the huge channel catfish, sword-nosed gar and the muskellunge, which is the fresh water cousin of the barracuda.

"You've got to be strong and careful for this," says a noodler in Arkansas. "A big cat can pull you into the water and a muskie could cut you to ribbons."

One of the most rewarding parts of noodling is serving the fish to guests at dinner. When a noodler tells his friends how he caught the fish, they seldom believe him. When he finally gets them convinced that he's not just telling them a big "fish" story they are invariably amazed and awed by his methods. Many an evening has been spent giving every painstaking detail of the noodler's favorite catch. Noodlers, like anglers who use the hook-and-line method, are not above talking about the one that got away.

Ready to roll up your sleeves and give noodling a try? The sport is slow and hard to learn, but the rewards in fish and admiring looks from your friends are worth it.

Remember the basic key— patience.

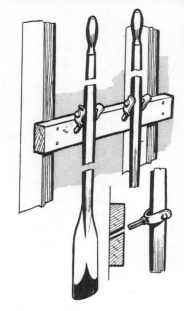

Dry storage in an open boat is always a problem. However, you can protect small items from rain and spray by carrying them in a screw-type jar mounted under a seat. It makes a fine place for extra matches, etc.

If you want extra insurance against losing that string of fish, attach a toilet float to the top clip. Then, if the stringer should come loose from the boat, you can retrieve it from the water easily.

To make a space-saving storage rack for your oars, just drill a couple of angled holes a few inches apart in a length of 2 x 4 and nail it to two studs in your garage. Hang the oars by their oarlock pins in the holes.

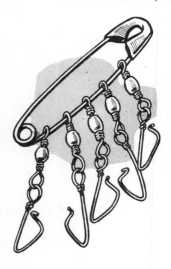

Next time you're cleaning your tackle box, keep three or four large safety pins handy. They make fine holders for snap swivels, hooks and even small lures, keeping them from getting scattered all over the box.

A hook extractor can easily be made by notching a length of ⅛-in.-dia. galvanized wire. To use it, follow the leader down the fish's throat, engage the hook in the notch, push it free and withdraw the hook.

NOTCH

Tips for the fisherman

Fishing lures won't become tangled when stored together in the tackle box if you wrap each one in a sheet of plastic or a plastic bag and secure it with a rubber band. This will also protect the lures from possible damage in the tackle box.

To avoid the discomfort of a wet seat when returning to your boat after a shower, wrap a grain sack or folded piece of canvas around the seat and pin the ends together underneath. This endless pad may then be pulled around to present a dry seat after rain.

Worms will stay healthier and livelier if you keep them in a reasonably large container. You can make a fine take-along worm can from a 2-gal. oil can by just cutting out the front. Worms won't bunch up as in a narrow can, and stay peppier.

Capacitor flash box

BY FRANK P. FRITZ

1

2 Components can be installed in any size box to fit the camera or special needs. The box can be mounted directly on the camera, above, or on a bracket, as shown here

■ MANY SHUTTERBUGS have synchronized or solenoid-operated flash cameras but either don't own flash guns or else have guns which are only powerful enough to fire one flash bulb at a time.

This low-cost, battery-capacitor flash box will fire several flash lamps simultaneously from a synchronized shutter or trip solenoids without flash and even some with flash (i.e., Heiland). It also saves bulbs because if the circuit is broken by the absence of a bulb in one flash lamp, a bad lamp or a switch in the "off" position, none of the lamps will fire. The box houses a 22½-volt battery with a capacitor in an R-C circuit, and the battery will last a year or more, depending on its use.

The flash box either can be mounted on the

flash gun tester: see testers, photo

1043

3   With a Speed Graphic, you may attach the box to the bottom of the camera and the reflector to the top, so the whole unit can easily be mounted on a tripod

6

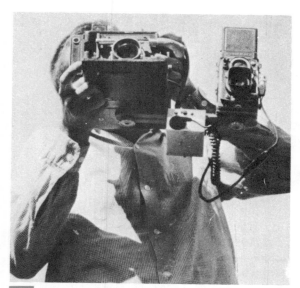

4   If you wish to take color and black-and-white shots simultaneously, you can mount a second camera on a bar connected to the first and attach the box between them

bottom of the camera, Figs. 1, 3 and 5, or on a bracket attached to the camera, Figs. 2 and 4. By mounting a socket and reflector directly on the camera or on the box, you have a simple one-lamp flash gun. You can obtain the mounting stud from any store which carries Graflex accessories.

For natural lighting or studio effects, all flash lamps may be located remote from the camera. However, when you use more than two lamps with a sync shutter you must plug them into a series-wired double socket formed by wiring two female plugs and one male plug together in

7   Dimensions of the box and layout of the components will depend on personal requirements. This one, and that shown in Fig. 6, are examples of the many possibilities

5

8 Top and bottom of the flash box contain holes for the tripod screw and camera mount

9 Pot-pie reflectors, above, and below, right, will help to reduce "hot spots." The commercial reflector, below, left, is wired in parallel and cannot be used in series setups where more than one flash lamp is desired. On such occasions, use pot-pie reflectors like that on the right

series. A common double socket is wired in parallel and thus cannot be used, nor can side-light flash guns not wired for B-C.

The box can be any size, Figs. 6 and 7, and holes for the flush-mounted female plugs cut with a radio socket punch. Follow the wiring diagram carefully, Fig. 11, adding the capacitor last to avoid possible damage from the soldering gun. To provide for tripod mounting, solder a small aluminum plate inside the bottom, using liquid aluminum solder, Fig. 8. Drill and tap a hole for the ¼-20 tripod screw and another hole in the top of the box for the ¼-20 camera mounting screw.

The "hot spots" so common when ordinary flash reflectors are used with a wide-range lens can be reduced by using homemade reflectors, Figs. 9 and 10. Cut a hole large enough for the socket of a midget flash-bulb adapter in the center of a small foil pie pan. Then cut a hardboard disk to fit the bottom of the pan, drill a hole for the adapter socket and glue the disk to the bottom of the pan. Insert the adapter in an ordinary light socket and attach it to a bracket or ball-clamp mounting. Finally, wrap the outside of the adapter with masking tape to insure a tight fit and push it into the hole in the pie pan. A slight increase in exposure may be necessary when using the reflector.

See also: cameras, used; darkroom light control; darkroom, portable; darkrooms; easel, enlarger; film dryer; floodlamp; photoflood control box; photography; testers, photo; timer, photo; timer light, photo.

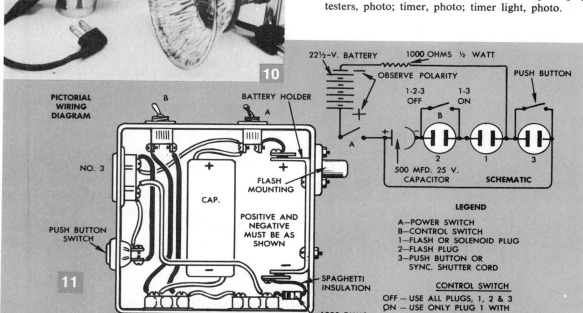

10

11

PICTORIAL WIRING DIAGRAM

NO. 3

CAP.

PUSH BUTTON SWITCH

NO. 2   NO. 1

B   BATTERY HOLDER   A

FLASH MOUNTING

POSITIVE AND NEGATIVE MUST BE AS SHOWN

SPAGHETTI INSULATION

1000 OHMS ½ WATT

22½-V. BATTERY   1000 OHMS ½ WATT

OBSERVE POLARITY   PUSH BUTTON

1-2-3 OFF   1-3 ON

B

A   2   1   3

500 MFD. 25 V. CAPACITOR   SCHEMATIC

LEGEND

A—POWER SWITCH
B—CONTROL SWITCH
1—FLASH OR SOLENOID PLUG
2—FLASH PLUG
3—PUSH BUTTON OR SYNC. SHUTTER CORD

CONTROL SWITCH

OFF — USE ALL PLUGS, 1, 2 & 3
ON — USE ONLY PLUG 1 WITH PLUG 3 TO SHUTTER OR PUSH BUTTON FOR SOLENOID USE

Blinker is small enough to put almost anywhere. You'll probably want to keep it at eye level or higher so it can be seen easily. Add a magnet to the case and you can just stick it in place the next time you have to change a tire, day or night

Pocket-sized blinker
will warn off traffic should
you break down on the highway.
Build it for a few dollars

Wiring is kept as uncomplicated as possible. As an additional help, you don't have to worry about the placement of the leads inside the case. If you desire, you can solder the lamps into the circuit and avoid using sockets, since the bulbs should last a lifetime

Lifesaver
in your glove compartment

BY FRED BLECHMAN

■ WHAT A TIME for a flat tire! Night, on a dark road in the middle of nowhere.

The problem is not in changing the tire, but in avoiding being hit by an approaching car whose driver doesn't see your disabled vehicle. Leaving your parking lights on is one solution, but this imposes a drain on the car battery.

Another possibility is to use a dry-cell battery powered flasher. But very often the batteries in these units are dead at the moment you need them most.

A better solution is to build the compact warning blinker described here. It plugs into the automobile cigarette lighter socket for power, provides two alternately blinking lights and takes up almost no storage space.

With about $4 cash and an hour's labor (probably less), you can have your own.

Construction is kept as uncomplicated as possible by using a preassembled transistorized flasher module. In all, there are only three electronic parts to interconnect. All parts are mounted in a small 3¼ x 2⅛ x 1⅛-inch box. If you use the aluminum case listed, be sure that none of the wiring contacts the case.

For best results, drill three holes in the face of the case for the module leads and cement the module to the front of the case again, mak-

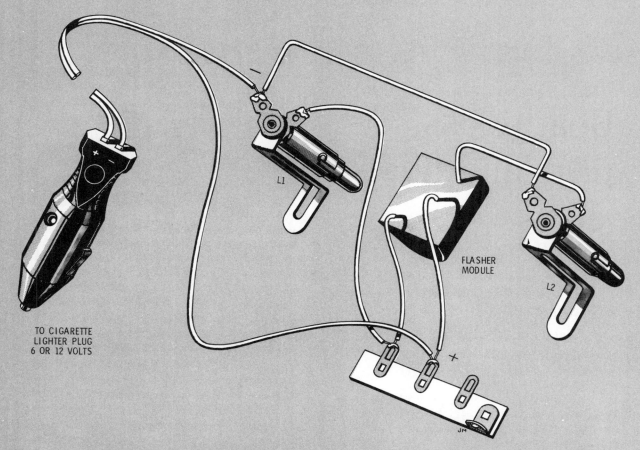

This large-scale pictorial diagram shows compete wiring in detail. The only connection to the flasher module that must be made is the middle lead as indicated. The other two can be reversed and the unit will still work. Don't let any leads touch the case

ing sure that these leads do not touch the case.

If you intend to use the unit with a car that has a 12-volt electrical system, use No. 57 or 1815 bulbs. For 6-volt systems use No. 55 or 47 bulbs. Be sure to wire the cigarette lighter plug (available at most auto parts stores) with the proper polarity, the hot side to the center prong and the ground to the remaining contact.

Attach a small permanent magnet to the case with epoxy glue. The magnet holds the unit on the deck or fenders. Glue felt to the bottom to prevent scratching.

The cord that connects the plug to the flasher is ordinary lamp cord and can be made any length. Normally about 10 ft. is enough. As a final touch, coat the bulbs with a light layer of red nail polish.

Chances are you'll never have to use this flasher. But you'll surely appreciate it should it ever be needed.

PARTS LIST

Dual Flasher Module (Lafayette 19C0106 or equiv.)
Cigarette Lighter Plug (see text)
L1, L2—6 volts: No. 55 or 47
        12 volts: No. 57 or 1815
Pilot Light Sockets (2) for L1 and L2
Case, 3¼ x 2⅛ x 1⅛ (Bud CU-3017A or equiv.)
Lamp cord, terminal strip, cement, miscellaneous hardware

See also: auto repair; brakes, auto; driving, snow; headlights, auto; mufflers, auto; shock absorbers; steering, auto; wheel alignment, auto; wheel bearings, auto.

Boat docks, piers and floats

BY GEORGE DANIELS

Twin docks connected by a crosswalk form an H-unit with a boat slip in the center. Note the roller-type bumpers on the slip sides to keep boats from rubbing

Buying or building one of
these units can add extra fun
and dollar value to your
waterside haven

■ WANT TO double the fun value of your lake-front vacation hideaway? A new boat dock or diving float will do it. The cost will be less than you probably expect, and you're likely to make it up in the resale value of your cottage.

If the idea of just dropping a ready-made unit into the water sounds tempting, you can get a 20-ft. floating dock 40 in. wide for about $150. Add another $50 and you'll have enough for a similar size all-steel pier with adjustable legs which adapt to any bottom contour. Costs given are those at the time of publication.

However, you'll save money by building your own pier or float. The lumber used in such units (especially piers) should be rotproofed and borer-proofed by pressure treatment with penta-chlorophenol or creosote. While you probably won't find this at most lumberyards, it's available on special order. Cost may run anywhere from a third more to double that of untreated lumber, but it's definitely worth every penny.

As for flotation, you can buy enough poly-styrene foam to support close to half a ton for about $30, and it will last indefinitely without paint or maintenance. If your budget is tight, three 55-gal. oil drums will do about the same

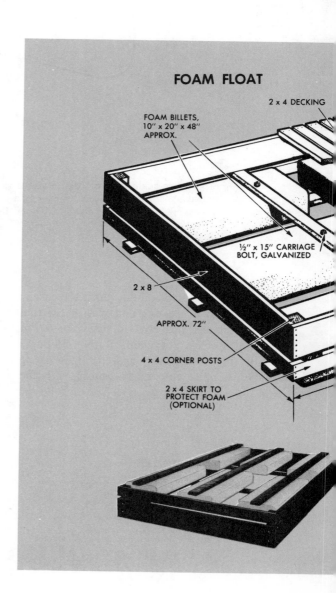

FOAM FLOAT

2 x 4 DECKING

FOAM BILLETS,
10" x 20" x 48"
APPROX.

½" x 15" CARRIAGE
BOLT, GALVANIZED

2 x 8

APPROX. 72"

4 x 4 CORNER POSTS

2 x 4 SKIRT TO
PROTECT FOAM
(OPTIONAL)

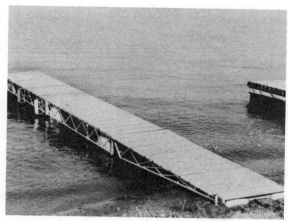

This budget-priced floating dock for sheltered waters uses pre-fab steel trusses with brackets designed to hold oil drums. 10-ft. section sells for $63

Pipe pilings hold this floating dock in line. If the water level changes, oversized sleeves ride up or down the pipes, allowing the float to rise or fall

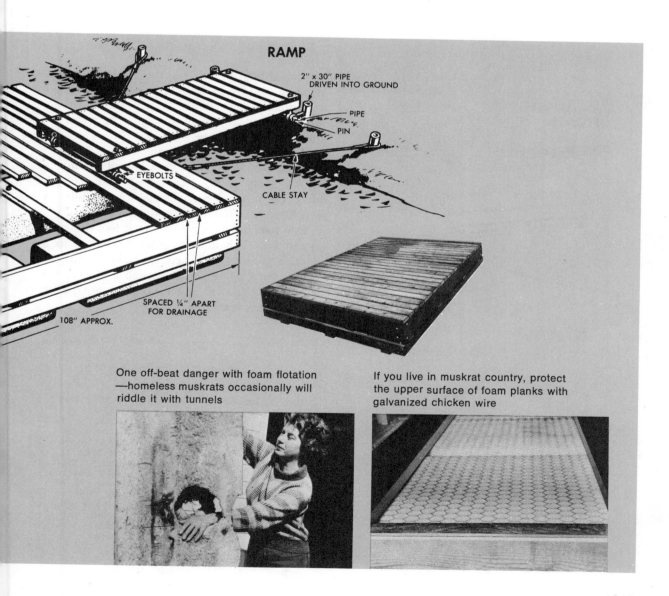

RAMP

2" x 30" PIPE DRIVEN INTO GROUND

PIPE

PIN

EYEBOLTS

CABLE STAY

SPACED ¼" APART FOR DRAINAGE

108" APPROX.

One off-beat danger with foam flotation —homeless muskrats occasionally will riddle it with tunnels

If you live in muskrat country, protect the upper surface of foam planks with galvanized chicken wire

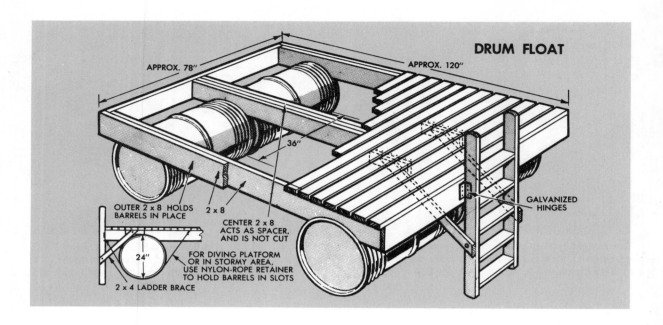

DRUM FLOAT

APPROX. 78"

APPROX. 120"

36"

OUTER 2 x 8 HOLDS
BARRELS IN PLACE

2 x 8

CENTER 2 x 8
ACTS AS SPACER,
AND IS NOT CUT

GALVANIZED
HINGES

24"

FOR DIVING PLATFORM
OR IN STORMY AREA,
USE NYLON-ROPE RETAINER
TO HOLD BARRELS IN SLOTS

2 x 4 LADDER BRACE

docks, piers and floats, continued

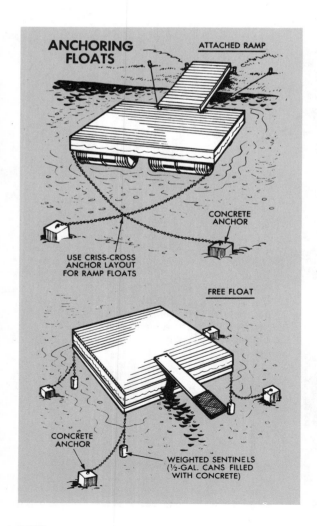

ANCHORING
FLOATS

ATTACHED RAMP

CONCRETE
ANCHOR

USE CRISS-CROSS
ANCHOR LAYOUT
FOR RAMP FLOATS

FREE FLOAT

CONCRETE
ANCHOR

WEIGHTED SENTINELS
(½-GAL. CANS FILLED
WITH CONCRETE)

job for around $10, if you don't mind seasonal painting and occasional replacement. A good compromise here might be galvanized drums which cost slightly more, but last longer and require less maintenance.

Piers built from scratch can cut costs from 30 to 50 percent, but plan on days instead of minutes for assembly work. Ready-made and pre-fab piers rest on tubular or channel-form metal legs which are adjusted to the bottom contour.

One type has an 8 x 8-in. metal foot designed to rest on the bottom; another terminates in a spiral auger bit that is actually screwed into the bottom by slipping a rod through a hole in the upper end. (You can buy this permanent type for use with home-built piers.)

FIGURING FLOTATION

Two factors determine how much weight a float can support: the weight of the lumber and the buoyancy of the flotation units. Douglas fir, a popular lumber, weighs about 34 lbs. per cubic foot. Thus, a 2 x 12 will have a running-foot weight of about 4¼ lbs.; a 2 x 8, just under 3 lbs.; a 2 x 6, just over 2 lbs.; and a 2 x 4 about 1¼ lbs. Use your lumber bill to estimate the total weight. As for buoyancy, a cubic foot of polystyrene foam will support 60 lbs. (figure 55 lbs. to allow a safety factor). A pair of 55-gal. oil drums will support about 770 lbs. in addition to their own empty weight of 50 lbs. each. So the drums and foam have about the same flotation values.

Trestle dock, the ultimate in simple, low-cost construction, is adequate for sheltered waters

Make the walkway by nailing 1 x 5s over 2 x 4s. Stagger 2 x 4s so the sections can be bolted together

There are a number of methods of driving homemade pilings. Simple pipe pilings can be sledge-hammered from an anchored boat. Wood pilings should have a square pyramidal point, like that of a soldering iron, for easier penetration; you can either "work" them into the bottom by tilting back and forth while applying pressure, or "bore" them in by drilling a hole near the top of each one for a hardwood dowel so that it can be turned.

In the fall, leg-type piers should be removed

from the water. Driven pilings can remain in place, though you may wish to remove the walkways. If the water level varies after ice has formed around the piers, this may tend to loosen them. You can minimize this effect by placing a few large rocks near the piling bases; when the water level drops these rocks will break through the ice, loosening its grip on the pilings so that they won't be pulled out of the bottom.

Floats, both home-built and ready-made, usually use either foam or drum flotation. An ordi-

To assemble, first put trestles in place, then bolt walkway sections to each other and to the trestles

Dock weight is enough to keep it from floating, but keep the walkway high above the water to play safe

Three tips on dock building: The spacer board (top) will speed up the job of nailing deck planking and assure even spacing; costs can be cut by using large, galvanized eyebolts and galvanized pipe (middle) to hinge the ramp to the float; worn-out firehose (bottom) makes a perfect dock bumper, and often you you can find plenty at your local firehouse

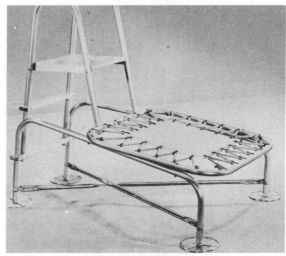

You can add plenty of bounce to a small diving float with this unit. You merely jump from the top step to the tension-mounted center section and bounce off into the water

docks, piers and floats, continued

nary 55-gal. oil drum weighs about 50 lbs. empty and will support approximately 385 lbs. While prices vary, you can figure on around $3.50 for a standard drum and about $5 for a galvanized one. Galvanizing almost doubles the life of the drum so that some last up to eight years. A 10 x 22 in. plank of polystyrene foam 9 ft. long replaces two drums. It can't rot, and marine borers won't touch it. While this foam costs more than twice as much as comparable drum flotation, its advantages are obvious.

Polystyrene foam has only two natural enemies: muskrats and seagulls. The best insurance against muskrats is described on p. 1049. As for the gulls, they won't actually eat the foam, but they do get a big kick out of pecking holes in it. However, paint the exposed portions of foam a brilliant orange and gulls won't touch it.

More dangerous to polystyrene foam are its man-made enemies—oil, gas, industrial chemicals and other solvents floating on the surface of the water. To protect the foam, build a wooden skirt that extends beneath the waterline all the way around your float. This will block out the harmful surface film. In areas of heavy contamination, you'll probably be better off using drums or ready-made metal pontoons. Or you might

check on a new type of buoyancy billets which are designed to resist this solvent damage.

Two home-built floats shown on these pages illustrate the general construction methods used with both types of flotation. While these small landing or diving floats may not suit your purposes, you can easily vary the dimensions to make narrow docks or large-area fun floats.

Anchoring a float is basically like anchoring a boat, but there are a couple of special rules to keep in mind. A float linked to a pier ramp should have two anchors at the outer end with the lines crisscrossed to insure lateral stability. A free float requires four anchors with the lines radiating out from the corners instead of crossing. And since the water around a float is a heavy-traffic area, lines must be deep enough to be out of the way of boat props and springboard divers, so rig weighted sentinels to them.

To cut costs, you can cast your own 18-in., 300-lb. concrete-block anchors in scrap-wood forms, embedding an eyebolt in the concrete before it sets. Your 4-anchor free float will be held in place with more than half a ton of concrete.

You can get a non-skid walkway by finishing with a weatherproof coating sprinkled with non-skid grit, available from any large paint-supply house. The best tool for spreading this grit? A salt shaker.

A boat dock or a diving pier requires work to build, but after all, building is half the fun of maintaining your vacation hideaway.

See also: boat handling; boats, buying; boats, used; games, boating; skin diving; swimming pools; water skiing.

Handy hooks soldered to the outside of a can in which you store bolts will hold nuts and washers, and make it easy to locate the size you want. Use ⅛-in. welding rod or coat-hanger wire to form the hooks.

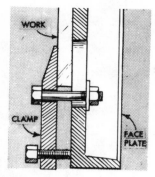

You'll find that the jaws from toolmaker's clamps make excellent straps for mounting work on a drill-press table or the face plate of a lathe.

When driving stakes to support the form for a concrete walk, insert a trowel into the ground and hold it against the side of the stake while it is being driven to keep it vertical.

This low-cost feeder is easily made from a coat hanger. Just pull the hanger straight until the two wires are parallel, bend up the lower end to form a right-angle projection, which is stapled to the perch, and wedge a ball of suet between.

A kerf wedge prevents binding when sawing thin panels. It's a shingle nail driven into a small block of wood which can be inserted above the saw when the cut is deep enough.

Use a tin can as a foolproof support for a campfire tripod. The crossed ends of the three legs should be wedged securely inside the can. A cooking container can be suspended from a wire hook slipped through a hole in the can.

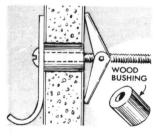

When mounting brackets on plaster walls with toggle bolts, the hole is necessarily larger than the bolt's diameter. For a snug fit, make a wood bushing from dowel the same diameter as the hole and slip it over the shank of the bolt.

A pickle jar is a perfect container for storing stainless-steel welding rods. The wide mouth makes it easy to remove the rods, and the cap provides a tight seal against moisture.

This swing-up support for a paste brush is a handy accessory for your pail. Drill a hole through the side of the pail just under the rim and attach a piece of stiff wire.

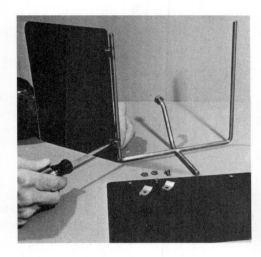

You'll get better pictures with this easy-to-make floodlight, complete with a diffuser and swinging "barn-door" light control vanes

Floodlamp with barn doors

BY MARTIN D. KOEHLER

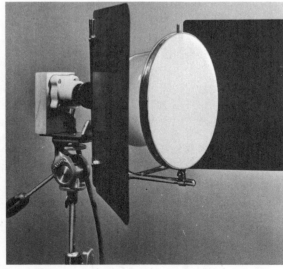

Ready for use, swinging vanes control background lighting and diffuser softens too brilliant light

■ FINE VARIATIONS of lighting for better pictures are possible with this controllable floodlamp which is easy and inexpensive to make. Two sheetmetal vanes permit delicate control of background lighting, a diffusing screen softens too brilliant light, and a pan head permits quick beaming of light where it is wanted, also locking the lamp into position.

The framework that holds the vanes and diffusion screen attaches to a steel plate which mounts on the pan head. The heart of the unit is an RFL-2 sealed-reflector floodlamp. This turns into a porcelain surface-type socket fastened to a wooden block held on the steel plate with screws. Tape the exposed terminals to prevent shocks or shorts and fit a through switch in the cord so the lamp can be turned on and off conveniently.

Drill and tap the plate for the screw of the pan head. Bend the forward end at right angles,

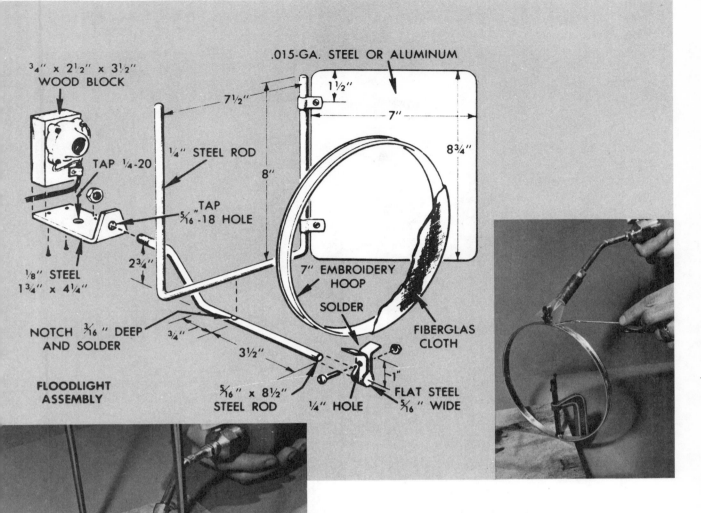

.015-GA. STEEL OR ALUMINUM

¾" x 2½" x 3½"
WOOD BLOCK

TAP ¼-20

1½"

7"

8¾"

7½"

¼" STEEL ROD

8"

TAP 5/16-18 HOLE

⅛" STEEL
1¾" x 4¼"

2¾"

7" EMBROIDERY HOOP

SOLDER

FIBERGLAS CLOTH

NOTCH 3/16" DEEP AND SOLDER

¾"

3½"

FLOODLIGHT ASSEMBLY

5/16" x 8½" STEEL ROD

¼" HOLE

1"

FLAT STEEL 5/16" WIDE

Brazing vane holder to support the rod after it has been notched. Apply C-clamps to hold pieces

then drill and tap it to take the threaded end of a 5/16-in. steel rod to which you braze the U-shaped vane holder. File a round-bottom notch across the rod to fit the vane holder and to provide good contact for silver soldering or brazing. This can be done with a gas (propane) torch and is just as easy as soft soldering, but provides a great deal more strength. Bend an offset in the rod to clear the lamp.

Make the vanes of 26-ga. sheet steel or aluminum. Round the corners, file off the sharp burrs, and paint the surface toward the light a matte black. Next, form the hinges from a piece of sheet steel about .010 in. thick (No. 30 ga.). These should be a friction fit on the holder so that the vanes will stay put in any position. Machine screws and nuts holding the hinges on the doors are turned to tighten or loosen the fit on the rod supports.

The diffusing screen consists of a 7-in. embroidery hoop and a piece of fiberglass cloth. Make the bracket from sheet steel about .040 in. thick (No. 18 ga.), forming it for a friction fit on the rod and making it adjustable for tightness with a machine screw and nut. Solder or braze the bracket to the embroidery ring as in the photo to complete the job.

See also: cameras, used; darkroom light control; darkroom, portable; darkrooms; easel, enlarger; flash box, photo; photoflood control box; photography; portrait photography; testers, photo.

A good example of what a ranch-type (pegged) hardwood floor can do for your living room

What you should know about hardwood flooring

BY W. CLYDE LAMMEY

Nowadays a hardwood floor comes to you almost ready-made. You just nail it down or stick it down with mastic

■ A FLOOR IS MANY THINGS to any household. Primarily it's the bottom of the room, a place to set foot when you enter, a basic setting for home furnishings. It should feel sure and solid underfoot, should complement any room decor and be easy to look at—for generations to come.

Like many other good things it doesn't come cheap, either in first cost or added taxes. But its initial cost is more than offset by the esthetic and the dollars-and-cents resale values it contributes to your home. And the service you get from a hardwood floor is measured in lifetimes.

That's because selected-oak flooring has a warmth and beauty and lasting solidity in its own right. It's more nearly mar and dent-proof than any wood that grows. You can roll pianos around on it. Wobbly casters may mar the finish, but not the floor.

Wood floors in homes have an early origin, date back to the latter days of the Dark Ages.

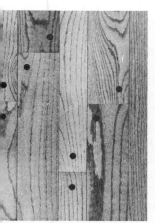

Left, a look at the mechanics of laying a hardwood pegged floor, using a nailer with auto feed. Notice how the craftsman has been careful to "break" the joints and select the boards so that he gets a uniform distribution of grain and color in the finished job. Above, the boards, or strips, come in random widths and thicknesses and are tongued and grooved on edges and ends

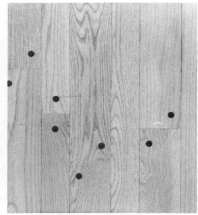

Samples of plank flooring in the pegged ranch type. Both are prefinished, that on the left in a darker shade which brings out the grain more strongly. Right, ranch flooring being laid over a concrete slab on false "joists" or screeds

Photos courtesy E. L. Bruce Co.

But it remained for the Early American colonials to popularize wood flooring—"puncheon" floors, they called them, great slabs split raw from the tree, adzed smooth, and held in place on sleepers with "trenails" (we've renamed these dowel pins).

And now with our driving penchants for modernization—and keeping up with the Joneses —we've selected and sawed and tongued and grooved—and imitated—until we have hardwood flooring in planks and boards and squares and oblongs to suit anyone's fancy. Although there are modifications and offshoots in design and type, present-day manufacturers of hardwood floorings stick pretty closely to four standard types, known generally as "strip," "plank," "parquet" (or pattern) and "block."

Strip flooring will be familiar to everyone as

1057

This homeowner is laying a laminated block floor over mastic. The mastic has been troweled to a uniform film and the grain of the blocks is alternated

Here's what he gets in the finished job, with furnishings in place. Of course, the wood squares, or blocks, are prefinished and are laid like floor tile

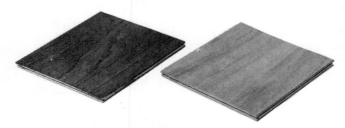

You can have your blocks in a light, natural finish or in a darker tone which brings out the grain. Blocks are commonly ¾ in. thick

hardwood flooring, continued

it's perhaps the most widely used. It consists of strips 1½ to 3½ in. wide and comes in random lengths and various thicknesses. The strips are commonly tongue-and-grooved, or side-matched, and also are end tongue-and-grooved to simplify joinery. Square-edged strips also are supplied.

Plank flooring is less readily available, is more or less custom-rated. Normally it consists of planks, or boards, up to 9 in. in width with square edges. It comes more commonly in random narrower widths and lengths with tongue-and-grooved edges and ends and some stylings come with dowels, or pegs, of a contrasting color inset in the boards. This product is usually factory-finished. Some types are available with the edges beveled slightly to simulate the cracks in old floorings.

Parquet or pattern flooring is perhaps the fanciest of all hardwood floorings. You'll see it in homes and apartments finished a cut or two above the common, both old and new. In general, it consists of short identical lengths laid in geometric patterns to produce squares, rectangles,

and herringbones. In older construction the strips were nailed down individually as a rule, but in later structures they are either set in mastic or laid as prefabricated squares or other shapes in a cement prepared for the purpose. The sizes of the squares or other forms vary, as do the thicknesses. The patterns usually are factory-finished.

Block flooring is just another version of parquet flooring, except that it usually comes in squares or rectangles and generally consists of a one-piece veneered surface, the block being laminated like plywood. The block design may consist of several parquet strips laid in a pattern of geometric form. In laying such squares (they are tongue-and-grooved so they fit edge-to-edge tightly) the direction of the grain is often alternated to produce an overall pattern which is pleasing to the eye.

Although oak is traditional and probably the most commonly laid of all floorings, newer flooring woods are coming into more common usage, such as beech, birch, hard maple and pecan. Although possibly less durable as "wear" floors, these woods do turn up flooring jobs of decorator beauty and eye-catching colors in a variety to match any decor.

Always get the manufacturer's work sheets and other instructional literature from your building materials dealer before you lay a floor, using any of the floorings. These will give you the recommended nail sizes, the cements or mastics to use, all the information you need for a do-it-yourself flooring project.

See also: acoustics; ceramic tile; epoxy paints; floor finishing; floor polisher; slate floors; tile floor.

Quieting squeaky creaky hardwood floors

BY STEVEN J. HOWARD

If you've been bothered by squeaky floors for a long time,
here are a number of cures you can use to quiet them

RECENTLY, I made a survey of 75 homeowners in my community. "Name the No. 1 nuisance in your house," I requested.

About half of the men complained of moisture problems (fogged windows or a wet basement), 40 listed leaky faucets—and 15 said: "My wife!" But *one* problem appeared on *every* list, and topped most of them: squeaky floors.

When I pressed the issue, I found that only a couple of these men had ever tried to *silence* those annoying squeaks. The rest assumed that a noisy floor—like taxes—is something you just have to put up with. This isn't true, of course. There are a number of ways to chase a squeak— without much of an investment in time or cash.

The trouble is widespread because of the way all floors are constructed—and because a natural enemy of wood is present in most homes, all winter long. This enemy is dry air. It pulls moisture from wood and causes shrinkage which, in turn, causes loose fitting. The result is bounce, sag, squeaks and creaks.

In times of high humidity—usually during the summer when your home isn't artificially heated —the winter-dried wood gains back some moisture, but never enough to counteract what's been taken from it. Once that wood shrinks, it seldom returns to its original tight-fitting form.

On the other hand, if a wood floor is laid too tight to start with, excess humidity can result in swelling, which causes the hardwood strips to buckle. This opens a gap between them and the subflooring—a gap which closes only when you walk over it; and it closes with a loud protest!

Basically, a floor consists of two layers, and a squeak can originate in either of them.

Manufacturers of wood flooring materials are all agreed that the most common sound-source is the movement of the tongue of one flooring strip in the groove of its neighbor, as the result of wood shrinkage or swelling.

If this is your problem, simple lubrication may

floors, slate: see slate floors

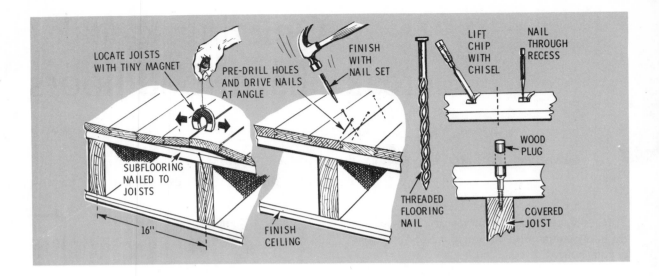

take care of the squeak—at least for awhile. Try squirting powdered graphite in the joints between flooring strips. If this doesn't work, force in a little liquid soap, using a clean oil can.

But suppose you live in a fairly new house—one where there's scarcely been time for the flooring to shrink. Yet recently, as you walk around, you notice a lot of barely audible squeaks. They're too many and too scattered to "lubricate"—the condition is simply a sign that the wood is starting to dry out.

These minor irritations can often be eliminated with a coat of penetrating floor sealer, brushed on with the grain. Work the sealer in between the floorboard joints as best you can, let it set a few

minutes, then wipe off the excess *across* the grain. Follow this up, next day, by flowing on floor finish across the grain, with only your final, light strokes brushed *with* the grain, for appearance.

Another source of squeaks and sags is a *subfloor* that dries out and shrinks away from supporting joists. Where you can attack the problem from a basement or a crawl space, have someone walk around on top, as you listen from below. This lets you spot the area of the noise. If there's a gap between floor and joist at that point, shim it.

Bridging is another possible source of noise. Where crossed pieces touch each other, they can rub, when weight is put on from above, produc-

PATCHING A HARDWOOD STRIP FLOOR

You can patch a stained or split board by removing it and putting in a new section. Measure off the damaged area—no less than 10 in. long—and drill a large hole at each end, in finish floor only. Chisel out old board, cut a new board for snug fit and nail at corners

If your floor is sagging under a weight such as a piano, stiffen it with solid bridging. Cut a 1 x 8 for tight fit and drive in place

SILENCING STAIR TREADS

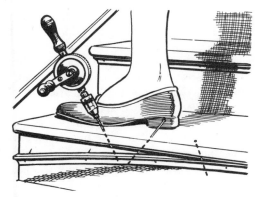

Indoor stairways often squeak because the tread rubs against the riser. This play is caused by inadequate nailing, which has let the tread lift. To close the gap, pry loose the molding under the tread's lip, have someone put full weight on it while you drill diagonally through the tread into the riser. Then drive 10d resin-coated nails in place, re-attach molding and remove weight

ing a chirp the way a cricket does with its back legs. After you find which pair of bridging is at fault, you shave the pieces apart with a saw.

While you're at it, make sure bridging is nailed tightly in place. Not all houses have bridging, but when it's used it's important to strengthen floor structure by keeping joists from twisting.

If floor strips are nailed directly to the subfloor, No. 10 round-head screws will usually do the job. First locate the squeaky board (or boards) by having someone walk on the floor above. You'll want to drill clearance holes that will pass the screw's threads through the sub-

flooring. To avoid breaking through the top surface of the finish flooring you'd better equip your bit with a depth stop. Round-head screws are used because the flat shoulder prevents sinking the head into the subflooring. You want the screw to enter the squeaky strip only far enough to get a good bite that will pull the board tight against the subflooring. Where the subfloor is ¾ in. thick, a 1¼-in. screw is best. If the subfloor is thinner stock, try a ⅞ or 1-in. screw.

Turn the screw up snug while your helper puts full weight on the strip from above. Drive in as many screws as necessary to stop the squeak—but let's be practical. If more than four or five screws placed about 4 in. apart don't do the job, you're either screwing into the wrong board or the squeak can't be conveniently eliminated in this manner.

There's one other thing to try before you give up the attack: Drill bigger holes through the subfloor—large enough to take the nozzle of a caulking or grease gun—and force thinly-mixed crack filler into the space between sub- and finish flooring.

how to spot sleepers

The caulking stunt won't work, of course, in those rare instances where hardwood flooring is laid on sleepers, creating a permanent space between the sub- and finish floor. Sleepers are staggered nailing strips, commonly laid on a concrete floor for the same reason you'd apply furring strips to a basement wall before you put up paneling. But you may encounter sleepers in above-grade floors in older homes. You'll know with the first pilot hole you drill: if the bit breaks free and jumps ahead after the first ¾ in., you're into sleeper space, and will have to tie down those squeaking floorboards with longer (probably 2-in.) round-head screws.

The problem of silencing floor squeaks is greater in homes where there's no basement or crawl space—or on the second floor, where you can't get at the subflooring because of the ceiling below it. Here, you must work from above, and your best bet is additional fastening. The big job is to find something into which you can drive nails, and this means locating nails already in the floor. You can do this with a small magnet hung on a string and moved along the squeaky floor board. When you feel or see a slight tug, you're over a nail—which means you're over the joist that the subfloor's nailed to.

Drill a small pilot hole through the flooring at an angle and into the joist. Drive in finishing

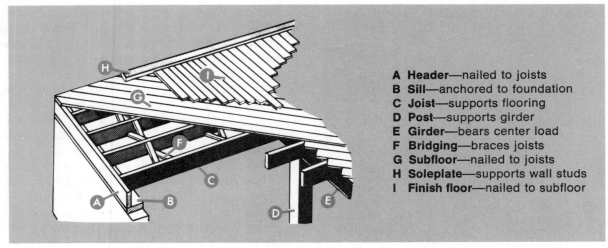

A **Header**—nailed to joists
B **Sill**—anchored to foundation
C **Joist**—supports flooring
D **Post**—supports girder
E **Girder**—bears center load
F **Bridging**—braces joists
G **Subfloor**—nailed to joists
H **Soleplate**—supports wall studs
I **Finish floor**—nailed to subfloor

This is the most common form of floor construction in older homes. In modern homes, the subflooring is often made of solid plywood panels, which are less likely to squeak. The subfloor may be diagonal across joists or at right angles to them. If the girder supports a load-bearing wall, the wall's sole plate may rest directly on it, and not on top of the subfloor. Bridging prevents canting of the joists

quieting squeaky floors, continued

HOW TO TIE DOWN BUCKLED FLOORING

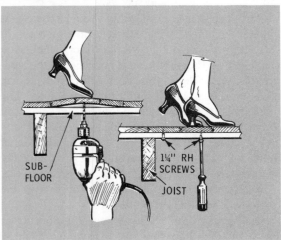

SUB-FLOOR

1¼" RH SCREWS

JOIST

nails and countersink them below the surface of the floor. Try at least two, but again, don't pepper the floor with nailheads. For better holding power, you may want to buy threaded flooring nails. There are two types—the spiral-thread, or a barbed-ring type. The small holes left by the nails can be filled with a wood filler.

If nailing doesn't do the job, maybe the maximum holding power of one or two screws will. Drill pilot holes to accommodate 1¼-in. flathead screws. Counterbore the holes to sink the heads and drive the screws firmly in place.

When squeaks resist these anchoring methods, perhaps your problem is greater than localized shrinkage or warp. A large part of the floor may be sagging under a weight that's too heavy for the existing supports. The solution to *structural* squeaks is to strengthen the floor. The simplest way to do this is to tie the joists together with solid bridging. Such a brace must be toenailed to both joists.

If this doesn't work, you may have to resort to floor jacks to support the sagging area. The best kind are the steel ones sold in lumber yards and home supply outlets. They're adjustable and can be shoved firmly up against the sagging area as much as is needed to level the floor. You can, of course, simply drive a 4 x 4-post in under the sag, if the situation makes this feasible.

If you live in an older home, wide cracks may have opened up between floorboards or, for that matter, floorboards may have suffered wood rot. Manufacturers have told me that wide cracks are a direct result of faulty workmanship in lay-

Cross-bridging that is butted tightly can cause a squeak when walked over. An easy way to separate the two pieces is to saw between them as above. If the bridging is loose, nail it tightly into place

Once a squeak is located, check to see if shrink or sag has opened a gap between the subfloor and the supporting joist. If so, drive a shim into it. A wooden shingle serves this purpose

ing the floor since little regard may have been given to moisture control.

Maximum protection against moisture can be afforded new flooring by back-painting the wood with a moisture-resistant paint, such as aluminum paint, prior to installation.

Suppose, though, that you're unlucky enough to have these gaps. You'll note that if this happens, the cracks open wider in the winter when wood has a minimum moisture content and become narrower in summer when wood becomes more moist. Is there anything to do about it?

I hate to tell you this, but the answer is "no" unless you want to start ripping out floorboards and installing a new floor.

"How about all those 'wonder' fillers," you might query, "Isn't there one that'll do the job?"

The answer is, "No." These products are good for many uses, but not this one and, in fact, may make the condition worse. When cracks develop, your best bet is to learn to live with them.

But you *don't* have to live with a floor that's spotted with stains, gouges, splits or rot. You can patch such areas with new flooring. The job isn't hard.

1. Measure off the damaged area and draw a line above and below it, at right angles to the side joints. If possible make *one* limit line the

end of the existing board, but if your patch is shorter than 10 in., it'll *look* like a patch.

2. With a large bit, drill a hole in each corner of the damaged section, close to the limit lines.

3. Use a sharp chisel to tap cuts across the strip, on the lines at each end, between the holes. Then split out the marred board, end to end, with the grain. Be careful not to damage the tongue and groove of adjoining pieces.

4. Cut a square-end piece of new flooring to the length of the finished hole. Naturally, if your floor is oak, you use a piece of oak—if maple, use maple. In order to sink this piece into place, you'll have to trim off the bottom flange of its groove to clear the tongue of the adjoining piece.

5. Insert the tongue of the patch-piece into the groove of its neighbor and press it down carefully. Seat it firmly by tapping with a hammer on a scrap block.

6. Nail each corner through pilot holes drilled slightly smaller than the finishing nails. Countersink the heads.

7. If the replacement piece is slightly raised above adjacent boards, plane or sand it down flush to the floor.

8. You can now match the patch to the color of the rest of the floor with stain, or crayon rubbed in with alcohol.

Thanks to modern
methods and materials
you can now "trade"
old floors for new
easily and economically

Trade in
your
old floor

■ WITH THE INCREASING POPULARITY of natural wood finishes throughout the home, chances are friend wife has been taking a long, hard look at her wood floors. Unless they're in real good shape, you can expect to hear, "We've just got to do something about these floors."

Happily, modern methods, equipment and materials make it possible for the average handyman to do a top-quality professional job with a minimum of fuss, bother and upset. What's more, if you use a fast-drying product, you can do the whole job in one day from sanding off the old

finish to moving the furniture back in. If you're planning to redecorate the whole room, finish all the other work except the final trim of the baseboards before you begin.

First step is a trip to your paint, hardware or tool-rental dealer. To remove the old finish you'll need a power floor-sanding machine, an edger to sand close to walls, a hand-scraper for corners and sandpaper. Machine-rental rates are reasonable, so is the cost of sandpaper. Better pick up a paint brush (or roller) unless you have one at home in good condition.

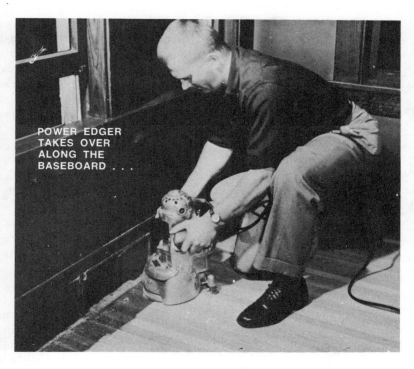

POWER EDGER TAKES OVER ALONG THE BASEBOARD . . .

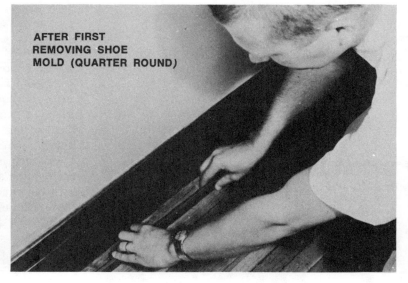

AFTER FIRST REMOVING SHOE MOLD (QUARTER ROUND)

Then there's the finishing material. You can choose from several types—shellac, varnish, floor seal or the new synthetic-resin chemical coatings. The properties of shellac and varnish are well known; chances are your present finish is one of these, probably shellac. Shellac is fast-drying, easy to use, wears well if waxed regularly and contact with water is avoided. Varnish is slower-drying, tends to scratch easily unless protected with wax, but outranks shellac in water-resistance and gloss.

Floor seals are designed to sink into the pores and seal the floor against the penetration of dirt, moisture, stains, etc. Because the surface of the wood remains unfinished, sealed floors require waxing for satisfactory appearance and wear. Like shellac and varnish, the synthetic-resin types are almost the opposite of floor seals in principle. They are *surface* coatings, and the object is to provide a surface so hard and tough that the wood itself never receives any wear at all. Most brands are fast-drying, should be applied (prefer-ably with a roller) rather than brushed on. The finish is attractive, durable and easy to keep

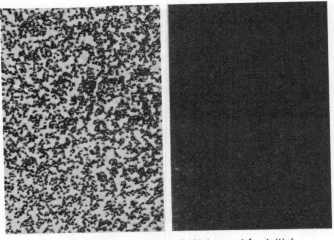

Coarse abrasive paper (left) is used for initial sanding. Second and final sanding is done with finer grades of abrasive

CHART OF SANDING OPERATIONS — OLD FLOORS

FLOOR	OPERATION	TYPE OF PAPER	
Covered with Varnish, Shellac, Paint, etc.	First Cut	Coarse	3½ (20)
	Second Cut	Medium	1½ (40)
	Finish Sanding	Fine	2/0 (100)

floor finishing, continued

Before sanding, go over entire floor and renail any loose boards, countersinking all nail heads. Sand between finish coats by hand, using fine paper

clean. And some brands never require waxing.

Because oak floors have an "open" grain, paste wood filler is sometimes used under shellac or varnish to provide a level finish. This practice is dying out, however, because a filler slows up the job (requires overnight drying) and adversely affects adhesion, often resulting in shorter finish life.

Once you've assembled all the necessary equipment and materials, you're ready to start. Clear out all rugs, furniture, drapes, etc. Remove shoe moldings along the baseboard (use care to avoid breaking), fasten any loose flooring boards, countersink exposed nail heads to guard against ripping sandpaper or damaging felt pad on the sanding drum.

Use the power sander with the correct grade of paper (see chart) to remove the old finish down to the bare wood. If you've never used one before, running the sander may be a little tricky, but you'll get the hang of it in no time. For best results, always sand with the grain or at a slight angle. Be careful not to stop the sander in one spot while it's running; this could gouge out a deep pocket.

finish-sanding

After removal of the old finish with coarse paper, two finish-sanding operations with finer papers are required. This insures a good, smooth surface, a "must" if you want a first-class job. After sanding, remove all the dust with a vacuum cleaner.

Final step is application of the finish. Follow manufacturer's directions to the letter. Unless instructed otherwise on the label, use a paint roller with an extension handle to apply the finish. You'll do the job faster, easier and better. Lightly hand-sand with fine paper between coats to cut off any raised grain.

How long will the job last? If manufacturer's recommendations are observed, most types of finishes will give several years' service under average traffic conditions. The harder, synthetic resin types will probably last longer with least care, especially those which require no waxing.

A point to remember is that resanding need never again be done provided the finish is not allowed to wear off down to the bare wood. When worn spots begin to show in heavy-traffic areas, "blend-patch" by applying another coat of finish to these spots. This way, you can end shabby floors—and major refinishing—forever.

See also: finishes, urethane; finishes, wood; floors; floor polisher; slate floors; tile, floor.

VACUUM DOES
BEST JOB OF
CLEANING UP

PAINT ROLLER WITH
HANDLE MAKES PLAY OF
APPLYING THE FINISH

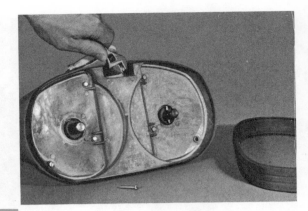

How to repair a floor polisher

BY JOHN PENNINGTON

■ DID YOU EVER SEE a household electrical appliance of which it could be said that all parts were completely worn out, no longer serviceable? That would be a rare thing. Most of them are swapped or junked when motors, bearings and many other parts are still serviceable—with a little fixing. Parts that are especially vulnerable to wear go faster, of course, an example being motor brushes. Normal wear is often greatly accelerated by simple neglect and by unusual operating conditions.

There is always the tendency to leave well enough alone when things appear to be working and there are no unusual mechanical noises to

attract attention. But take a look at the insides of the floor polisher in Fig. 1 and you'll see what usually happens after a time when you continue to polish what you thought were clean floors.

Here the accumulation of dust, lint and no telling what else has almost reached the point where it could conceivably provide a path for an electrical short. The lesson to be drawn from this exhibit is simply to clean up the floor polisher periodically and also give it the once-over to discover any parts that may be showing undue wear.

Be careful with press-fit assemblies or those which use twisted tabs to attach stamped-metal parts. As a rule-of-thumb when repairing or giving routine maintenance to a floor polisher, as with any appliance, take it apart only to the point necessary to get the job done. Going further will only complicate the reassembly job and raise the likelihood of running into trouble.

A vacuum cleaner will come in handy when removing dust and dirt and be helpful following

4

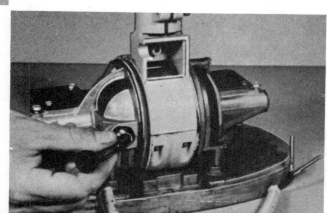

5

6

any dress-up sanding you give the commutator.

When you dismantle a polisher, Fig. 6, be especially careful when removing the handle. Usually you loosen a clamp at the base, unplug the cord and slip the handle out of a socket. Then you remove the cover, or housing, by backing out several small screws having either slots or hex heads, Fig. 2. As a rule you'll find the commutator, Fig. 3, in good condition, that is, it will be a uniform color. Usually it's best to just wipe it with a clean, soft cloth as you turn the armature by hand. If the commutator seems to be rough or slightly pitted, then it's permissible to clean it with very fine sandpaper.

It's always a good idea to remove the brushes, Fig. 5, and examine them for wear and chipping at the edges. Usually it's the rule to replace brushes worn shorter than ⅜ in. Always replace both brushes, even though one may appear to be in good condition.

Floor polishers are pretty much the same in general design. The motor usually is mounted between two vertical shafts, or spindles that carry the brushes. These spindles are driven by bevel gears from the armature shaft. These gears run in oil or light grease contained in reservoirs. In older polishers it is a good idea to remove the covers of these reservoirs and check the oil level, or the amount of grease they contain, Fig. 4. The amount should conform to the manufacturer's specification but if you do not have this and added lubricant appears necessary, then it is best not to fill the reservoirs more than about two-thirds full; never full, as the lubricant will be forced out through the oil seals. After completing the routine checks, replace parts and reassemble in the reverse order. Be especially careful to draw all screws uniformly tight.

See also: appliances; electrical wiring; floors; floor finishing; guarantees; testers, electric.

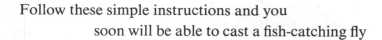

Learn fly casting in just 60 minutes

BY LAWTON CARVER

Follow these simple instructions and you
soon will be able to cast a fish-catching fly

■ IT'S ABOUT TIME somebody exploded the fiction that it takes at least five years to become a competent fly fisherman.

Fully mastering the art of fly-casting can take years, and I know experts who have been at it most of their lives and are still learning. But a complete novice can learn enough in one hour to cast a fly out onto a lake or stream, and if the fish are rising he'll catch his share.

Ellis Newman, a soft-spoken, burly outdoorsman who divides his time between giving trick casting exhibitions at sportsmen's shows and operating a fishing camp at Livingston Manor, N.Y., has devised a teaching method that is simple and infallible.

The basic idea in fly-casting is to drop an imitation fly on the surface of the water so that it

Exhibition fly-caster and teacher, Ellis Newman, works with a student, keeping the rod in the correct position for the overhead cast

looks like the real thing to a wary but hungry trout. The rod and the line are the tools for getting the fly out there. The function of the reel is simply to store the line and to take up the slack as you fight the fish.

The fly line is specially designed for its task. It is heavy to compensate for the lack of weight on the end, and it is tapered down to the end where it attaches to the fine silk or monofilament leader to which the fly is tied. For fishing dry

flies the line is treated to float on the water.

A fly rod is generally longer than a bait casting or spinning rod, the eyelets are larger to allow the line to run freely, and it has more "whip" to the end, increasing the catapulting action.

The beginner can equip himself with a complete outfit, rod, reel, line, leaders and an assortment of flies, for as little as $25. And with Newman's simple system, which we illustrate here, you can teach yourself. You don't even need a stream or a lake. You can practice on a lawn or a rooftop in the city.

The proper stance is of primary importance. Make believe you are going to make a cast. The left foot goes out, as though you are going to throw a ball, and the body twists slightly to the right. This is wrong!

Rather stand with your feet planted on an imaginary line about 12 in. apart. Move the right foot forward until the heel is level with the toe of the left foot. Now go through an imaginary cast. Note how the arm goes straight up and down and there is no twisting of the body. This position will also eliminate the possibility of the excess line, which is held in the left hand, getting tangled with the rod or reel.

This stance is vitally important for the beginner. *The right foot always forward of the left.* This, of course, is reversed if you are left-handed.

Now you are ready to take up the rod. Hold it lightly, but firmly, in the right hand, the thumb resting on the top. Point it straight out before

OVERHEAD CAST

A — Right foot forward, let two rod lengths of line drift on the water ahead of you. Stand relaxed, the rod tip held above the horizontal

B — Press the elbow against the right side. Forearm and wrist are stiffened. Bend forward at the waist and the rod tip will come down toward the water. Prepare to count "ONE"

C — The right elbow should be tight against the side. The arm bends at the elbow as you count "ONE" and snap your body upright, bringing the rod up sharply over the head and lifting the fly off the water. The line is now traveling above your head

D — Stop! Don't move! Freeze the rod and body as you shout, "AND—," giving the line time to straighten out

E — Shout "TWO," and snap the body forward, bringing the rod down sharply to just above the horizontal. The arm bends at the elbow, but the forearm and wrist are rigid and the elbow is tight against the side

you, the tip angled slightly above the horizontal. Now strip some line off the reel with the left hand, holding it in loops about 18 in. long.

By flipping the tip of the rod and letting loose of some of the line, you can get about 20 ft. of line out on the water. Take up the slack with your left hand.

You are now ready to attempt your first cast which will be a *roll* cast.

This is a technique used on streams or lakes where trees and heavy brush prohibit the use of the overhead cast. Most fly fishermen add this cast to their repertoire after they have experienced the problem of insufficient casting room, but Newman uses it as a starter because it is easy and enables the beginner to get the feel of both the rod and the line.

Standing with the right foot advanced, the rod held out horizontal to the ground and about 20 ft. of line floating directly out ahead of you,

ROLL CAST

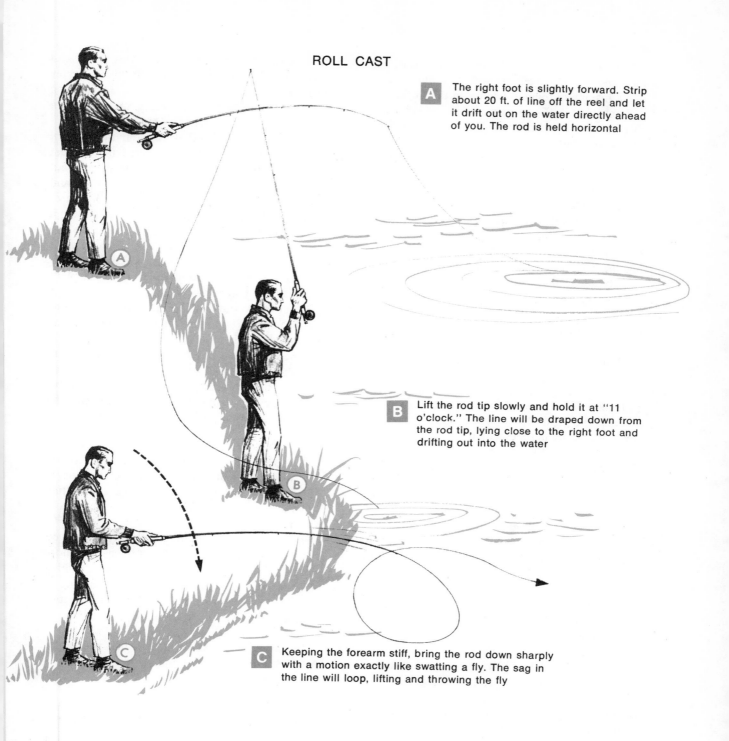

A The right foot is slightly forward. Strip about 20 ft. of line off the reel and let it drift out on the water directly ahead of you. The rod is held horizontal

B Lift the rod tip slowly and hold it at "11 o'clock." The line will be draped down from the rod tip, lying close to the right foot and drifting out into the water

C Keeping the forearm stiff, bring the rod down sharply with a motion exactly like swatting a fly. The sag in the line will loop, lifting and throwing the fly

slowly lift the tip of the rod, drawing the line toward you. Hold the rod so that the tip is above and behind your head, in a position that would be pointing to the numeral "11" if it were the hand of a clock. The line will drape down from the tip of the rod and run close to your right foot. (See illustration B on this page.) Press your right elbow close to your side. Now, with the forearm and wrist as rigid as possible, bring the rod down sharply with exactly the same motion

as you'd use swatting a fly. *Do not bring it down below the horizontal.* The sag in the line will go into a loop, neatly picking the fly off the water and dropping it again well beyond the rod tip.

That's all there is to the roll cast. It sounds easy and it is. It is also an extremely practical cast used by the experts in close quarters.

The overhead cast is almost entirely a matter of timing, and you can learn it in a few minutes.

What you are attempting to do is pick the fly

off the water, swing it back over your head, and then shoot it out over the water, letting it drop like a live insect touching down on the surface.

Slack line can be a problem in the overhead cast because it is line that is not under control. Learn to avoid this in the beginning and it will not become a problem as you gain in casting proficiency. Instead of yanking the fly into the air from wherever it and the line might be, lower the rod tip and take up the slack in loose coils with the left hand until the rod tip and line are as near as possible in a straight line toward the fly. Then slowly pull the fly toward you by lifting the rod tip to the proper position—angled slightly above the horizontal.

Now try the overhead cast. The right foot is advanced. The rod is slightly above the horizontal (Fig. A, page 1072). About two rod lengths of line are out before you. There is no slack in the line.

The following movements will seem exaggerated, but they are Newman's method, designed to teach control from the very beginning.

Press the right elbow tightly against the side, the upper arm perpendicular from shoulder to waist. Bend slightly forward from the waist (Fig. B). The forearm and wrist are kept rigid. There is no bending of the wrist.

count aloud

Count, "One!" Shout it aloud. Snap your body erect, throwing your head back. This will automatically bring the rod up, concentrating any movement in the elbow. Stop the rod in the position that would have the tip pointing to the numeral 10 on the face of a clock (Fig. C).

Freeze in that position!

The line is in the air and traveling back over your head.

Shout, "And!" This gives the line a full second to get fully straightened out behind you (Fig. D).

Shout, "Two," and snap your body forward, bending slightly at the waist, the elbow still tight against your side. The rod automatically returns to the position, angling slightly above the horizontal (Fig. E). The line descends to the water, the fly following it to land like a bug from the blue.

The timing is everything. "One—And—Two." If the line is snapped back before it has fully straightened, the result will be like cracking a whip. The line will not go out and the fly could snap off. If you wait too long the line drops behind you.

Run through the overhead cast until you get the feel of the timing. You can do this by making false casts. Before the line and fly hit the water bring it back up again, counting aloud, keeping the line in the air and working up a rhythm. "One—And—Two—And—One—And—Two."

When you have this down to your satisfaction, take a few loops of line in the left hand. Repeat the overhead cast, keeping the fly in the air, but now let out a little more line from the left hand on each false cast. As the length of line increases so must the length of the pause that allows it to straighten out. When all the slack is in the air, send it out and let it hit the water. This is the whole reason for the overhead cast, working the line out to the desired length that will place the fly where you want it to land.

Don't try to put out too much line. A fly line is 90 ft. long, but most stream fishing is done within a distance of 50 ft.

When you have the feel of the timing you can stop the exaggerated body movements and cast with just the arm. But remember: *no wrist movement!* The arm, from shoulder to hand, must be used like two rods with a hinge at the elbow.

gentleness is an art

A principle of fly casting is to lay the line on the water as gently as possible, so as not to frighten the fish. This is where you are getting into the "art" of fly casting, and it comes from practice.

You will also want to put the fly on target. This is the part that makes fly casting more pleasurable than other types of fishing. Catching fish becomes secondary to the fun of learning to put the fly where you want it. You can practice this on the lawn or rooftop, with a teacup as target.

In one hour you'll be able to fish with a fly. After that there is no limit to how skillful you may become—by practicing.

Ellis Newman can put out the full 90 ft. of line without a rod, using only his bare hands. He can cast with two rods in one hand. I've watched him cast simultaneously with a rod in each hand, and then alternate the rods so that he's in the back cast with one and the forward cast with the other.

This is the epitome of the art, but Newman is the first to admit that it doesn't impress a fish. Dropping a fly in the current so it looks like a free lunch is the important thing—and the easiest.

See also: bait, fishing; bass fishing; boats, buying; fishing; ice fishing; lures; pram; trolling motor.

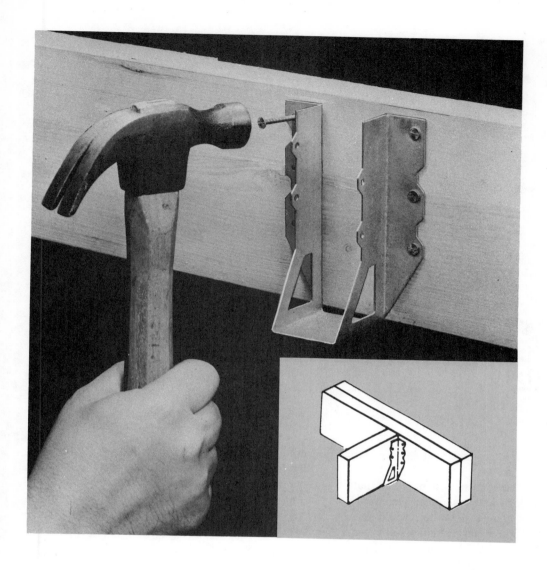

Engineered nailing simplifies framing

BY ARTHUR MAHER

Rejects from a kid's Erector Set?
Wow, how they help the builder!

front suspension: see ball joints, auto

■ CALLED "Building Specialties" in the trade, these sheet-metal fasteners now make it possible for the amateur to frame a house as strong as a bridge. With them, toenailing becomes a thing of the past for fastening studs, joists and rafters. Butted members become "welded" together, so to speak, to make the joining of a house 50 percent or more stronger. And there is less chance of splitting the members while nailing.

The devices go by the names of joist hanger, framing anchor, post base, rafter anchor, etc.. In most cases, they are made of 13 to 18-ga. galvanized steel and cost so little that ten dollars or so can buy enough for a good-sized room addition. Prospective homebuilders will find these fasteners raise the price of a dwelling comparatively little when added to the building specs, yet

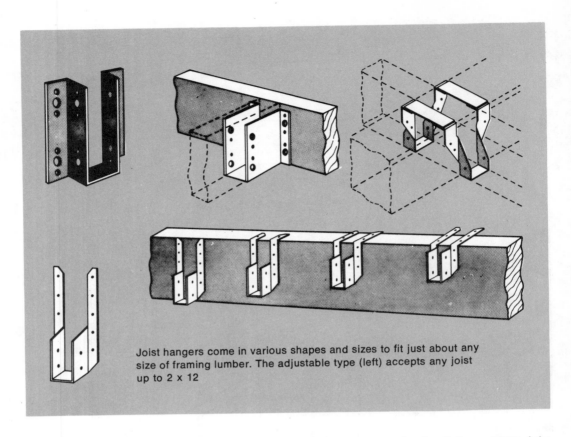

Joist hangers come in various shapes and sizes to fit just about any size of framing lumber. The adjustable type (left) accepts any joist up to 2 x 12

are well worth the additional cost in the extra strength gained.

For an idea of how these fasteners can help you, consider the joist hangers above. Ordinarily, to butt floor joists against a timber, you'd have to toenail with 10d or larger nails—not easy without a lot of practice. And in many cases, you'd need a ledger strip, and might even have to notch each joist to fit the ledger. With joist hangers, all you do is nail the hangers to the timber, insert the joists and drive in more nails. The nails, which go in pre-drilled holes in the hangers, may be only 1½ in. or so long and are often supplied with the hangers. Ledger strips are out altogether, and each joint is stronger than a toenailed joint.

Joist setters are said to be 3½ times stronger than toenails. You nail them to the sill, then insert joists as shown below without nails

With joists in place, level their top edges by raising the back panels of the joist setters to insert shims. Then drive nails into the joists

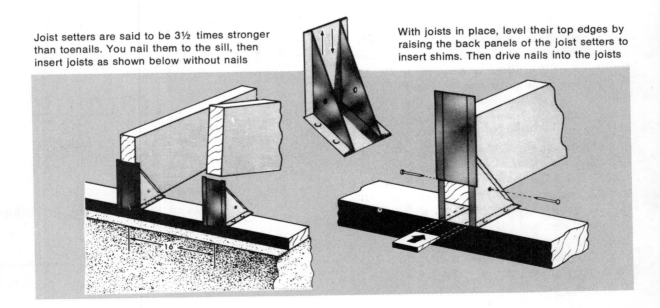

1076

This is because loads bearing on the joint are resisted by what engineers call the shear strength of the nails (the force required to break the nails). With toenails, the loads act against the nails' withdrawal strength, which is much weaker.

Besides the joist hangers, there are a wide variety of fasteners that act in a similar way to anchor studs to the shoe plate, the top plate to the studs, rafters to the studs or top plate, etc.

Other fasteners do more than merely simplify

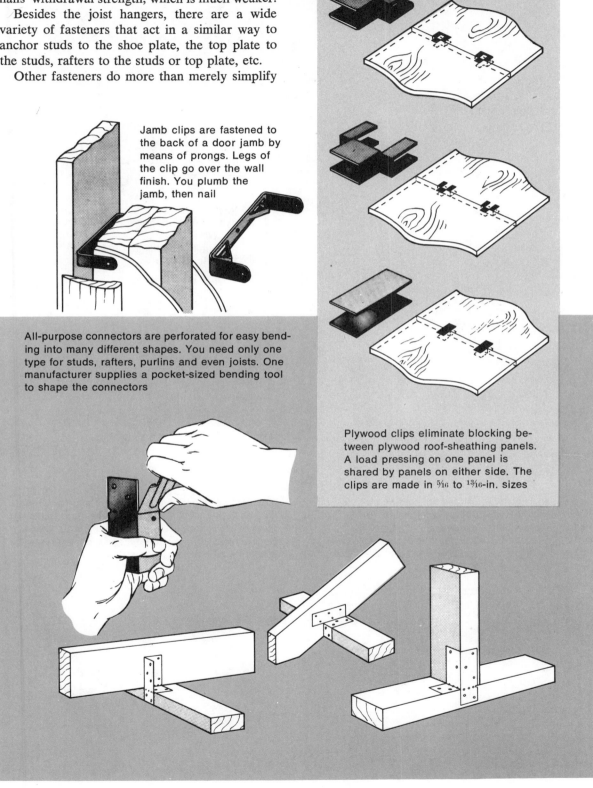

Jamb clips are fastened to the back of a door jamb by means of prongs. Legs of the clip go over the wall finish. You plumb the jamb, then nail

All-purpose connectors are perforated for easy bending into many different shapes. You need only one type for studs, rafters, purlins and even joists. One manufacturer supplies a pocket-sized bending tool to shape the connectors

Plywood clips eliminate blocking between plywood roof-sheathing panels. A load pressing on one panel is shared by panels on either side. The clips are made in $5/16$ to $13/16$-in. sizes

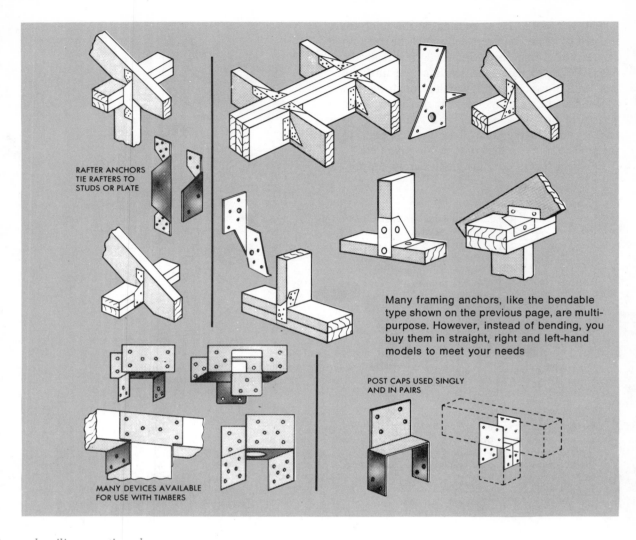

RAFTER ANCHORS
TIE RAFTERS TO
STUDS OR PLATE

Many framing anchors, like the bendable type shown on the previous page, are multipurpose. However, instead of bending, you buy them in straight, right and left-hand models to meet your needs

POST CAPS USED SINGLY
AND IN PAIRS

MANY DEVICES AVAILABLE
FOR USE WITH TIMBERS

engineered nailing, continued

Line-a-joist stretches joists by splicing into single units. Positive (downward) bending of ordinary joists concentrates flexing at centers. Negative bending of spliced joists counteracts positive bending, which results in more even flexing of the wood

Metal stair stringers let you put in a stairway in as little as 20 minutes. You nail stringers to basement walls or other support, then slide in 2 x 10 treads. Double-headed (removable) staging nails go into the treads through holes in the stringers

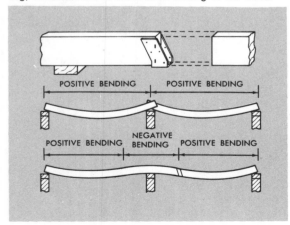

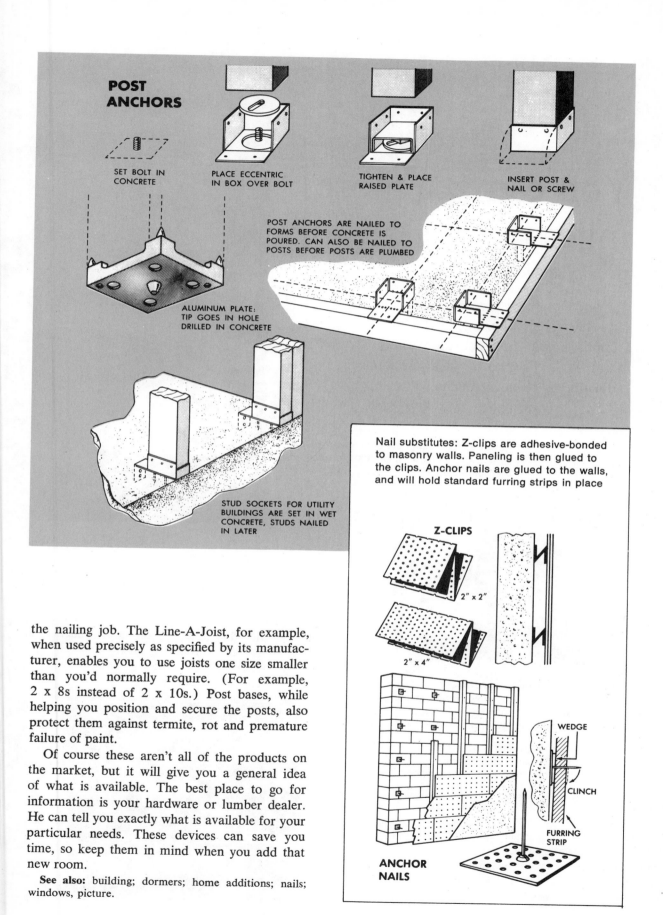

POST ANCHORS

SET BOLT IN CONCRETE

PLACE ECCENTRIC IN BOX OVER BOLT

TIGHTEN & PLACE RAISED PLATE

INSERT POST & NAIL OR SCREW

ALUMINUM PLATE: TIP GOES IN HOLE DRILLED IN CONCRETE

POST ANCHORS ARE NAILED TO FORMS BEFORE CONCRETE IS POURED. CAN ALSO BE NAILED TO POSTS BEFORE POSTS ARE PLUMBED

STUD SOCKETS FOR UTILITY BUILDINGS ARE SET IN WET CONCRETE, STUDS NAILED IN LATER

Nail substitutes: Z-clips are adhesive-bonded to masonry walls. Paneling is then glued to the clips. Anchor nails are glued to the walls, and will hold standard furring strips in place

Z-CLIPS

2" x 2"

2" x 4"

WEDGE

CLINCH

FURRING STRIP

ANCHOR NAILS

the nailing job. The Line-A-Joist, for example, when used precisely as specified by its manufacturer, enables you to use joists one size smaller than you'd normally require. (For example, 2 x 8s instead of 2 x 10s.) Post bases, while helping you position and secure the posts, also protect them against termite, rot and premature failure of paint.

Of course these aren't all of the products on the market, but it will give you a general idea of what is available. The best place to go for information is your hardware or lumber dealer. He can tell you exactly what is available for your particular needs. These devices can save you time, so keep them in mind when you add that new room.

See also: building; dormers; home additions; nails; windows, picture.

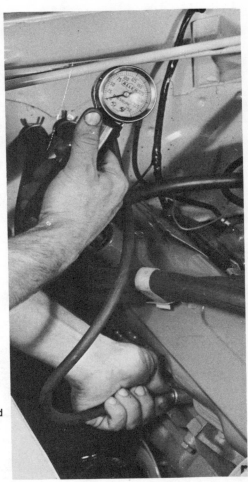

You can get more miles per gallon

BY MORTON J. SCHULTZ

There's no shortage of techniques
to help improve your fuel consumption.
They range from mechanical
adjustments to acquiring new
driving habits that save fuel

Power thieves within the engine can be detected with a compression test (as above) and a vacuum gauge test

Test vacuum advance by moving the breaker plate to full advance. Cover opening with finger. Plate should not move when finger is lifted

An over-long accelerator pump stroke delivers too much fuel to the engine. Measure the stroke and adjust it to specifications

■ "WHAT DO YOU FIND to be the major causes of excessive fuel consumption in modern cars?" was a question asked of 200 top mechanics in the New York metropolitan area.

Two answers stand out:

1. The way drivers drive.

Precise fuel consumption can be established only with a gauge of the type shown above. It's tapped into the fuel system while the car is run over a planned course of known length

2. Mechanical letdowns which rob the engine of power or add to the normal resistances a car must buck.

The experts also pointed out that many drivers whose cars are delivering quite satisfactory mileage are convinced they're driving "gas hogs"— simply because they employ a faulty method of calculating gas consumption.

Unless your car is mechanically perfect, and unless you're an expert driver, there's little doubt you *can* increase your miles-per-gallon. How much will depend on the adjustments you make to your car—and the *re*adjustment you make in your own driving habits.

Let's concede that right away some drivers will ask, "Is it worth it?"

Well, from a mechanical standpoint it is, because the same conditions which reduce mileage are also those which rob your car of power and performance and lead to big repair bills.

As for a driver's ability—or willingness—to form new gas-saving driving habits . . . that's another matter. Some people will refuse to cut their highway speed by five miles an hour no matter how much gas they'd save.

You must find out how much fuel your car is now using *with you driving*. A mileage test conducted by an expert will not show the same results that it will with *you* behind the wheel. However, having an expert drive the car after he observes your driving will give you the chance to get a comparison in mileage between his driving and yours. And he may offer you some good advice for improving your driving habits.

The *only way* to determine accurately how much gas a car is using is with a gas-per-mile gauge connected into the fuel system while driving over a *planned* test course. For those who might scoff at the above statement, read what engineers of a leading national automotive service

FUEL SYSTEM GAS ROBBERS

Beware of a fuel system that delivers more gas to an engine than it needs. Listen for faster-than-normal idling; look for black smoke from the exhaust pipe when car is started. Cause may be poor fuel-to-air ratio.

LOOK FOR—

- ☐ High fuel-pump pressure
- ☐ Dirty air cleaner
- ☐ Too-rich choke adjustment
- ☐ Improper adjustments of:
  idle setting
  fast-idle screw
  accelerator pump stroke
  anti-stall dashpot
- ☐ Too-high carburetor float level
- ☐ Internal carburetor damage such as worn jets and faulty power valve
- ☐ Binding in the accelerator linkage

IGNITION SYSTEM GAS ROBBERS

You are not getting the full benefit from your fuel if a weak spark delivered to the cylinders fails to completely burn the gas. Unburned gasoline which reaches the cylinders is then lost through the exhaust pipe.

LOOK FOR—

- ☐ Leaks in the high-tension cable
- ☐ A weak coil
- ☐ Worn, dirty, fouled or incorrectly gapped spark plugs
- ☐ Faulty ignition timing
- ☐ Incorrectly adjusted or worn distributor breaker points
- ☐ An inoperative distributor spark advance unit

more miles per gallon, continued

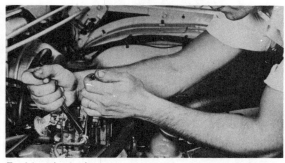

Fuel lost by leakage or evaporation is wasted. Check all the lines up to the carburetor and tighten any loose connections, especially those at the carb

A clean crankcase valve helps to avoid wasted fuel. To clean or replace it, remove the cover and pull off the vent line. Check the manual before starting

said recently about odometers as instruments for checking gas mileage:

"An odometer is not an accurate meter for recording engine use because engine idle time is not recorded. Both speedometer and odometer rely on a cable driven by the transmission. Thus, if the vehicle is not in motion, neither the speedometer nor the odometer can operate."

Now, here's the bombshell:

"Therefore, in consulting the numbers on the vehicle's odometer it is recommended that about *2000 miles be added to each 12,000 miles showing on the odometer to account for the time the engine has spent idling.*" (The italics are added.)

In other words these engineers estimate that in 12,000 miles of driving some 2000 miles' worth of gasoline is wasted by the engine in idling! That's a lot of fuel.

Of course gas is wasted in other ways as well. There is no way to estimate, for example, how much gas you lose just by evaporation when the car is not used for some time. General engine fatigue as well as particular mechanical failures are important factors too.

According to the rough estimate of one car owner's fuel consumption, he was getting an unsatisfactory 13 miles to the gallon. He decided to check this out a little more scientifically.

He took the car to a mechanic buddy of mine

ENGINE/POWER TRAIN GAS ROBBERS

The engine and power train are prime sources of fuel loss. Often the trouble can be traced to the valves. Regular maintenance and particular adjustments in this area can help save much fuel.

LOOK FOR—

- ☐ Compression loss
- ☐ Burnt or sticky valves
- ☐ Improperly adjusted valves
- ☐ A defective crankcase ventilation regulator valve
- ☐ A frozen manifold heat control valve
- ☐ A restricted exhaust system
- ☐ Improperly adjusted automatic transmssion

AREAS OF GAS LEAKS

Leaks account for most of the gas that's lost before it reaches the engine. Stop leaks by battening down on connections and sealing up seams. The most likely places where leaks will occur are . . .

HERE—

- ☐ In the fuel line where it connects to the carburetor
- ☐ In the fuel line where it enters and leaves the fuel pump
- ☐ In the seams of the gas tank filler neck
- ☐ At the gas tank cap
- ☐ In the gas tank itself

who had an accurate gas-per-mile gauge calibrated in tenths of a gallon. They tapped the gauge into the gas line between fuel pump and carburetor and conducted the so-called *bottle test*.

The car was taken on four different runs of equal distance. It was not allowed to sit still and idle except where traffic conditions and red lights forced natural stops. Readings on the corrected odometer were taken before and after each run.

The test course included (1) a drive at highway speed in one direction; (2) a drive over the same highway in the opposite direction (to equalize the effects of any head or tail winds); (3) a drive through a light-traffic urban area; and (4) a drive through a heavy-traffic business district.

Each run was conducted, where possible, at posted speed limits. The resulting readings were then added up and averaged to get the correct gas mileage.

The results of this test showed that the car was getting 18.2 miles per gallon—or 5.2 *more* miles per gallon than had been estimated—thus proving the unreliability and inaccuracy of those off-the-cuff estimates previously referred to.

This kind of test will cost you a few dollars, but it's worth it—especially if you discover that your car's not the gas burner you thought it was.

A driver who wants to save gas keeps two "gas-gulping" facts in mind: (1) The more the accelerator pedal is hit, the more gas is wasted; (2) the more a car's engine is allowed to idle, the more gas is wasted. In other words, stop-and-go driving around town consumes much more gas than highway driving.

Here are some ways you can stretch your fuel dollar by using intelligent driving techniques. Try one or more of them for a week or two, then check your mileage again to see how much —or if—your fuel bills have been reduced.

● *Avoid needless idling.* Three minutes with the engine idling and the car standing still uses as much gas as driving one-half mile at 30 miles per hour. Repeat: *avoid needless idling.*

● *Use a steady foot on the accelerator pedal.* When starting from a standing stop, press the gas pedal slowly and steadily. Avoid jackrabbit starts—and stops, too. "Flooring it" and then backing off burns up gasoline which isn't needed for acceleration in the first place. Maintain steadiness of acceleration and deceleration at cruising speeds as well. Don't run up on the tail of the car ahead only to have to brake down because you can't go anywhere anyway.

● *Use correct passing procedure.* Never run up on the car ahead, slam down on the brakes, then hit the accelerator pedal to pass. Start the

Valve lash of cars with mechanical valve lifters and valve clearance of engines with hydraulic lifters should be checked periodically

pass well back of the car ahead to permit yourself a smooth swing out and in again.

● *Drive at moderate speeds.* Once the car shifts into driving gear, gas consumption increases as speed increases. Stay within posted speed limits; these are considered "moderate" as well as safe.

● *Don't brake unnecessarily.* Try to time traffic lights, for example, so you can keep rolling without stopping. You'll use more gas by stopping and starting again than if you can manage to coast to the light just as it turns green; then reapply a steady pressure on the gas pedal while you're still moving.

When you must stop, let your engine act as a brake. When approaching a stop sign, for instance, let up on the gas pedal at a sufficient distance from the sign to allow the engine to slow the car so only a minimum use of brakes is needed. This conserves not only gas, but also the brakes.

● *With a manual shift car, use your brakes instead of the clutch when waiting for a traffic light on an uphill grade.* "Riding" the clutch and revving the engine to keep from stalling wastes gas and increases clutch wear. Shift into neutral (or keep the clutch disengaged) and use the brake.

● *Never fill the gas tank to the top, especially in hot weather.* Gas expands as it heats up and may overflow a brimful tank. Always leave an air space of a few inches between the top of the gas and the top of the filler neck.

A car isn't a greased rod moving through a vacuum. Forces reacting against its forward motion act to hold it back. These forces (resistances) are both *natural* and *mechanical*.

In the first category are included such elemental forces as head winds, snow, mud—and hills (gravity).

A car's inherent mechanical resistances include the weight of the vehicle, friction generated by its movement through the air and the friction of the tires on the pavement.

Bucking all these resistances is engine go-power. A gas-efficient engine will overcome resistance by using a minimum amount of power. Just one mechanical flaw which reduces peak power means the engine must furnish just that much *more* power to overcome these forces. In generating this power the engine uses gas. So in your own attempts to increase gas mileage, bear the following two considerations in mind:

1. Reduce to a minimum those resistances over which you have control.

2. Maintain the car at peak mechanical efficiency so it can achieve maximum performance using minimum power.

aim for peak efficiency

An important point in maintaining engine efficiency is to insure that no gas is lost by leakage because of a break in the sealed fuel system.

Tire pressure, too, is an important governing factor in fuel consumption. With less tire surface in contact with the road, less friction exists, thus less gas is consumed. This *doesn't* mean you should jam 45 lb. of air in your tires. However, slight overinflation—about 5 lb. over recommended pressure—is acceptable in most cases. *Under*inflation will substantially reduce tire life.

Wheels that are out of alignment are another cause of fuel-frittering friction. So is a hung-up brake that puts a drag on the wheels.

The mechanical failures that can rob your engine of power and cause it to waste gas are too numerous to discuss individually. We've done the next best thing by listing the most common causes in troubleshooting check-off charts on pages 1082 and 1083. If you discover your car is a gas-burner and are satisfied your driving habits are not at fault, spend a couple of Saturdays on the repairs and adjustments indicated on the check-off lists. The effort you put into this area of car maintenance now *may* pay off with a saving of $100 or more in gas and repairs over the next year's driving.

See also: auto repair; carburetors, auto; idling, auto; ignition system, auto; speedometers.

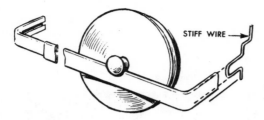

A convenient holder for two or three pot covers can be made from a flat curtain rod. The potholder may be hooked to a panel of perforated hardboard by bending a piece of wire to fit inside as shown.

To remove a tight fitting cap from a large diameter jar, wrap a damp towel around it to serve as a handle for easier and surer grip.

A small funnel makes a fine substitute for an egg separator. Break the egg into the funnel; the white will flow through the spout, leaving the yolk to be emptied into a separate container.

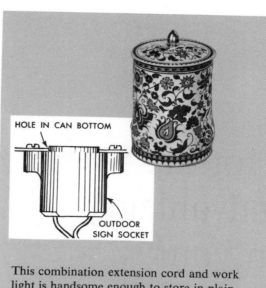

This combination extension cord and work light is handsome enough to store in plain sight. You make it from a fancy candy tin. Fit a socket in a hole in the bottom and attach a 25-ft. lamp cord. A three-way socket permits plugging-in a portable tool. The bulb, cord and socket all store inside.

Hot-dip galvanizing in your own kitchen

Weatherproof those shop-made parts
and fittings with a coating of
zinc right in your own kitchen and
protect them from the elements

■ IF YOU THINK OF GALVANIZING as strictly an industrial procedure, you're dead wrong. Any home craftsman can use this process. You can obtain pure zinc in bar form from any metals supply house. As for equipment, you'll need a plumbers' furnace and melting pot which can be purchased at almost any local hardware store or by mail order.

In addition to these, you'll have to stop at a drugstore to pick up some sal ammoniac (ammonium chloride) and hydrochloric acid. The commercial grade of hydrochloric acid, usually labeled "muriatic acid," is cheaper and works just as well for pickling.

The first step in galvanizing is to clean the metal thoroughly. You can burn off paint or an old coat of zinc with a torch or the flame of the plumbers' furnace, but grease and oil should be removed by boiling the part to be galvanized in a solution of sodium carbonate. Almost any photo supply store stocks this chemical. (Don't substitute baking soda; that's sodium *bi*carbonate.) For average cleaning, mix about two tablespoonsful per quart of water and boil for five to ten minutes.

After boiling, rinse the part thoroughly in

Cleaning the metal to be galvanized is the first step in the process. Old paint or previous galvanizing may be burned off, but grease and oil must be removed by boiling it in a solution of sodium carbonate

Pickling in acid completes the cleaning. Leave the parts in an acid bath until the metal has a uniform gray tone, indicating that it is thoroughly clean. Be sure to wear rubber gloves when working with acid

Rinsing removes all traces of the acid. Place the parts in a shallow pan of cold water in your kitchen sink and turn on the tap. This will keep the water circulating and speed the rinsing job

Drying after rinsing is a safety measure, since any moisture left on the metal will flash into steam on contact with the hot zinc and this may cause the molten metal to spatter. Use a hair dryer for drying

warm water to remove all traces of the solution. Then dry it with a clean towel or a stream of warm air (from your wife's hair dryer, for instance). From this point on, *do not touch the metal with your bare hand.* The invisible grease smears from your skin will inhibit the plating.

Pickling, or bathing the part in acid, is actually a second cleaning operation which removes all oxides, leaving the metal perfectly clean and ready for the zinc. Pour enough hydrochloric acid into a glass dish to cover the part and slide the part under the surface gently to avoid splashing. Be sure to provide proper ventilation.

It may take an hour of soaking in the acid bath to remove every last bit of oxide. The metal will have a uniform gray tone when clean, but even though it may look clean allow an extra five or ten minutes to be absolutely sure. Then take the part out of the acid and place it in a pan of cold water under an open tap so that the running water will rinse away any acid remaining on the metal. After rinsing, dry the part thoroughly.

Acid-cleaned steel will begin to oxidize immediately upon removal from the bath, so you should have the pot of molten zinc prepared before removing the part from the pickling. Zinc

Before dipping, skim off the worst of the oxidation scum floating on the surface of the zinc and sprinkle a little sal ammoniac on the molten metal to act as flux; immerse the part immediately after

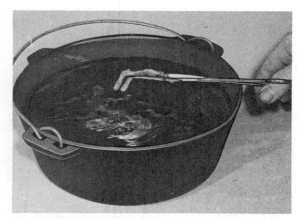

Plunge the zinc-coated part into cold water immediately after withdrawing it from the zinc bath. If a heavier coating is desired, return it to the zinc bath a second time, assuring good protection

GALVANIZING TIPS

If the zinc doesn't adhere well, your trouble can probably be traced to one of the following:

1. *Kind of steel*—Mild steel and forgings are easier to galvanize than other types.
2. *Cleanliness*—Remove *all* grease and oil before pickling.
3. *Poor pickling*—Leave part in acid long enough so that no spots of oxide remain.
4. *Poor quality zinc*—Happens rarely. Be sure to use "electrolytic" zinc.
5. *Temperature of zinc bath*—Keep it well above the melting point of zinc.
6. *Duration of zinc bath*—Allow part to come up to temperature of zinc.
7. *Oxide deposits*—Skim zinc bath thoroughly and sprinkle enough sal ammoniac over surface to clean it, then submerge part immediately.

melts at a temperature of 787 deg. F., but for good adhesion it should be heated to 820 deg. F. Be sure the room is well-ventilated.

Molten zinc oxidizes rapidly, forming a yellowish-green scum on the surface. For a bright clean galvanizing job, avoid getting any of this oxide on the metal. Just before immersing the part, skim off the worst of this scum with an old spoon and then sprinkle a little sal ammoniac on the molten metal. When the surface is clean, thrust the part into the pot.

The part should remain in the zinc bath until its temperature comes up to that of the zinc. With the parts shown here in the photographs, a couple of minutes was sufficient. Naturally, heavier parts would require longer periods. When the part is ready to come out, reach into the pot with tongs and get a good grip on it, but don't bring it above the surface. Then use the procedure mentioned above to remove oxide from the surface of the zinc and lift the part out. Hold it over the pot for a moment to let the excess zinc flow off, then plunge it into cold water. If a heavier coating is desired, dry the piece thoroughly and repeat the zinc bath.

See also: rust prevention; rust removal; sandblasting; tumbling machines.

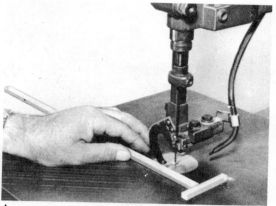

A permanent magnet of the bar type is just the thing to use as an adjustable cut-off stop on your jigsaw. Say you need to cut a number of equal lengths from a small strip. Place a rule on the table, measure the required distance from the side of the blade, and drop the permanent magnet on the table with its edge at the measured point. Then place the workpiece with the end against the edge of the magnet and move into the blade.

Large pipe caps, such as those on oil-tank filler pipes, require use of a pipe wrench for removing and replacing. Not everyone has a pipe wrench handy when needed for such a job. Solve this problem by having a ½-in. nut welded to the cap. This permits use of any small end wrench or adjustable wrench when removing or replacing the cap. To prevent the nut from filling with water and rusting, turn a bolt of the same diameter into the nut, cut it off flush and peen it over.

You don't need to build a demagnetizer to demagnetize small tools such as screwdrivers. You have one right in your tool kit. Just connect your soldering gun, close the switch and insert and withdraw the blade of the screwdriver between the two arms that form the tip. This does the job in a hurry and leaves your tools ready to use.

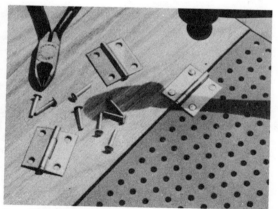

Installing hinges on doors or panels of thin materials, such as ¼-in. plywood and perforated hardboard, is difficult and often impossible because screws won't hold. Rivets solve this problem nicely. Just use ordinary aluminum rivets and rivet washers. Drill holes in plywood for the rivets to exact size.

Cornstalk feeding station for pheasants should be wired securely to small tree for support. It offers both food and shelter in extremely cold, stormy weather when the normal food supply is covered with deep snow

Game-bird savers

BY W. CLYDE LAMMEY

When the hunting season ends,
the birds still face survival
problems from lack of food

game cart: see carts
game-room table: see pool tables

■ IN ANY REGION where heavy snowfalls and prolonged periods of severe cold are likely during the winter months, non-migrating game birds by the hundreds and often by the thousands may die of starvation. This is especially true of the ground feeders who must rely on seeds, grain scatterings from fall harvesting and, in forested regions, on mast, such as acorns, berries and certain small nuts. In some seasons game-bird losses from a lack of food during long spells of severe weather can greatly exceed the normal take of natural predators, and may even wipe out entire local bird populations, so it is important to make game-bird feeders as plentiful as possible if

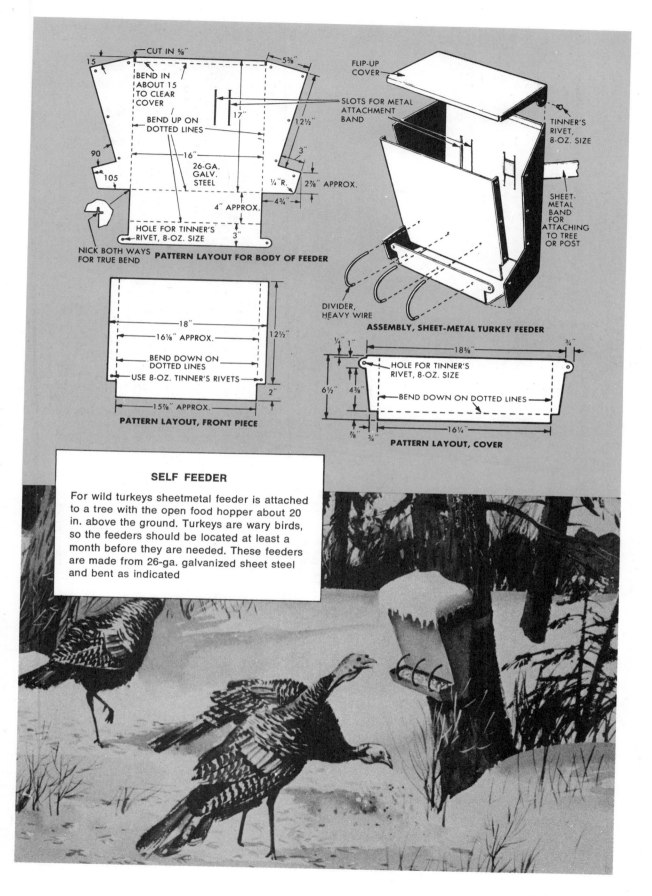

CUT IN ⅝"

BEND IN ABOUT 15 TO CLEAR COVER

5⅜"

SLOTS FOR METAL ATTACHMENT BAND

15

BEND UP ON DOTTED LINES

17"

12½"

3"

90

16"

26-GA. GALV. STEEL

105

¼" R.

2⅞" APPROX.

4" APPROX.

4¾"

NICK BOTH WAYS FOR TRUE BEND

HOLE FOR TINNER'S RIVET, 8-OZ. SIZE

3"

PATTERN LAYOUT FOR BODY OF FEEDER

FLIP-UP COVER

TINNER'S RIVET, 8-OZ. SIZE

SHEET-METAL BAND FOR ATTACHING TO TREE OR POST

DIVIDER, HEAVY WIRE

ASSEMBLY, SHEET-METAL TURKEY FEEDER

18"

16⅛" APPROX.

12½"

BEND DOWN ON DOTTED LINES

USE 8-OZ. TINNER'S RIVETS

2"

15⅞" APPROX.

PATTERN LAYOUT, FRONT PIECE

¼" 1"

18⅝"

¾"

HOLE FOR TINNER'S RIVET, 8-OZ. SIZE

6½"

4¾"

BEND DOWN ON DOTTED LINES

⅞" ¾"

16¼"

PATTERN LAYOUT, COVER

SELF FEEDER

For wild turkeys sheetmetal feeder is attached to a tree with the open food hopper about 20 in. above the ground. Turkeys are wary birds, so the feeders should be located at least a month before they are needed. These feeders are made from 26-ga. galvanized sheet steel and bent as indicated

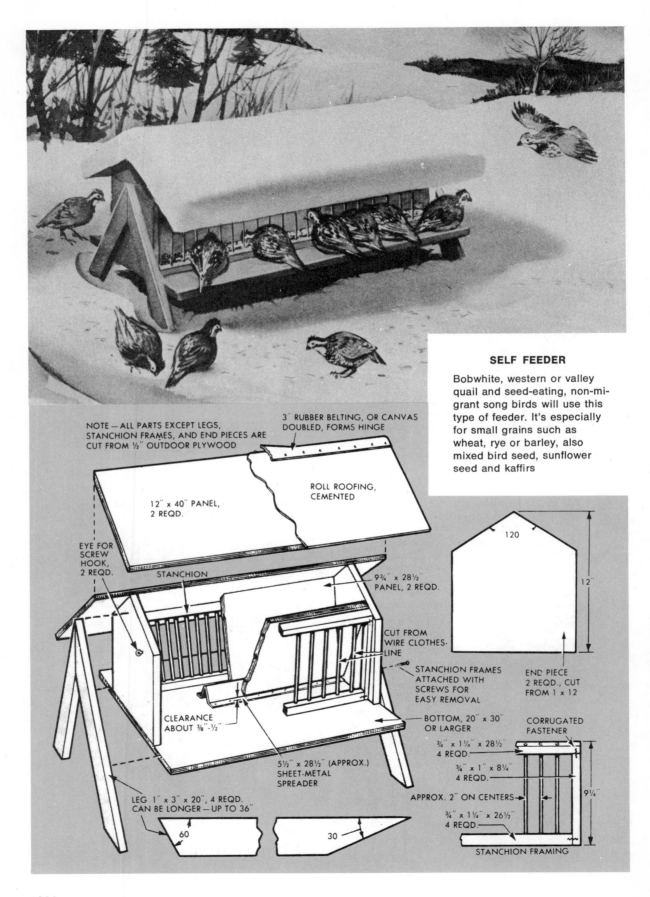

SELF FEEDER

Bobwhite, western or valley quail and seed-eating, non-migrant song birds will use this type of feeder. It's especially for small grains such as wheat, rye or barley, also mixed bird seed, sunflower seed and kaffirs

NOTE — ALL PARTS EXCEPT LEGS, STANCHION FRAMES, AND END PIECES ARE CUT FROM ½" OUTDOOR PLYWOOD

3" RUBBER BELTING, OR CANVAS DOUBLED, FORMS HINGE

12" x 40" PANEL, 2 REQD.

ROLL ROOFING, CEMENTED

EYE FOR SCREW HOOK, 2 REQD.

STANCHION

9¾" x 28½" PANEL, 2 REQD.

CUT FROM WIRE CLOTHES-LINE

STANCHION FRAMES ATTACHED WITH SCREWS FOR EASY REMOVAL

CLEARANCE ABOUT ⅜"-½"

120

12"

END PIECE 2 REQD., CUT FROM 1 x 12

BOTTOM, 20" x 30" OR LARGER

5½" x 28½" (APPROX.) SHEET-METAL SPREADER

CORRUGATED FASTENER

¾" x 1¼" x 28½" 4 REQD.

¾" x 1" x 8¼" 4 REQD.

9¼"

LEG 1" x 3" x 20", 4 REQD. CAN BE LONGER — UP TO 36"

60

30

APPROX. 2" ON CENTERS

¾" x 1¼" x 26½" 4 REQD.

STANCHION FRAMING

String ear corn on a length of heavy wire and support the wire between two sturdy shrubs with one end of the wire attached to a spring to maintain tension, keeping the corn above the snow. All feeders will attract other birds, even some undesirables. This cannot be avoided

we are to maintain them in any numbers.

The time to get game-bird feeders built and located is long before they are needed. As a rule truly wild game birds (those hatched in the wild) are extremely wary and won't approach newly placed feeders until they become accustomed to them by long association. This means that feeders should be placed at least a month before heavy snows and cold are due. And to make sure that the feeders will be strategically located where most needed, one must know the daily range of the birds, their feeding habits morning and evening, where they roost and how far they may range in seach of food during any single day. This is easily determined by observation or from landowners, most of whom will gladly grant you permission to locate feeders on their properties.

There are several pointers which are important to the placement of the feeders and these should be observed if the birds are to receive the most benefit from the effort. As a rule, individual feeders should be located near natural cover frequented by the birds, such as a ditch or a small waterway overgrown with shrubbery in which birds normally shelter during stormy winter weather. In the open near a thicket or at the edge of a wooded area also is usually a good location. But before you locate the feeder take careful note of the immediate area, and keep in mind the quarter from which the most severe storms are likely to come. Don't place the feeder

where drifting snow may cover it completely and remember to place it far enough from heavy cover so that predators will be forced into the open before they can come within striking distance of feeding birds. In some cases it may be best, because of an otherwise favorable location, to place the feeder close to natural cover and then erect a length of temporary woven-wire fencing which will force predators to make a detour and thus reveal themselves in time for the birds to get airborne. A few long stakes and a discarded length of poultry netting are all the materials you need for this protective screen against predators. Also, the feeders should, so far as possible, be placed in areas not frequented by livestock, since they could easily be trampled and destroyed before the birds would benefit from them. Where this is unavoidable, it may be advisable to fence a small area in which to place the feeder. Get your landowner friend's permission before building a fence enclosing even a small area.

Several different types of feeders and feeding stations suitable for nearly all common non-migratory, ground-feeding game birds are shown here. Some of these are simple affairs that can be assembled in a few minutes, largely from materials immediately at hand. The cornstalk station is an example. Gather sufficient stalks to make a large shock. Stand them at an angle around a small tree and wire the tops tightly to the tree trunk as illustrated. Spread the stalks

Quickly improvised station for feeding prairie grouse, chukar partridge, pheasant; also suitable for quail and other smaller birds. Canvas or plastic supports tree branches to protect the feed from drifting snow

when severe winter storms sweep their ranges in the plains states. A feeding station built of twigs can help these birds survive the severest winters. To make it, cut forked "posts" from small saplings and drive them into the ground, spacing 3½ to 5 ft. each way over-all and standing to a height of about 15 to 18 in. Lay poles in the forks and cover with a sheet of heavy plastic. Pile on trimmings from shrubs and small trees to make it appear as a natural brush pile with the opening on the leeward side of the prevailing winds and storms. Scatter a good supply of small grains such as wheat, oats or barley inside the enclosure and sprinkle a few grains outside to attract the birds. They will soon locate the feeder and once association overcomes their wariness you will have regular patronage.

turkeys increase range

Wild turkeys are increasing their range due largely to protective and propagation measures of various clubs and state conservationists. Normally, in the southern turkey ranges particularly, the birds can make it through the average winter without any outside help. But there are seasons when a line of feeders in the mountain ranges of the wild turkey could mean the difference between few or no birds the following spring and a normal or increasing turkey population. One feeder for turkeys which seems to meet most of the requirements is shown on page 1091. Turkeys are extremely wary birds and it will likely be some time before they finally visit your feeders. Once feeders are placed, don't move them. Any of the small grains are acceptable as food, also hazelnuts and even small acorns, if they can be gathered in sufficient quantity.

For recommended feed grains and other foods contact your state department of conservation. They also may have special recommendations for winter feeding of game birds in your locality, and have available late surveys of bird populations. This information should be helpful in carrying out your feeding program.

In addition, you will find that all feeders, of course, will attract other birds, even some undesirables such as crow and starlings. This cannot be avoided.

With the simple materials needed for these projects, and the slight amount of time it will take to construct them, you'll find the effort very rewarding, especially when the bird population in your area increases.

See also: birdbath; bird feeders; birdhouses; bird photography; pheasant hunting.

apart to form an opening on the leeward side of prevailing winds and storms. Form a hopper for ear corn from woven-wire fencing. Such a feeder provides food and even shelter for pheasant, prairie grouse and others. Another quickie feeder especially suited to pheasant in some localities is the ear-corn "string" at the top of page 1093. A length of fairly heavy wire is forced through the cob of each ear of corn and tensioned between two shrubs with loops of wire and a strong coil spring. Three to five ears of corn can be strung in this fashion.

The self-feeder shown and fully detailed on page 1092 is especially suited to bobwhite, valley quail and even seed-eating, non-migrant songbirds. As dimensioned, it's about minimum size but can be made larger and the legs can be extended from the length given in the directions in the illustration to 30 or even 36 in. to keep the feeder above deep snows. Use outdoor plywood and solid stock combined and when finished, stain the exposed parts with a gray shingle stain to give a weathered appearance. The feeder should be placed where it is not easily overturned by wind (or livestock). In some cases it may be advisable to anchor the four legs with stakes driven into the ground.

Although both are hardy and resourceful birds, the native prairie grouse—also called prairie chicken—and the "immigrant" chukar partridge often suffer greatly from lack of food

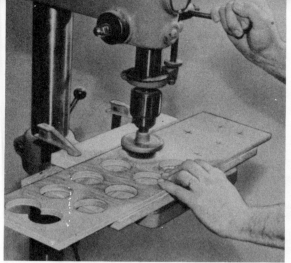

The hole saw is perfect for making the cutouts in the upper half of your Mancala board. If you don't have one, use a jigsaw for this job. To cut out scoring bins with a hole saw, make two overlapping hole cuts and trim the waste to leave a smooth side

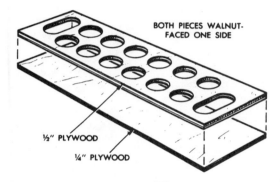

BOTH PIECES WALNUT-FACED ONE SIDE

½" PLYWOOD

¼" PLYWOOD

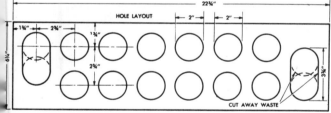

22¾"

HOLE LAYOUT   2"   2"

1¾"   2¾"   1¾"

6¼"   2¾"   3¾"

CUT AWAY WASTE

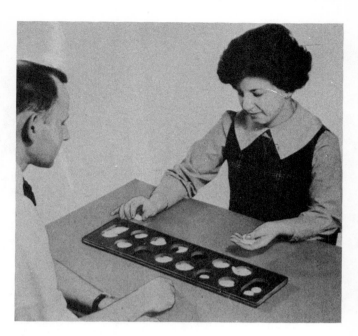

Africa's most popular game has caught on in the United States. You can join in by making a playing board in your home workshop

Mancala

BY VOLTA TORREY

THE NATIONAL GAME of Africa, known as "Mancala," has caught on with Americans.

You can join in the fun by making a Mancala board in your home workshop. All you have to do is follow the details below.

One of the oldest games in the world, Mancala is played by two people. The object is to capture the most counters. Each player places the same number of counters (coins, marbles, etc.) in six holes on his side of the board.

You can start with six counters and use more as you gain proficiency.

To begin the game, the first player picks up all the counters from any one of his six holes and distributes them to his right, placing one in each hole. If the last one lands in his scoring bin, he gets another turn, but otherwise the turn passes to his opponent.

If he has enough counters to go beyond his scoring bin, after dropping one there, he proceeds from right to left along his opponent's side of the board. When he can go around the other end (skipping the other player's scoring bin) and drop the last counter in any empty hole on his own side of the board, he captures all the counters in the hole opposite.

The game of Mancala is over when all the holes on either side of the playing board are empty. The player with the most counters in his scoring bin is the winner. Mancala can be enjoyed by everyone except for the smallest youngster.

See also: billiards; bowling; chess board; games, boating; games, children's; pool tables; puzzle; railroad model; road racing, model; targets.

Anyone for skittles?

BY CLIFFORD B. HICKS

■ FOR CENTURIES, Englishmen have gathered in pubs to play skittles—a miniature sort of bowling game. The object is to send the top spinning through the "rooms," knocking down skittles (pins) as it goes. Point values in the "rooms" can shave 10 points off your score or boost it by 100. The game may be played for a predetermined number of turns or simply with each player taking a turn to see who gets the highest score. You needn't go to England to try it—it's easy to make your own board.

A 4 x 4-ft. sheet of ½-in. plywood will provide adequate material. After cutting the base and walls, mark and cut the dadoes; if your shop lacks a power saw, simple butt joints may be used.

An optional step is to cement a scrap of plastic laminate or tempered hardboard to the inner face of the end wall, where the hole for the top will be cut. Without this protection, the top will eventually wear away a cradle to brake its spin.

After cutting all doorways—a job you can speed by careful stacking of the blanks—sand edges smooth. A coat of shellac thinned 50 percent with alcohol, followed with two coats of enamel makes a durable finish. Brushing is easier if you prefinish the parts before you glue and nail them together.

The smoother the finish on the floor, the longer the top will spin, so give it extra care and attention. Sand carefully between each coat of shellac

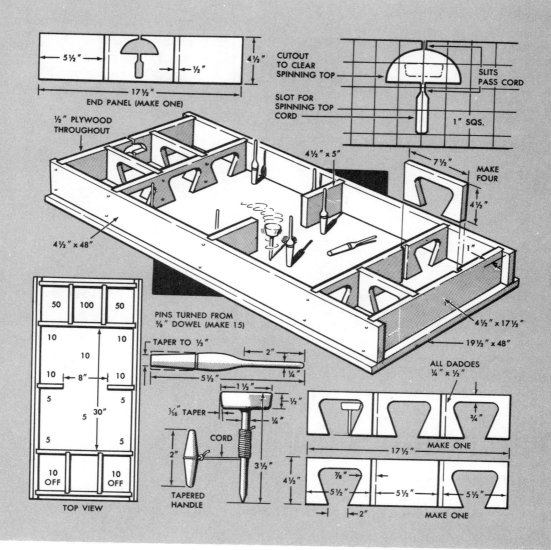

5½"   ½"   4½"

17½"

END PANEL (MAKE ONE)

½" PLYWOOD THROUGHOUT

CUTOUT TO CLEAR SPINNING TOP

SLOT FOR SPINNING TOP CORD

SLITS PASS CORD

1" SQS.

4½" x 5"

7½"

MAKE FOUR

4½"

4½" x 48"

1"

PINS TURNED FROM ⅝" DOWEL (MAKE 15)

4½" x 17½"

19½" x 48"

ALL DADOES ¼" x ½"

50	100	50
10		10
	10	
10	8"	10
	30"	
5	5	5
5		5
10 OFF		10 OFF

TOP VIEW

TAPER TO ½"

2"

5½"   ¼"

1½"

½"

¹⁄₁₆" TAPER   ¼"

CORD

2"

3½"

TAPERED HANDLE

4½"

¾"

17½"   MAKE ONE

⅞"

5½"   5½"   5½"

2"

MAKE ONE

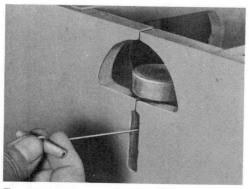

To spin the top, wind the cord around its stem, then feed the free end down through the slits as you lower the top into the position shown above. Hold the top snugly against the end wall with your left hand, releasing it at the same moment you give a sharp, smooth tug to pull the cord out through the slot

and enamel; then apply a paste wax and buff it to a hard finish before assembly.

If you have a lathe, turning the skittles will present no problem. The alternative is to use straight sections of dowel. These have a greater tendency to block doorways than do the turned pins, but they are usable. So are toy bowling pins.

If you don't have a lathe but do have a portable drill, you can make a true-spinning top by driving a ¼-in. dowel in a tight-fitting hole in a hardwood disk and then chucking it in the drill to true the disk with a sharp wood chisel. It's important that the top be made of hardwood since it takes quite a battering as it bounces off the walls. Strong black thread makes a good cord and should be about 12 in. long with a pull handle tied at the end. Happy skittling!

The highball handicap race is a real test for a pair of skillful boat drivers. Run too close together and you'll break the beach ball, disqualifying your team. This should be done at slow speeds since there is danger of a collision and damage to the boats

Water games for boaters

BY PATRICK K. SNOOK

Are you tired of the same old Sunday afternoon cruises?
Then try some of these fun-filled, skill-building water games

■ MANY BOATING CLUBS are solving the problem of those midsummer what-do-I-do-with-my-boat-now doldrums by borrowing ideas from sports-car clubs.

Predicted-log competitions, a nautical adaptation of the automobile rally, has picked up thousands of fans over the past couple of years and is already a red-letter date on many club calendars. However, few people have heard of a more recent but equally appealing borrowing—the boaters' "gymkhana."

A sports-car gymkhana is run on a twisting road course marked off into sections with flags or pylons. Actually, it's just a series of tests—acceleration, braking, backing, driving through a narrow slot, etc.—and the winner is determined by timing each contestant's run, then subtracting any penalties picked up along the way.

Boaters have taken this general idea, added a few special wrinkles of their own and come up with a number of games which are ideal for livening up your midsummer outings.

The rules and instructions for eight of these games follow:

SLALOM. Use anchored balloons or plastic bleach bottles to mark off a twisting slalom course. These should be located in pairs so that they form "gates" through which the boat must pass. For a fast course, make the gates wide and locate them farther apart; if you want to make things more difficult, use narrow gates spaced only a boat length or two apart.

The actual event is run against time, with the contestant idling up to the first gate and pouring on the power at a signal from the starter. Over-running the markers or leaving the course earns a time penalty, and the fastest time wins.

For a little extra excitement, try a flying start

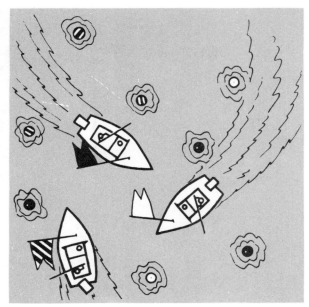

In crowded water, balloon popping can be dangerous. In all events, make sure you have enough open space for safe maneuvering

The plug check is an easy dockside contest particularly good for the gals, though all outboarders should know how to do it

Pop-and-run is a modern version of Moby Dick, using balloons instead of whales. While many variations are possible, the basic idea is to pop all of the balloons with the harpoon

The shear-pin switch tests your speed at pulling up and locking the motor, removing the shear pin, then getting motor started again

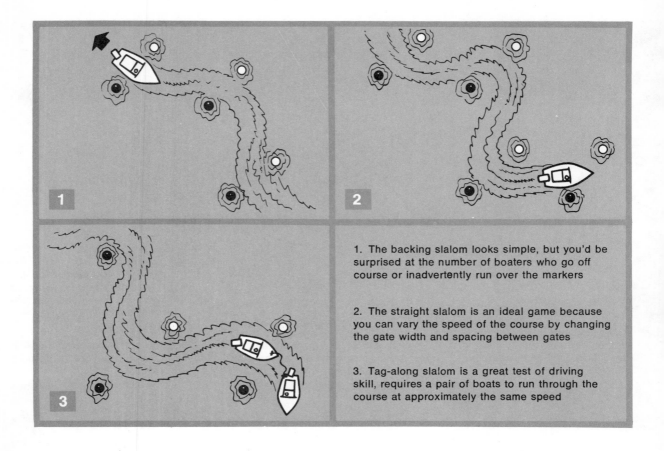

1. The backing slalom looks simple, but you'd be surprised at the number of boaters who go off course or inadvertently run over the markers

2. The straight slalom is an ideal game because you can vary the speed of the course by changing the gate width and spacing between gates

3. Tag-along slalom is a great test of driving skill, requires a pair of boats to run through the course at approximately the same speed

water games for boaters, continued

First mates can be a big help, and many of the clubs have events for husband-and-wife teams

on a tight course and increase the penalty times.

BACKING SLALOM. Reverse maneuvering requires a considerable amount of skill, particularly in close quarters, so a slalom variation based on this aspect of boat handling is a real test and has a great deal of spectator appeal.

The competing craft is brought up to the starting gate and shut down. When the starter's flag drops, the contestant must fire up the engine, turn the boat around and back through the course. As in a regular slalom, over-running a marker or leaving the course is a penalty offense.

TAG-ALONG SLALOM. Here's one that requires two boats. You can use the same basic slalom course, but the gates should be wider and the turns less severe.

Tie a 10-ft. length of very light cord or ribbon between the transom of the lead boat and the bow of the No. 2 craft. After positioning the boats at the starting gate, both engines must be shut off. Then, at the starter's signal, each driver starts his engine, and the boats make a follow-the-leader run through the course.

The object, of course, is to make the fastest time without breaking the string between the two boats. This can be quite a challenge, particularly while accelerating. Snapping the ribbon means disqualification for the team.

HIGHBALL HANDICAP. This is a tough one, and like the "tag-along," requires two boats. The boats take up a position some distance from the starting line and get under way, running side by side. Next, a large plastic beach ball is positioned between the inside gunwales. This is a little tricky, and several false starts are par for the course.

When the team has the ball set, they signal the starter and head through the starting gate. Once on the course, the ball cannot be touched. Fastest time wins, and dropping or breaking the ball disqualifies the team.

It's a good idea to have an adequate supply of balls on hand if you plan to try this one.

QUICK PICKUP. This event tests skill in close-in maneuvering and the use of a boat hook. A number of bleach bottles are scattered about 100 yds. apart, and at the starter's signal, each team (one driver and one hook-handler) retrieves the bottles.

Interesting variations? Number the bottles and pick them up in sequence. Or paint them different colors and start the teams together, each one picking up only one color.

POP-AND-RUN. All you need is a good supply of balloons and some lightweight poles sharpened on one end. Either set the balloons adrift or anchor them with stones and lengths of light string. The object is to break all the balloons and get back to the starting line in the fastest time. See "quick pickup" for possible variations.

PLUG CHECK. In this dock-side game, the contestant must remove the shroud, disconnect a sparkplug wire, remove the plug and hold it over his head, then reverse the procedure and wind up by starting the engine. With tyros, better stop at the plug-over-head point to make sure that the plugs don't go back in crossthreaded.

SHEAR-PIN SWITCH. Same idea as the above. However, heaving the engine up requires a little muscle, so this should be a men-only competition (or husband-and-wife teams, with mother doling out the tools and shouting encouragement).

And so it goes. You can probably come up with at least as many game ideas of your own. Have fun!

See also: boat handling; boats, buying; boats, used; floats and docks; games, adult; games, children's; skin diving; water skiing.

Racing through the wide starting gate, two boats enter the twisting course for a tag-along slalom run. If the ribbon joining the two boats snaps, they're out of the race. Winners have to be good helmsmen

Roll-a-ball

Here's a game for both children and adults that provides a real challenge to coordination, fast reflexes and a delicate touch

BY C. L. WIDDICOMBE

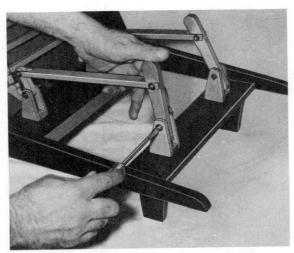

Assemble the activating linkage with steel washers between all moving parts and under the peened-over bolts. Keep contact points waxed

■ YOUNGSTERS worn out by the "creative" toys and push-button monsters they got for Christmas will find *this* game a welcome relief. It's plain fun, with emphasis on coordination, not education.

It's as simple to construct (mostly from scraps) as it is to play. The principle is to zigzag a large marble or steel ball from the starting position shown above through the pivoting parallel bars to the base. You've got to manipulate the levers skillfully to avoid inclining the bars so much that the marble shoots past the projecting catch-end of the next-lower bar. And even when you master this, you must reverse the pitch at just the right moment to send the caught ball in a new direction. If you seesaw the bars too much, the ball just rocks back and forth at the center. When you've mastered this, add a second ball at the top when the first is halfway down.

To protect the pivoting mechanism, the panel on which the bars are mounted is set in a grooved frame. Softwood can be used for this frame and for all base members, but the bars, pivot strips, levers and linkage should be cut from maple. Finishing of the bars is important, since the ball

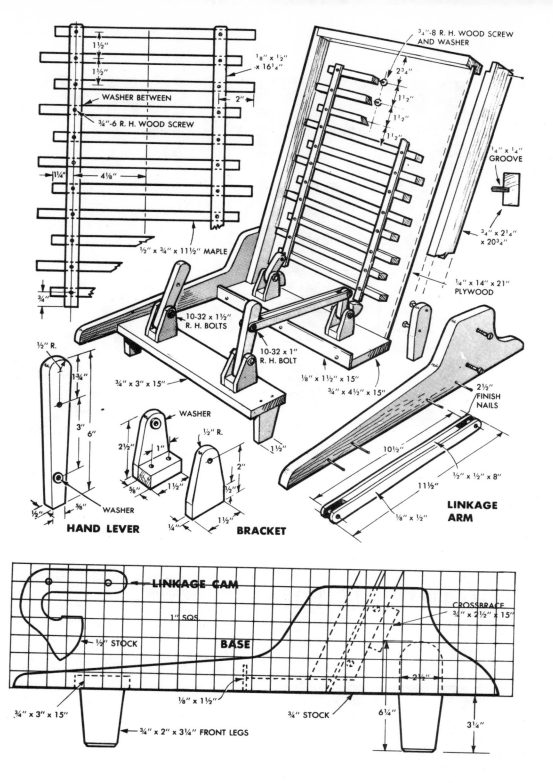

¾"-8 R. H. WOOD SCREW AND WASHER

¾"-6 R. H. WOOD SCREW

WASHER BETWEEN

1½"

1½"

⅛" x ½" x 16¼"

2"

2¾"

1½"

1½"

1½"

¼" x ¼" GROOVE

¾" x 2¼" x 20¾"

¼" x 14" x 21" PLYWOOD

1¼"   4⅛"

½" x ¾" x 11½" MAPLE

¾"

10-32 x 1½" R. H. BOLTS

10-32 x 1" R. H. BOLT

⅛" x 1½" x 15"

¾" x 4½" x 15"

¾" x 3" x 15"

2½" FINISH NAILS

HAND LEVER

½" R.

1¾"

3"   6"

½"   ⅜"   WASHER

WASHER

2½"   1"

⅝"   1½"

½" R.

2"

½"

1½"

1½"

¼"   **BRACKET**

1½"

10½"

11½"

½" x ½" x 8"

⅛" x ½"

LINKAGE ARM

← LINKAGE CAM

1" SQS

½" STOCK

BASE

CROSSBRACE ¾" x 2½" x 15"

¾" x 3" x 15"

⅛" x 1½"

¾" STOCK

← ¾" x 2" x 3¼" FRONT LEGS

2½"

6¼"

3¼"

must roll freely. Apply linseed oil, then two coats of shellac, rubbing each with steel wool. Then brush on flat varnish and rub it smooth when dry.

When you fasten the bars to the back panel, place washers between them and the plywood—and don't draw the screws snug. The screw holes in the plywood should let them turn freely. Attach the pivot strips so the entire assembly will respond freely to any movement of the cams. A

playing tip: When you grasp the levers, keep the cams in constant pressure against the lower ends of the pivot strips. Apply wax to these contact points to cut down friction and make the parts move freely.

See also: bicycle; boomerang; clothes dryer; games, adult; games, boating; kites; magic; merry-go-round; playground equipment; road racing, model; sleds; stilts; toboggan; toys; tree houses; unicycle.

Watching lights run up the ladder as levers are compressed is amusing (and builds muscles)

Kids can ring the bell with this
amusement-arcade game

Grip gauge tests young muscle men

BY C. SINAPI

An inside view of the grips shows how the movable one pivots on the dowel

■ YOUR YOUNG MUSCLE MAN will get a big kick out of this grip tester made along the same lines as those found in amusement arcades. Easy to build, the device consists of five flashlight bulbs, a 6-v. lantern cell, a doorbell and a simple switching arrangement.

The lower end of the movable hand grip connects to one terminal of the battery so as to close the circuit to the various lamps as it makes contact with the stationary lugs. A compression spring holds the hand grips apart until the spring is overcome by squeezing, causing the different bulbs to light. When the top bulb lights, the bell rings to add to the fun.

The toy consists of a slotted-top box which houses the doorbell, battery and levers, and an electric scoreboard which is labeled (bottom to top) with such appropriate words as ZOMBIE, GO HOME, KID STUFF, MUSCLES and BOILERMAKER. The terminal lugs are spaced on the leg of the fixed lever as sketched on next page, and secured with screws.

The five bulbs are merely pressed in undersize holes drilled in the ⅛-in. panel—no sockets are used. They are wired together following the diagram, one wire being soldered to the side of each bulb and the other to the very end.

1104

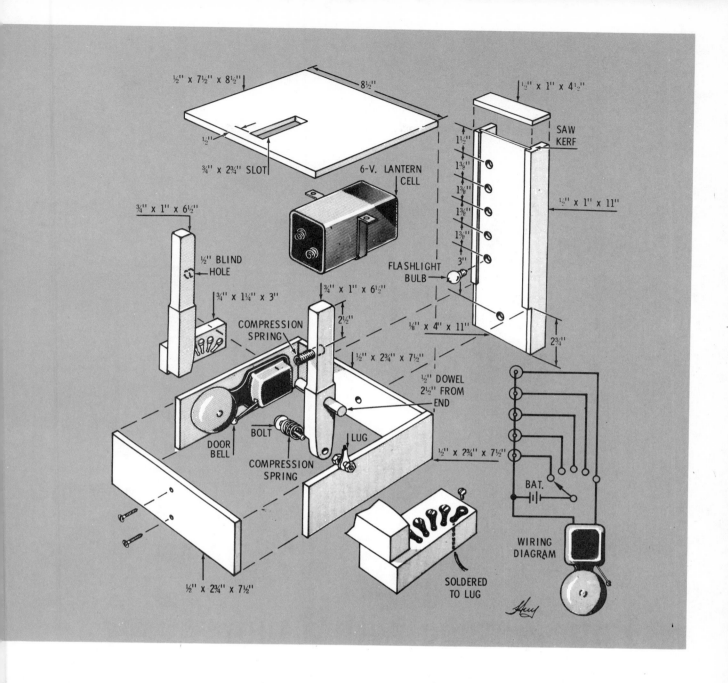

½" x 7½" x 8½"

8½"

½"

¾" x 2¾" SLOT

6-V. LANTERN CELL

½" x 1" x 4½"

SAW KERF

1½"

1⅜"

1⅜"

1⅜"

1⅜"

½" x 1" x 11"

¾" x 1" x 6½"

½" BLIND HOLE

¾" x 1¼" x 3"

FLASHLIGHT BULB

3"

⅛" x 4" x 11"

2¾"

COMPRESSION SPRING

¾" x 1" x 6½"

2½"

½" x 2¾" x 7½"

½" DOWEL 2½" FROM END

DOOR BELL

BOLT

COMPRESSION SPRING

LUG

½" x 2¾" x 7½"

BAT.

WIRING DIAGRAM

SOLDERED TO LUG

½" x 2¾" x 7½"

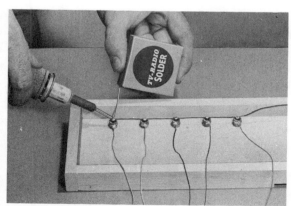

Panel lights are flashlight bulbs pressed into undersize holes. Solder the bases to the wires

A bottom view of the toy shows how the parts fit inside the base. Wiring enters a hole in the back

To come up with something
really new in garages, we called
on architects to design one, and then
on two authors to build it

Patio garage with a flair

BY MANLY BANISTER, with
DICK CHILSON

■ DATING BACK TO THE DAYS when a shed took
over as shelter for the horseless carriage, the
lowly garage has remained pretty much the same
in design and purpose. It has been a cold, cheer-
less, utilitarian kind of place. Except when it's
moved up to the front and made a part of the
house, this structure still leads a detached sort
of life.

Deciding that it was high time to do something
about making the lonely garage take a more important role in family affairs, we tossed the challenge at a New York architectural firm. We asked
that they look at the garage with different eyes,

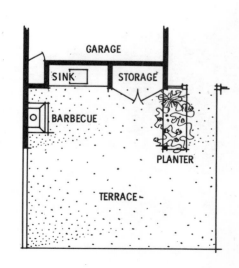

GARAGE

STORAGE   ☐ SINK

BARBECUE

PLANTER

TERRACE

PLANTER

These are two deluxe variations on the master patio-garage plan that is blueprinted on the next two pages. They elaborate on the "outdoor kitchen" treatment of the garage's patio end. Note that in these sketches, the roof projects over the patio but that the eaves line is carried all the way out. In the original plan, the peak of the roof juts out to a point over the patio. Added features in these models include a hooded brick barbecue or a metal unit hung from a brick wall

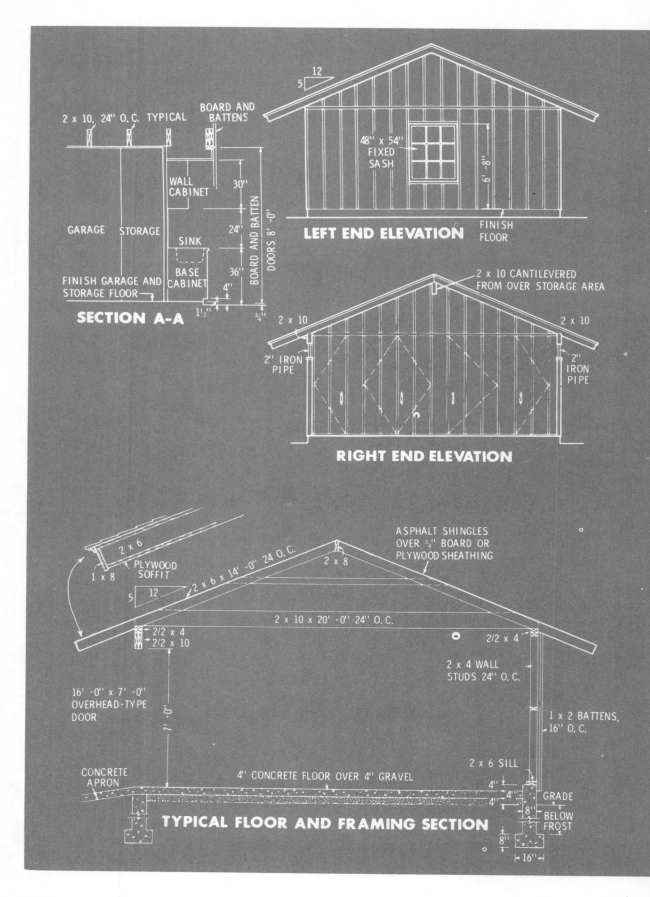

2 x 10, 24" O.C. TYPICAL

BOARD AND BATTENS

WALL CABINET

30"

GARAGE   STORAGE

SINK

24"

BASE CABINET

36"

BOARD AND BATTEN

DOORS 8' - 0"

FINISH GARAGE AND STORAGE FLOOR

4"

1½"

¾"

SECTION A-A

48" x 54" FIXED SASH

6' - 8"

LEFT END ELEVATION

FINISH FLOOR

2 x 10 CANTILEVERED FROM OVER STORAGE AREA

2 x 10

2 x 10

2" IRON PIPE

2" IRON PIPE

RIGHT END ELEVATION

2 x 6

PLYWOOD SOFFIT

1 x 8

2 x 6 x 14' -0' 24 O.C.

2 x 8

ASPHALT SHINGLES OVER ¾" BOARD OR PLYWOOD SHEATHING

5   12

2/2 x 4
2/2 x 10

2 x 10 x 20' -0" 24" O.C.

2/2 x 4

2 x 4 WALL STUDS 24" O. C.

16' -0" x 7' -0" OVERHEAD-TYPE DOOR

7' -0"

1 x 2 BATTENS, 16" O. C.

2 x 6 SILL

CONCRETE APRON

4" CONCRETE FLOOR OVER 4" GRAVEL

4"

4"

4"

GRADE

BELOW FROST

8"

TYPICAL FLOOR AND FRAMING SECTION

8"

16"

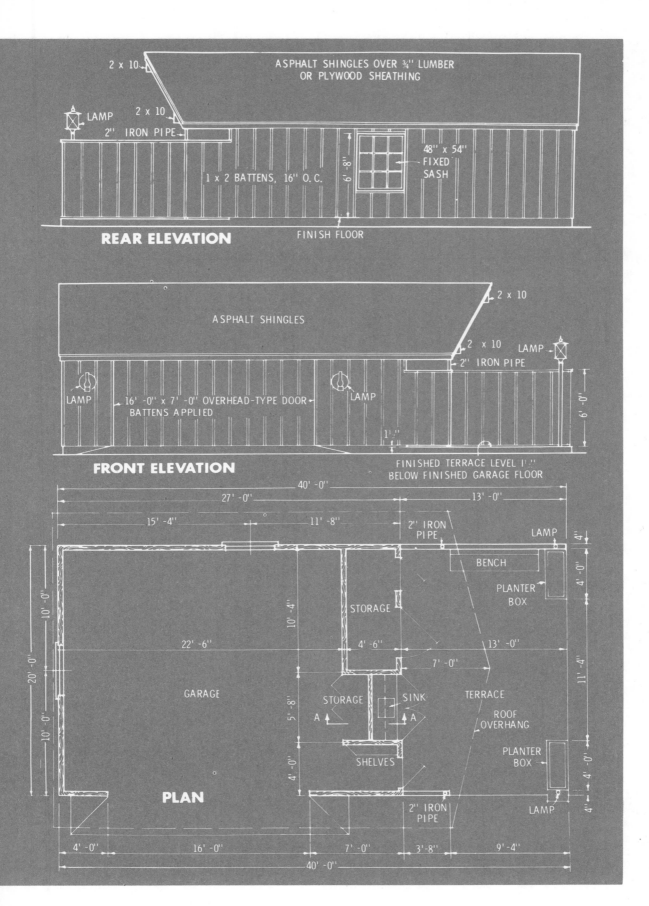

ASPHALT SHINGLES OVER ¾" LUMBER
OR PLYWOOD SHEATHING

2 x 10

LAMP
2 x 10
2" IRON PIPE

1 x 2 BATTENS, 16" O.C.

6' -8"

48" x 54"
FIXED
SASH

REAR ELEVATION

FINISH FLOOR

2 x 10

ASPHALT SHINGLES

2 x 10
LAMP
2" IRON PIPE

LAMP
16' -0" x 7' -0" OVERHEAD-TYPE DOOR
BATTENS APPLIED

LAMP

6' -0"

1½"

FRONT ELEVATION

FINISHED TERRACE LEVEL 1½"
BELOW FINISHED GARAGE FLOOR

40' -0"
27' -0"
13' -0"
15' -4"
11' -8"
2" IRON
PIPE
LAMP
4"

BENCH

PLANTER
BOX

4' -0"

10' -0"

10' -0"

STORAGE

10' -4"

20' -0"

22' -6"
4' -6"
13' -0"

11' -4"

GARAGE

7' -0"

10' -0"

STORAGE

5' -8"

SINK

A

A

TERRACE

ROOF
OVERHANG

SHELVES

PLANTER
BOX

4' -0"

4' -0"

PLAN

4' -0"

2" IRON
PIPE

LAMP

4' -0"

4' -0"
16' -0"
7' -0"
3' -8"
9' -4"
40' -0"

1109

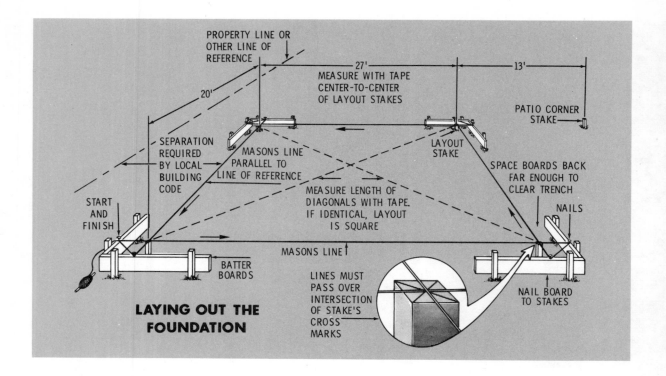

PROPERTY LINE OR OTHER LINE OF REFERENCE

27'

13'

20'

MEASURE WITH TAPE CENTER-TO-CENTER OF LAYOUT STAKES

PATIO CORNER STAKE

SEPARATION REQUIRED BY LOCAL BUILDING CODE

MASONS LINE PARALLEL TO LINE OF REFERENCE

LAYOUT STAKE

SPACE BOARDS BACK FAR ENOUGH TO CLEAR TRENCH

START AND FINISH

MEASURE LENGTH OF DIAGONALS WITH TAPE. IF IDENTICAL, LAYOUT IS SQUARE

NAILS

BATTER BOARDS

MASONS LINE

NAIL BOARD TO STAKES

LAYING OUT THE FOUNDATION

LINES MUST PASS OVER INTERSECTION OF STAKE'S CROSS MARKS

patio garage with a flair, continued

and then turn it into a gay fun center, with special emphasis on outdoor dining and entertaining.

The architects went to work, and from the fresh, exciting new concepts you see here, you know they have succeeded. The commonplace garage has at last come into its own.

It now takes over a dual role in family living by making cookouts twice the fun and by sheltering the family automobile when a garage can serve no other seasonal purpose. In addition to just plain space, the garage now contributes a sink-and-cupboard alcove, a storage wall for patio furniture, and a wind screen for privacy.

Now, with a sparkling new design in hand, we had to prove our point that the building of a garage is within the ability of any handy guy. So

PATIO SLAB IS FORMED AND POURED FIRST

The foundation trenching is done to the depth and width required by local code. Note that no foundation is laid under the 6-ft. door space in the left foreground. This trench was 12 x 12-in.

Here the front corner of the patio form shows how the batterboard was left in place to align bulkhead that is set into the foundation trench. The 2x4 in the right foreground defines the edge of the patio

The opposite end of the bulkhead has been blocked up, staked and leveled. The patio is now fully outlined. The sod showing in the left front corner of the photo must be skinned off before pouring

This is a view of the garage foundation just prior to pouring concrete. It is braced against the pressure of pour by means of cleats that bridge the trench, nailed to the bulkhead, and a staked-down 2x6

Before pouring concrete, plant the posts in foot-square pits after wiring them to each other and bringing the plastic cable under the bulkhead to tie into the garage wiring

After hosing down the soil, pour the concrete direct from the readymix truck, coaxing it with shovels for an even fill to the top of the form boards. The mix used in all concrete work is 1:3:4

Rodding off after the pour is accomplished by "sawing" a 2x4 across the top of the form. The loosely-set lamp post is plumbed after the concrete stiffens

Jitterbugging levels and smooths the pour, and forces heavy gravel under the surface. You walk backward, tamping rapidly with a steel grille on a pipe handle

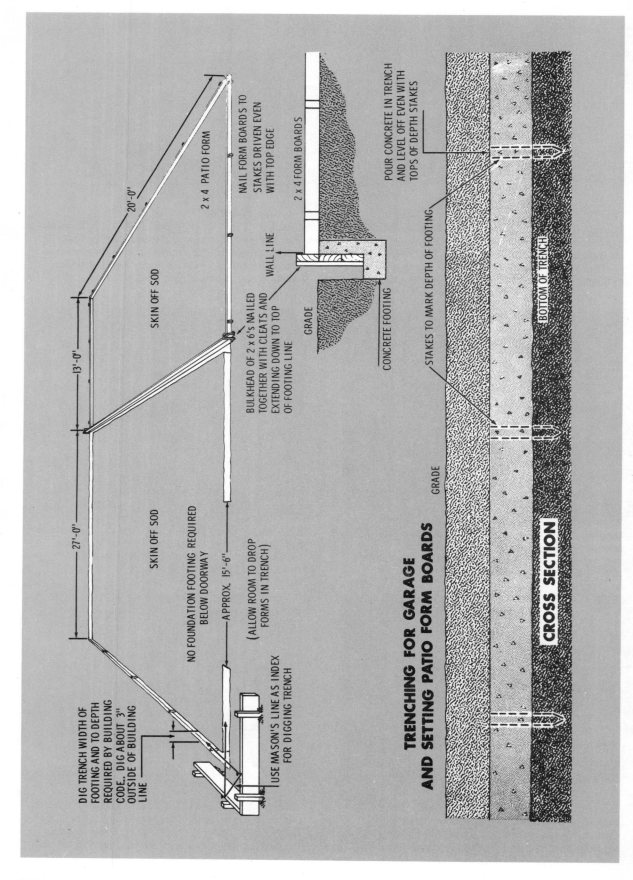

DIG TRENCH WIDTH OF FOOTING AND TO DEPTH REQUIRED BY BUILDING CODE. DIG ABOUT 3" OUTSIDE OF BUILDING LINE

USE MASON'S LINE AS INDEX FOR DIGGING TRENCH

NO FOUNDATION FOOTING REQUIRED BELOW DOORWAY

SKIN OFF SOD

APPROX. 15'-6"

(ALLOW ROOM TO DROP FORMS IN TRENCH)

SKIN OFF SOD

27'-0"

13'-0"

20'-0"

2 x 4 PATIO FORM

NAIL FORM BOARDS TO STAKES AND DRIVEN EVEN WITH TOP EDGE

BULKHEAD OF 2 x 6's NAILED TOGETHER WITH CLEATS AND EXTENDING DOWN TO TOP OF FOOTING LINE

WALL LINE

2 x 4 FORM BOARDS

GRADE

POUR CONCRETE IN TRENCH AND LEVEL OFF EVEN WITH TOPS OF DEPTH STAKES

CONCRETE FOOTING

STAKES TO MARK DEPTH OF FOOTING

GRADE

BOTTOM OF TRENCH

CROSS SECTION

TRENCHING FOR GARAGE AND SETTING PATIO FORM BOARDS

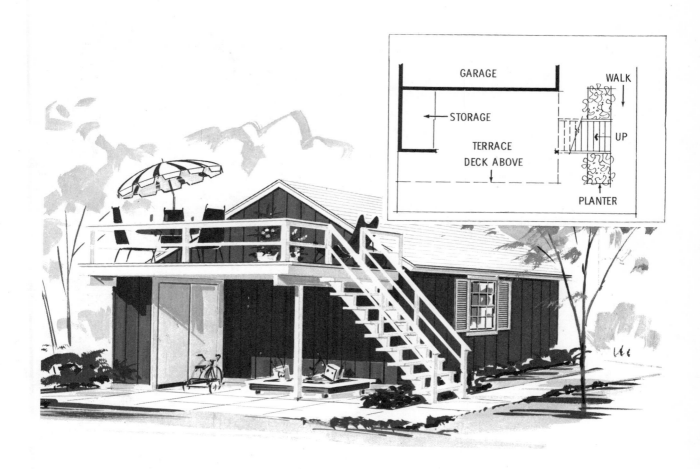

Another variation of the original plan has a solid end wall with a storage L that supports one end of a sun deck. The deck offers shelter for the sandbox and outside storage area

we commissioned Manly Banister, author of many craft articles, to build the test model.

Here in his own words, Manly takes over and tells how he and a friend built the Patio-Garage from the first shovel of dirt to the last swing of the paint brush:

Knowing little about actual building construction myself (I'm an avid workshopper) and never having been involved in a major building project before, I secured the services of a neighbor, Dick Chilson, who's a building contractor. I'll be passing along his practical tips on the right way to do things, in case you don't have a pro next door.

Dick believes in doing the job right by avoiding slipshod shortcuts, and in building for permanence. So if you're looking for a solidly build structure, join us. And then, when one of these days you walk on the roof of your new garage, you'll find it as solid underfoot as the concrete foundation.

Working from the architects' blueprints (which are reproduced on pages 1108 and 1109), Dick planned and executed the framing and rough construction, and I attended to siding, the garage door and the patio walls, nailing battens, and all the rest of the finishing work. Framewise, the garage is erected the same whether you cover the side walls with boards and battens as I did so it would match my house, or face it with siding or shingles. With boards and battens, however, you can forget about wall sheathing, which isn't true in the case of siding or shingles if you want a good job. But the choice is up to you.

In staking out the garage and patio floor plan, you work from a property line; in my area, the building must set 5 ft. inside this line. Check with your local planning commission for code requirements in your locality. There may be other considerations, too, such as setback from the street, total number of square feet built on the

patio garage with a flair, continued

BILL OF MATERIALS
The garage shown on page 1124

The following is the builder's list of all materials required to construct garage. This includes such optional details as the bench and planter boxes, and redwood-stained board-and-batten siding. The list is offered here for guidance in estimating your local costs, and in ordering lumber and supplies. For PM's garage, the lumber was supplied by Western Wood Products Association (formerly, Western Pine Assn.) and was all Douglas fir, except where otherwise specified; all grades were Construction or Standard, except where noted.

LUMBER

50	2x4 x 16' (Studs)
1100 lineal	2x4 (Framing)
70 lineal	2x6, pressure-treated (Mud sill)
34	2x6 x 14' (Rafters)
2	2x6 x 8' ⎫ clear (Garage door framing)
1	2x6 x 18' ⎭
6	2x6 x 10', clear (Frieze boards)
2	2x6 x 16' clear (Swept-back facing rafters)
16	2x10 x 20' Ceiling Joists; Door headers in patio wall)
2	2x10 x 12' (Headers over windows)
2	2x12 x 18' (Lintel beam)
2	2x8 x 18' (Ridge board)
6	1x8 x 18' (Fascia board, cabinet work, door jambs, etc.)
130 lineal	4x4 (Framing for privacy screen)
1200 bd. ft.	1x8 shiplap (Roof, attic deck)
50 lineal	1x5, clear (Patio wall, doorways, etc.)
216 lineal	1 x 12 (Shelving)
12	1x2 x 8, clear (Slats for bench seat)
14 lineal	2x12, clear (Bench back and legs)
1	4x4 x 6', clear (Bench feet)
32 lineal	2x12, pressure-treated (Planter boxes)
1	2x4 x 10', pressure-treated (Box feet)
1	1x24 x 6' Laminated pine (Sink cabinet top)
110	1x8 x 8' t&g pine paneling (Wall cover for storage and sink compartments, garage entry, closet)
6	1x4 x 12' ⎫ Sway braces, etc.
6	1x4 x 14' ⎭
1600 lineal	1x12, rough-cut, tight knot Western Red Cedar (Siding, Patio-wall doors, fences, battens)

NAILS

50 lbs., 16d Box
25 lbs., 8d Box
16 lbs., 16d Box, Galvanized
10 lbs., 8d finishing
3 lbs., 8d finishing, Galvanized
1 lb., 6d Box, Galvanized
¼ lb. 2" Concrete Nails

ROOFING

9 squares Asphalt Shingles
1 Starter Roll
3 Rolls 15-lb. Building Paper
30' Special Metal Edging (Overhang end of roof)
30' 1½" Sheet Metal Angle Roof Edging (Other gable)
10# ⅞" Roofing Nails
Gutters and Downspouts

FINISHING

Redwood Stain, 9 gallons

PLUMBING

16"x20" Plain Sink with Fittings
⅝" o.d. Copper Tubing Water Line, as required, for
1½" Pipe for Drain, as required

ELECTRIC WIRING

12-2 Underground Cable w/ground, as required, for lighting system, wall outlets
12-2 Indoor Cable and 10-2 Indoor Cable with ground, as required, for wiring inside garage
Two post lamps
Two porch lights
Boxes, lighting equipment, switches, duplex outlets, etc.

After jitterbugging, smooth the concrete with a homemade bull float, made by nailing a 2x6 across the end of a long 2x4

½" x 10" BOLT
1¾"
2¼"

Once the slab has set up and has been finished with hand floats, tap the foundation bolts into place. These will anchor the privacy screen

lot, etc. Get the details before carrying your planning too far. And remember, too, that you will probably have to obtain a building permit.

Now, with the legal questions out of the way, get out the big tape measure and get to work. Drive stakes at the four corners of the garage and at the two outside corners of the patio.

Your next step is to square up the layout, and this is best done by use of batterboards and masons' line, as directed in the sketch on page 1110. Since at least one of your building walls is to be parallel with a property line, work from this line to square up the rectangle. Stretch the masons' line from corner to corner as shown in the drawing, so that the cord passes over the center of each stake. The cords cross to provide index points at the stakes. Measure with a steel tape from stake to stake around the perimeter of the garage area only (the patio area is not concerned in this layout).

Measurements should read exactly 20 ft. on both widths and 27 ft. on both lengths. If any measurement is off, shift one or more stakes and cord-crossings to bring measurements true. When this is done, measure across both diagonals as indicated in the drawing. If these two measurements are unequal, the rectangle isn't square. Shift the cords as required, and re-measure. When all side measurements read true and both diagonals are the same length, the layout is square. Leave the batterboards up throughout the construction, for reference, and use the masons' line as a guide while trenching for the foundation.

check footing depth

Consult your local building authorities about requirements for the concrete foundation. These vary from area to area because of climate. The foundation footing must be laid below frost-level and the thickness of the foundation wall depends on code specifications. In my home town, Portland, Ore., 12 in. below grade is sufficient, with a footing 12 in. wide and 6 in. deep; the foundation wall can be a minimum of 6 in. thick, so we saved quite a bit of money on both concrete and labor by adhering to the local code instead of the architects' blueprint. But in some areas, their recommended foundation dimensions may be required. After trenching, use a transit-level to check out the depth to make sure the bottom is everywhere level. (The building trade calls this "shooting a few grades.")

The only preparation the area inside the forms received was the "skinning off" of the sod. Since we started construction at the height of the building season, we couldn't line up a bulldozer to do this scraping, so we cleared the patio area with hand mattocks. You'll be better off if you have a dozer in, first thing, to scrape and level the plot before you so much as drive a stake.

Your first concrete pour will include only the patio slab and the foundation footing for the garage. This took about 5 yds. of concrete in my case, but will be more if a heavier, deeper footing is planned. The patio slab is to be 4 in. thick, so use 2 x 4s for the form, staking them out to the dimensions shown on page 1112.

Keeping in mind that the patio slab is to be 1½ in. lower than the garage floor, we constructed a bulkhead to hang down the middle of the foundation trench along the left side of the patio slab, as shown in section on page 1112. For emphasis in this sketch, the bulkhead projects above the form boards, but if you wish to use it as a bearing edge when rodding off the patio pour (as in bottom-left photo, page 1111) it must set flush with the top edge of the form, then be raised 1½ in., later.

For drainage, the patio form was laid with a pitch of ⅛ in. per 18 in. (the length of our level) away from the garage.

When we were ready to pour, we called in the county inspector for an OK, and the concrete was ordered for the next morning. Since the weather was dry, we reeled out the hose that night and wetted the area and forms thoroughly. We hosed down again the following morning. A dry base sucks moisture out of the concrete mix, and you're in for endless trouble if you let this happen.

To start the pour, feed concrete—a barrowload at a time—into the trench in front of the bulkhead. The concrete flows *under* this suspended panel and is leveled off at footing depth along its opposite side. Keep adding concrete until the trench on the patio side of the bulkhead is filled flush with the ground line.

the "lucky-seven" steps

The step-by-step photos, starting on page 1110, provide an account of the pouring and finishing of the patio itself. In brief, the "lucky-seven" steps toward professional slab work are: (1) pour and spread the concrete; (2) rod off to level the pour; (3) consolidate the mix by "jitterbugging"; (4) smooth with the bull float. Then, when the concrete has set sufficiently to bear a man's weight on knee and toe boards, the finishing steps begin: (5) go over entire surface with a wooden float; (6) after considerably more setting up, smooth and equalize the surface with a rectangular steel trowel; (7) a considerable time later, when the concrete is firm enough not to erode away, go over the surface with a rubber float (sponge rubber on the bottom of a wood float—a special finishing tool) to roughen the surface so you won't slip on it in rainy weather. To assure a neat corner on the two outside edges, your final finishing step is to run an edger between the not-yet-set-up pour and these form boards.

You'll note that we poured my slab directly on the ground, without reinforcing of any kind. Where frost-heaving is likely, you'll probably want to lay welded wire fabric in the pour to prevent cracking.

As soon as you've laid the patio slab, pour the garage footings in the trenches to a depth of

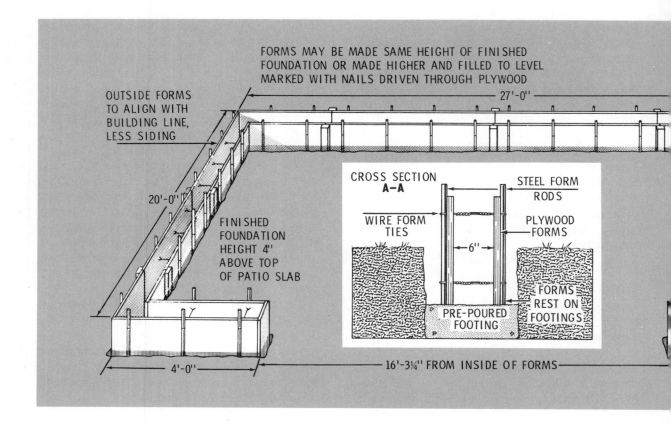

FORMS MAY BE MADE SAME HEIGHT OF FINISHED FOUNDATION OR MADE HIGHER AND FILLED TO LEVEL MARKED WITH NAILS DRIVEN THROUGH PLYWOOD

OUTSIDE FORMS TO ALIGN WITH BUILDING LINE, LESS SIDING

27'-0"

20'-0"

FINISHED FOUNDATION HEIGHT 4" ABOVE TOP OF PATIO SLAB

CROSS SECTION A-A

STEEL FORM RODS

WIRE FORM TIES

PLYWOOD FORMS

6"

FORMS REST ON FOOTINGS

PRE-POURED FOOTING

4'-0"

16'-3¼" FROM INSIDE OF FORMS

6 in. (previously driven stakes mark this depth) and jitterbug to smooth and level them out.

A clean-working mix—which we used throughout—is 1:3:4; 1 part cement, 3 of sand and 4 of gravel. The proportions may vary in other localities, owing to climatic conditions. Consult your ready-mix concrete supplier.

Be sure to insert foundation bolts along the rear edge of the patio slab for tying down the privacy screen. Also locate a hook-bolt for the tie-down under the eave-beam post at the front corner of the garage. The dimensions of this welded tie-down unit (to be detailed later) require that the bolt be positioned 1¾ in. from the *front* edge and 42½ in. from the *garage* edge of the patio. To safeguard against the patio cracking under the support beam, I dug a 12 x 12 x 12-in. hole here, before pouring the patio, so that the concrete, flowing into it, would create a footing. The hook bolt is then embedded in this footing.

To assure proper curing, keep the pour damp for at least a week after initial set.

Once the footing work is finished, you can spend only a short time enjoying that feeling of accomplishment and discussing your progress with interested neighbors. Then you have to get back to work, because now it's time to erect

forms on top of the garage-wall footings so that you can go ahead with the pouring of foundation walls.

The forms sketched at the top of the page and shown in the photo on the next page were erected by a contractor we called in to speed up construction. They consist of plywood panels tied together by wire "tourniquets" with eyes at both ends that pass through holes in the panels and are secured with vertical steel rods. This assembly merely sits on top of the footing, and is held erect and centered by braces nailed to stakes.

After the poured concrete has set, the rods are withdrawn and the panels stripped off. The lower tie wires are, of course, left embedded in the wall; before back-filling, the protruding eyes are clipped off on each side with wire cutters.

Since the forms shown were not custom-made for this job, they stand much taller than our foundation requires; if you build your own, you'd probably want to level them off at the height of the desired wall, regardless of how deep your footings might be—not only to save form material, but so you could pour the forms *full,* and rod-off along their top edges. When oversize forms are used, as shown here, nails are driven through the panels, along a leveled chalk line—then the

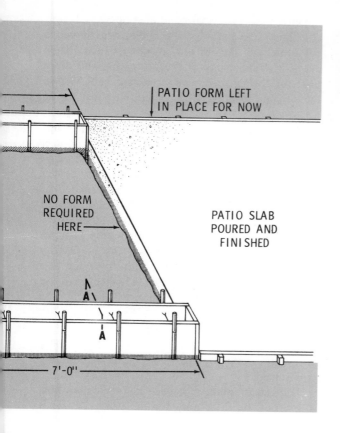

PATIO FORM LEFT IN PLACE FOR NOW

NO FORM REQUIRED HERE →

PATIO SLAB POURED AND FINISHED

A

A

A

← 7'-0" →

Foundation forms are needed for the back and the end walls, and for the two short walls that flank the 16-ft. door. The form shown in the picture is higher than necessary for a 12-in. foundation

concrete is poured to this level and the nails pulled out before the mix sets.

Of course, you can avoid erecting forms at all, if you prefer to lay a foundation of concrete block. In this case, you'd want to dig a wider footing trench so that you could get into it to lay your first course. Here, again, the depth of the footings would dictate the number of courses.

Whatever your method, you need a wall that stands an accurate 12 in. above your highest grade. Start from that point and adjust the form panels with a level—or, where the panels are over-height, scribe your pour line around the entire foundation, again checking with your level. To bridge the 16-ft. door opening, hang a straight-edged plank from the top of the "bulkheads" at the ends of the two short wall forms.

Whatever the height of your forms, these bulkheads should be level with the top of the poured wall, and should be only tacked temporarily across the form panels. When the suspended 2 x 6 straightedge is leveled by means of adjusting the form bulkheads up or down, nail the latter firmly in place.

The foot-above-grade wall allows for 4 in. of gravel fill, a 4-in. slab and 4 in. of foundation above the finished floor.

The best way to pour concrete into the forms is directly from the chute of the mixer, if you can position the truck to reach. It's a two-man operation; one holds a plywood panel against the far side of the form, opposite the end of the chute, to direct the flow into the form, while the other rams and spreads the concrete for a solid fill, using a length of 2 x 4.

When the pour is completed and leveled, but before it sets up, insert ½ x 10-in. foundation bolts no farther apart than 8 ft. to provide for tying the building down.

Assuming you've already stripped the sod from the area that is now enclosed by forms, you're ready to strip the forms from the poured foundation walls and spread a layer of gravel over the floor area, to within 8 in. of the top of the foundation. *Never pour concrete directly on sod.* The sod eventually rots out, leaving a space for settling, and the sagging slab will crack. Incidentally, I used no reinforcing such as welded-wire fabric, because my area is not subject to frost heaving. Where winters are more severe, you should reinforce the concrete to prevent cracking.

Now's the time to dig a trench for the electrical wiring, and to bring it up inside the foundation

Level the foundation form at the door gap by hanging a plank between bulkheads and adjusting till level

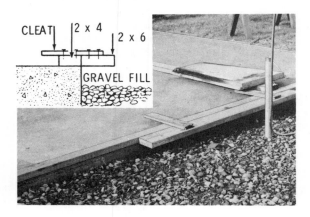

patio garage with a flair, continued

through 1-in. electrical conduit topped by a suitable box. The paths of the cables are shown in color on the sketch on bottom of next page, along with the paths of the water line and drain pipe for the sink. I brought power cables from the service entrance of my house to just inside the 16-ft. door.

I trenched 18 in. below grade and laid approved two-wire No. 12 underground cable in a bed of sand, covering it with more sand. The water line was buried in the same trench, before backfilling, while the drain pipe was trenched to a special drywell—in my case, a simpler method than tying it into my home drainage system.

The cables from the post lamps were brought across the garage footing before the patio slab was poured; these are now fed into a switch box located inside what will be the entrance from the garage to the patio. This switch will be wired to the entry box after the walls are erected.

Check the gravel level with a mason's line stretched across it; a dish in the middle can play hob with calculations for the amount of concrete you'll need.

The floor plan, detailed below shows how to lay out the floor area for the pour. Divide it in half with a 2 x 4 "floating screed" staked in place, and prepare a 2 x 4 rod for leveling the slab. The rod must be long enough to bridge half the area. Close the door gap with a 2 x 4 staked in flush with the inside face of the foundation wall.

Since the garage floor is to be 1½ in. higher than the level of the patio slab, lay a 2 x 4 on top

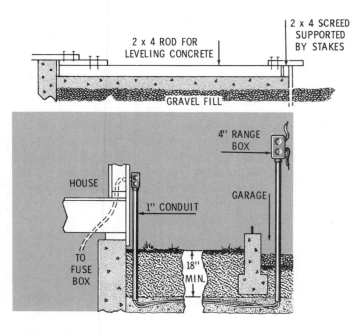

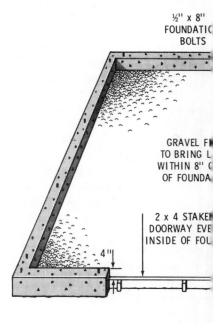

Because the drainpipe and water line stick up, rod off to this point of patio, then fill rest of form

Bull float smooths the surface after entire patio side has been poured, rodded off and jitterbugged

Once the second half of the pour has been jitter-bugged, the screed comes out. Bull float to close gap

The step-in bay at patio edge is finished off with a rubber float after removing cantilevered 2x6

HOW GARAGE FLOOR WAS POURED AND TROWELED

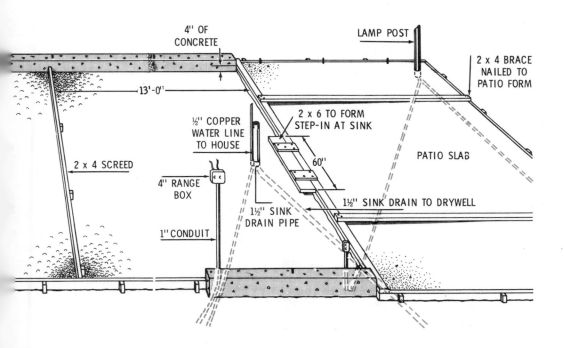

4" OF CONCRETE

LAMP POST

2 x 4 BRACE NAILED TO PATIO FORM

13'-0"

½" COPPER WATER LINE TO HOUSE

2 x 6 TO FORM STEP-IN AT SINK

60"

PATIO SLAB

2 x 4 SCREED

4" RANGE BOX

1½" SINK DRAIN TO DRYWELL

1½" SINK DRAIN PIPE

1" CONDUIT

Anchor the mud sill to the top of the foundation wall by drilling it to take protruding bolts, dropping it over them, and turning the nuts tight

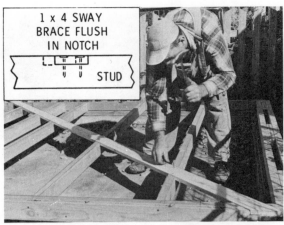

1 x 4 SWAY BRACE FLUSH IN NOTCH

STUD

Assemble the end wall flat on the slab. Here a sway brace is nailed into notches angled across the outer edges of the studs to let brace into frame

patio garage with a flair, continued

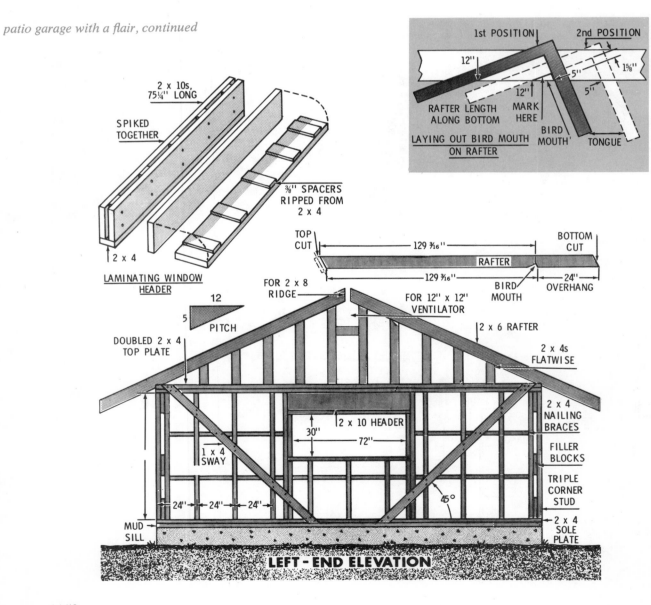

2 x 10s, 75¼" LONG

SPIKED TOGETHER

⅜" SPACERS RIPPED FROM 2 x 4

2 x 4

LAMINATING WINDOW HEADER

1st POSITION   2nd POSITION

12"   12"   5"   1⅝"   5"

RAFTER LENGTH ALONG BOTTOM   MARK HERE

BIRD MOUTH   TONGUE

LAYING OUT BIRD MOUTH ON RAFTER

TOP CUT   129 ³⁄₁₆"   BOTTOM CUT

RAFTER

129 ³⁄₁₆"   24" OVERHANG

BIRD MOUTH

FOR 2 x 8 RIDGE   FOR 12" x 12" VENTILATOR

12   5   PITCH

2 x 6 RAFTER

2 x 4s FLATWISE

DOUBLED 2 x 4 TOP PLATE

2 x 4 NAILING BRACES

2 x 10 HEADER

30"   72"

FILLER BLOCKS

1 x 4 SWAY

TRIPLE CORNER STUD

24"   24"   24"   45°

MUD SILL

2 x 4 SOLE PLATE

LEFT - END ELEVATION

Raise the wall onto the sill and nail the soleplate to it after setting it plumb by means of two side braces. These are attached with one nail so they'll pivot as they follow, preventing collapse if the men should stumble

of the slab along the edge and hold it there with 2 x 4 braces nailed to the patio form on the far side. To form the step-in bay for the sink compartment, measure in 4 ft. from the front edge of the patio, then cantilever a 2 x 6 over the fill (photo and inset sketch, page 1118).

Our concrete was the same 1:3:4-mix used for the patio. The center screed simplifies both pouring and leveling, since you do half the area at a time. First, the half on the patio side is poured, leveled, jitterbugged and bull-floated; then all these operations except the last are repeated for the other half. Before bull-floating the entire area, pull out the screed. If any areas look low, shovel on more concrete and bull-float it down. As the concrete sets up, work it first with the wood float, then with a metal trowel. Don't overwork it until it's glass-smooth, since this makes for hazardous walking. When the concrete has set up enough to be firm, carefully lift away the 2 x 4 form along the patio; this uncovers the bay recess so you can work it with a rubber float.

Your concrete work is now completed—except that if the weather's warm and dry, you'll want to prevent too-rapid curing by spraying the slab with a hose periodically for at least a week.

By now you'll have ordered the lumber from the bill of materials. Be sure to stack it someplace handy, organizing the pieces in the order they'll be used. If my delivery men are any gauge, your lumber (Idaho White Pine, Western Red Cedar and Douglas Fir) will be dumped with the mud sill material on the bottom and the shiplap for the roof on top. A few hours spent sorting lumber (including the shiplap by length) saves time and vexation later.

Now, cut all foundation-wall studs to length. You'll need 32 studs 92 in. long. Cut only one from each 16-ft. 2 x 4 and lay what's left aside; you'll use these pieces later, as studs for the patio wall. (Since that wall doesn't sit up on a foundation, the studs must be longer.) The photo on page 1123 shows how an 8-in. circular saw can be used to gang-cut the 92-in. studs

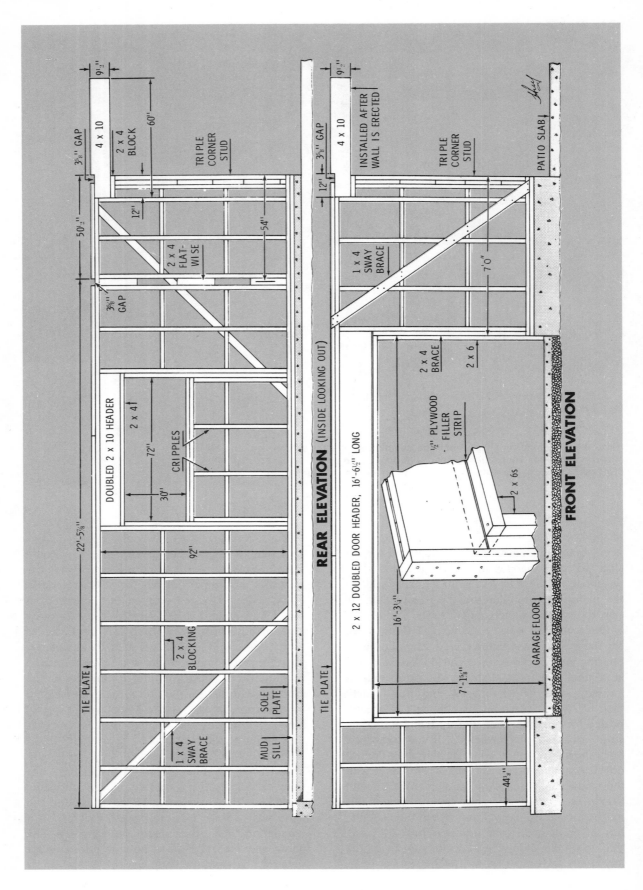

REAR ELEVATION (INSIDE LOOKING OUT)

FRONT ELEVATION

from the 16-footers. For working convenience, line up four saw horses on the floor of your garage.

You'll note from my framing plans on pages 1120 and 1122, and from the photo on page 1121, that I substituted horizontal sliding-sash windows for the conventional fixed-sash type indicated on the architect's elevations. Whatever your choice, be sure to have the sash on hand before framing the openings.

At this point, I figured how many pieces of the 1 x 12 Western Red Cedar siding I'd need for the back wall and the garage-door wall, and cut them to length. You'll note that the siding on these eave walls extends from the top of the tie plate to 4 in. below the top of the foundation.

When I'd cut all the siding I thought I'd need for my early work, I sliced some battens from the same 1 x 12 cedar. I cut these overlength, then trimmed them as needed when I nailed them on, later, after the walls were up. A radial arm or bench saw is essential for fast, accurate cutting of these 2-in. battens. If you don't have access to such a tool, you can, of course, buy ready-cut 1 x 2 battens.

All this assumes that you wish to reproduce the appearance of the garage presented here. The board-and-batten treatment complements many styles of homes and provided an ideal match for

A portable circular saw makes fast work of gang-cutting studs from 16-ft. 2x4s laid edge to edge and scribed across with a carpenter's square

The concrete slab now serves as a platform for assembling the back frame, outer face up, so the siding can be applied before the frame is raised into place

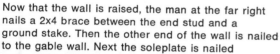

Now that the wall is raised, the man at the far right nails a 2x4 brace between the end stud and a ground stake. Then the other end of the wall is nailed to the gable wall. Next the soleplate is nailed

patio garage with a flair, continued

my own, but the garage framing could be covered equally well with bevel siding, shiplap clapboard or sheathing and shakes.

Following the three framing plans, you start by bolting each wall's mud sill to the foundation. Also, cut 1⅝ x 12-in. notches in the 4 x 10s that form the beams for the patio roof extension, though these won't be installed until the eave walls are up.

Begin actual assembly with the "triple corner studs" for all three walls. Note that the eave walls require triple studs on the patio ends only, since their opposite ends tie into the triple stud of the gable wall.

Frame the gable wall first. When the framing's done, rest the soleplate on the mud sill before nailing on the projecting siding. Though two of us would have been able to "walk" the wall upright, calling in another neighbor simplified the task, since he was able to keep the wall from falling while we planted the 2 x 4 "draggers" —those braces attached to the sides with a single nail so they'll follow the wall up—and muscled the wall into alignment with the mud sill. This aligning is easy: When the siding is snug against the foundation, it's safe to anchor the soleplate to the mud sill with 16d nails.

Note that in all three wall plans there's a double row of horizontal blocking equally spaced

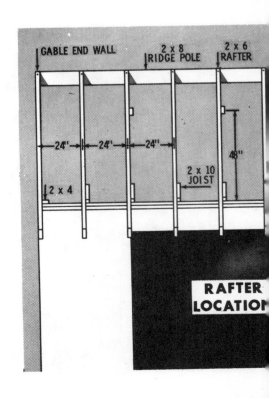

1124

Positioning the joists is a two-man job. They rest on and are nailed to the top plates of eave walls and are spaced 24 in. o.c. End bevels match roof pitch

The ridge pole is installed in sections as rafters go up. The man at the right is leveling the ridge by means of a marked upright extending from the floor

between soleplate and top plate. With a plywood "skin" or horizontal siding, you'd need only one row, but vertical boards call for more support, so I nailed each board at top, bottom and twice in between, along both edges. I used 8d box nails, since the heads would be covered when the battens were applied with 16d galvanized nails.

In applying tie plates of the eave walls, note that 3⅝-in. gaps are left in three places for tie plates of the patio wall. Once the roof boards are applied, you won't be able to nail these crossties in place, so it's a good idea to insert 3-ft. lengths of 2 x 4 now, nailing so they project inward from

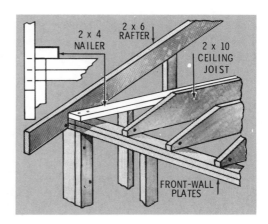

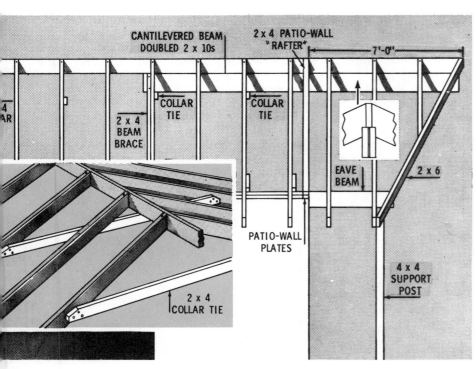

1125

More rafters are added, being nailed to the joists and the ridge pole. Note temporary support at the floor

The cantilever beam is held in place by collar ties and a beam brace, topped with the ridge-pole extension

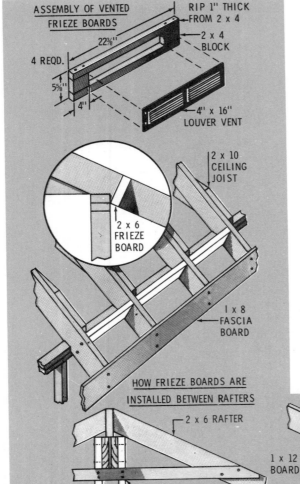

ASSEMBLY OF VENTED FRIEZE BOARDS

RIP 1" THICK FROM 2 x 4

22⅜"

2 x 4 BLOCK

4 REQD.

5⅝"

4"

4" x 16" LOUVER VENT

2 x 6 FRIEZE BOARD

2 x 10 CEILING JOIST

1 x 8 FASCIA BOARD

HOW FRIEZE BOARDS ARE INSTALLED BETWEEN RAFTERS

2 x 6 RAFTER

2 x 4 COLLAR TIE

2 x 4s SPIKED TO RIDGE BEAM AND JOISTS

2 x 10 JOIST

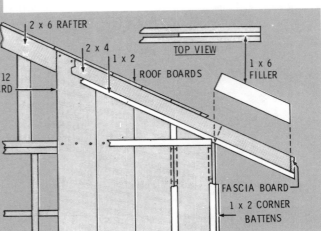

2 x 6 RAFTER

2 x 4

1 x 2

TOP VIEW

ROOF BOARDS

1 x 6 FILLER

1 x 12 BOARD

FASCIA BOARD

1 x 2 CORNER BATTENS

the eave walls. Later, you'll tie them into the patio-wall framing.

As the walls go up, they must be plumbed with a level and plumb-bob, secured in this position with braces nailed between the frame and nearby structures, trees or ground stakes. Also tie them to each other with temporary braces until you can roof them over. They form quite a pocket for a heavy wind.

With three of the walls up, you can begin to see the whole project taking shape. Now, instead of tackling that more-tricky fourth wall (with its patio-kitchen alcove) we go directly to the roof.

You'll need enough 2 x 10s to space your joists 24 in. on centers; the boards should be delivered to you in exact 20-ft. lengths, so the only cutting they'll need is the bevel at each end to match the slope of the roof. That same sketch shows a 2 x 4 "nailer" set against the gable rafters, so that it caps the joint between the doubled top plates of the meeting walls. I installed this in place of a more-expensive joist, to provide backing for a future ceiling. But if you're likely to install a floor, instead, you'll need a joist here.

A portable power saw, like this 8-incher, zips through siding stacked three deep and several wide

Frieze boards are toenailed between the rafters. The sketch on page 1126 shows the details

Information on cutting rafters for a ⁵⁄₁₂ pitch was given previously. Since they're identical, you only need lay out one, to use as a pattern. Every other pair of rafters is braced with a 2 x 4 collar tie. (Some builders tie only every *third* pair.) The five photos, page 1126 and this one, show how the 2 x 8 ridgeboard (or "pole," as my contractor friend and co-author terms it) is extended, in several sections, as more rafters are installed. At the patio end, the ridge treatment alters because of the 7-ft. cantilevered thrust of the roof peak beyond the end wall. As shown in the side view on pages 1124 and 1125 and the front-view detail, 1126, this beam is supported beneath the ridge pole on two 2 x 4 collar ties, and by the 2 x 4 braces that are anchored to a joist at rafter No. 11. I was able to secure a 4 x 10, 14 ft. long for this beam, but if you're not so lucky, you can "laminate" one by spiking two 2 x 10s together, as you did for door and window headers—except that here the ⅜-in. spacer between the 2 x 10s should be in one 4-ft. piece, so that no gap will show along the bottom of the exposed beam.

The ridgeboard is run out on top of this cantilevered beam—both to provide a nailer for the rafters and to eliminate the under-peak roosting of small birds. It stops short of the beam's end, however, just enough to create a rabbet to take the thickness of the angled facing "rafters."

Once all 16 pairs of full rafters are in place, nail a fascia across their vertical ends. Take care to drive the nails at an upward angle so they'll follow the grain of the rafters and not "point out" under the eaves. The sketch on page 1126 also shows how we nailed 2 x 6 frieze boards *between* the rafters; unlike the fascia, these were set square with the rafters, so they are at an angle to the wall. These are set snug against the doubled top plates of both eave walls, sealing out

Now 2x6 facings, with angle cuts at the top end, are nailed on. They butt each other, not the ridge pole. A 2x4 prop under the beam end supports you during roofing. Two short jack rafters are nailed next

the weather. But because I intend to insulate my garage for winter use as a workshop, I spotted louvered vents in several of the frieze boards—plus foot-square vents in both gables—to provide air circulation above my insulated ceiling.

This is a good idea, too, if you plan to install a floor for attic-type storage. This treatment of the overhang, incidentally, is not the one suggested on the architect's blueprints. There, the rafter ends are left square (which sets the fascia board at an angle to the wall) and the overhang is boxed in by means of a plywood soffit. But unless exposed rafters are objectionable, you'll find our method practical—and less expensive.

The sketch on page 1126 also shows how to finish the outside of the gable wall with 2 x 4 roof-line trim and a horizontal batten. Note in the sketch below that a filler piece must be inserted between the rafter and the 2 x 4 trim at the overhang, to make up for the thickness of the board siding that's sandwiched between.

You're now ready to apply your roof boards,

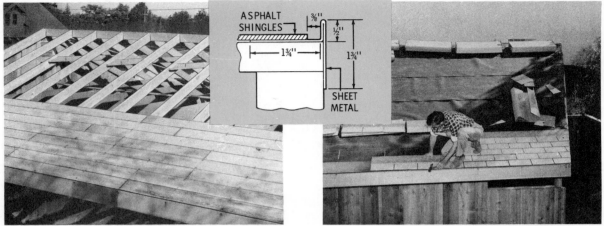

Work toward the ridge when applying shiplap, with the open lap at the upper edge. At each rafter, drive an 8d nail through the lap, another through opposite edge

Start shingling at the front corner to minimize waste caused by angled edge of roof. Cut shingles back to form a runnel (see inset) to channel run-off

as shown on page 1126. Just cut the Douglas fir shiplap to size with a portable circle saw, and nail it down, seeing that all end joints fall over a rafter—yet are staggered so that no more than two joints line up in a row.

Work from eave to ridge—and toward the patio overhang, letting the boards project beyond the angled edge. You can trim these flush when the roofing's done by snapping a chalkline and running your circular saw along it.

With the shiplap in place, go inside the garage and nail a 2 x 4 cleat all the way across the underside of the roof (called patio-wall rafter, page 1125) to provide a nailer for the patio wall framing. Though we won't be detailing the construction of this wall just yet, you must install this cleat before shingling so that you can drive nails through the shiplap and clinch them from above. You locate the cleat by means of those short tie plates we nailed into the gaps left in the "dap" of the eave-beam extensions.

Now, cover the roof with 15-lb. building felt. You'll need three rolls. But before applying any asphalt shingles, you should add the sheetmetal "gutter" along the edges of the swept-back overhang, to keep roof water from dripping off the

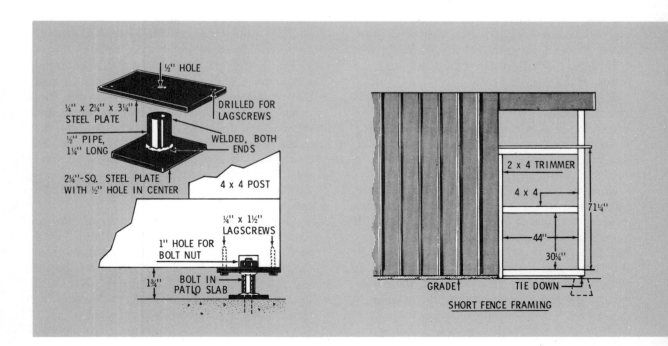

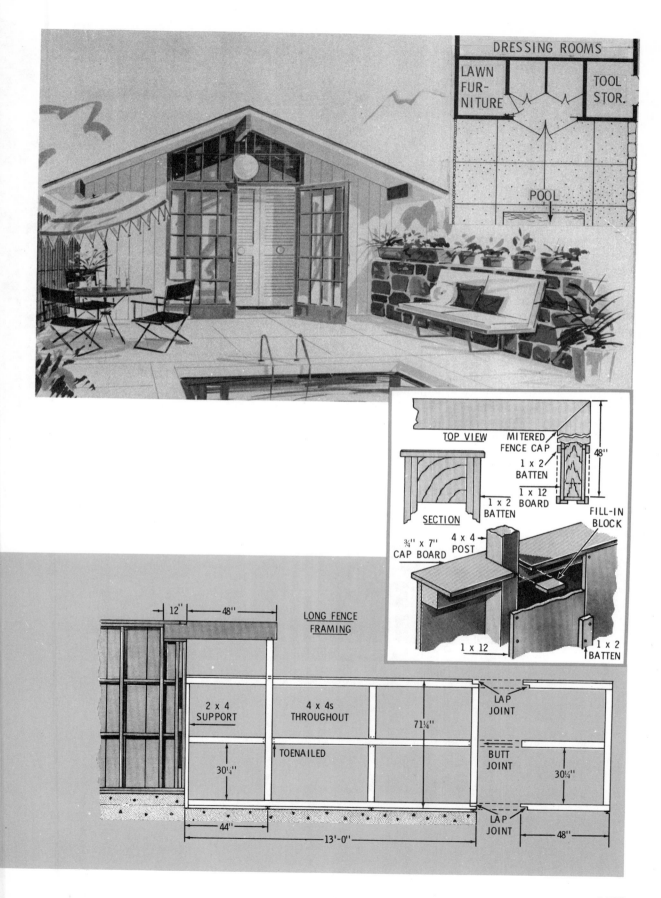

DRESSING ROOMS

LAWN
FUR-
NITURE

TOOL
STOR.

POOL

TOP VIEW

MITERED
FENCE CAP

1 x 2
BATTEN

1 x 12
BOARD

48"

SECTION

1 x 2
BATTEN

FILL-IN
BLOCK

¾" x 7"
CAP BOARD

4 x 4
POST

1 x 12

1 x 2
BATTEN

12"   48"

LONG FENCE
FRAMING

2 x 4
SUPPORT

4 x 4s
THROUGHOUT

71¼"

LAP
JOINT

TOENAILED

BUTT
JOINT

30¼"

30¼"

44"

13'-0"

LAP
JOINT

48"

patio garage with a flair, continued

angled edge. Bend a 4-in.-wide strip into a lop-sided T-shape to fit over the edge of the roof boards and the facing rafter.

To ready yourself for shingling, distribute the packages across the roof, so you'll always have a supply at hand as you move along. The first row (at the eaves) is laid over a strip of 12-in.-wide roll roofing.

Once we got the garage space under cover, work could progress at a more cheerful pace, without racing our local rainy season. We turned our attention to the patio privacy fences, and if you compare our details with the architect's blue-prints, you'll see we made a few more changes. First, we added a 4-ft. return to the right end of the rear fence; by having it turn the patio corner, we not only increased privacy, but buttressed the fence against Oregon's heavy winds. I didn't tie the corner lamppost into the wall.

Nor did I follow the architect's specification of iron-pipe supports for the eave beams. I substituted 4 x 4 posts, which were simpler to incorporate into the fence framing. The same board-and-batten surfacing used on the garage walls was

Gaps between the boards needn't be uniform since battens hide them, but errors in alignment compound

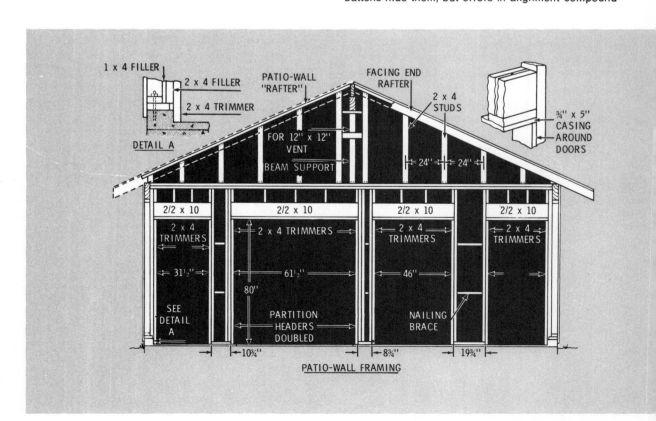

PATIO-WALL FRAMING

extended to the fences—but was applied to *both* sides of the framing.

Both the long, rear, corner-turning fence and the short front one (which runs only to the support post) are anchored to the concrete by means of tie-downs welded from steel plate and ½-in. pipe, as shown in the detail on page 1128. The size of the plates isn't critical, as long as they're not wider than the fence-timber. The bottom plate, however, should be smaller, to facilitate driving 1½-in. lagscrews up into the timber after the unit has been dropped over anchor-bolts previously embedded in the patio slab. At the time you drill 3/16-in. pilot holes for the lagscrews, bore other, larger holes far enough into the bottom timber to accept the projecting bolts and nuts. You need only one tie-down unit for the short fence—directly beneath the support post; you'll remember that we provided a 12-in.-deep footing here when we poured the patio. The opposite end of this fence is tied into a 2 x 4 trimmer nailed to the triple corner stud of the eave wall. The long rear wall is anchored to the garage the same way, and again, you'll want a tie-down under the eave-beam support—and under the three other 4 x 4 posts.

You have come far enough along now so that

The gable framing of the patio wall has the studs installed sideways for easier toenailing to the under-roof cleat. Beam support ties into framing for vent

you could make use of both the garage and the patio. But, as you can see from the sketch of the finished garage and from the floor plan, that missing end wall is the feature that gives the whole project its punch. It contains a sink alcove flanked by big storage closets, one of which is also the garage entry. It's an exciting design.

So by this time, you're getting impatient to get on with that fourth wall that gives the garage its special distinction. Look at the sketches again for a few moments before going on. Note that

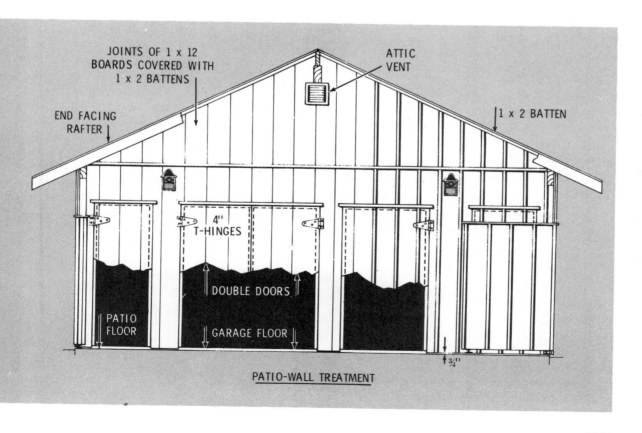

JOINTS OF 1 x 12 BOARDS COVERED WITH 1 x 2 BATTENS

ATTIC VENT

END FACING RAFTER

1 x 2 BATTEN

4" T-HINGES

DOUBLE DOORS

PATIO FLOOR

GARAGE FLOOR

3/4"

PATIO-WALL TREATMENT

Wall X runs parallel to the patio wall. This view from inside the garage (below) shows how it sets between the storage closet (left) and the entry partition (right). Note wall X inset in the drawing below

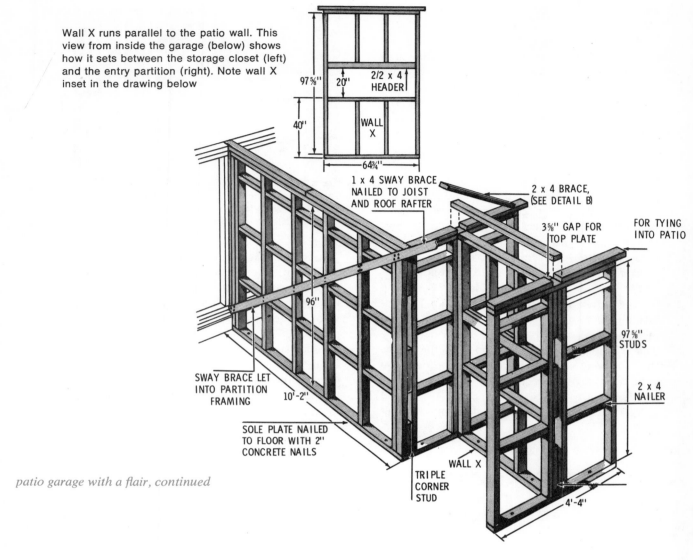

97⅝"
20"
2/2 x 4 HEADER
40"
WALL X
64¾"

1 x 4 SWAY BRACE NAILED TO JOIST AND ROOF RAFTER

2 x 4 BRACE, (SEE DETAIL B)

3⅝" GAP FOR TOP PLATE

FOR TYING INTO PATIO

96"

97⅝" STUDS

2 x 4 NAILER

SWAY BRACE LET INTO PARTITION FRAMING

10'-2"

SOLE PLATE NAILED TO FLOOR WITH 2" CONCRETE NAILS

TRIPLE CORNER STUD

WALL X

4'-4"

patio garage with a flair, continued

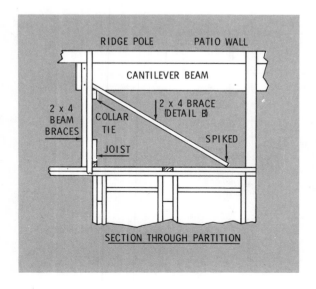

RIDGE POLE   PATIO WALL

CANTILEVER BEAM

2 x 4 BEAM BRACES

COLLAR TIE

2 x 4 BRACE (DETAIL B)

JOIST

SPIKED

SECTION THROUGH PARTITION

this wall is a two-faced, dual purpose wall that provides practical storage *inside* the garage while turning a face of fun toward the patio.

When we put up the roof, we went right past that missing wall (and on out 7 ft. over the patio) because the wall is compartmented in a way that requires a number of partitions, and it's simplest to erect it last. So, for this reason concentrate on that patio wall. The quickest way to grasp its construction is to refer to the floor plan of the architect's blueprint. As we've noted earlier, when we tackled the actual construction, we made certain changes you won't find on that blueprint. One of these involves the four door openings in the patio wall; to simplify framing, the architect called for 8-ft.-high door panels. Since we raised the top plate all around, if we'd made our doors full height, they'd have been even taller, and I felt such panels would be un-

The quickest way to make a pair of doors for the sink compartment is to assemble a single panel, larger than the opening, attaching braces with 6d nails at a slant so they won't penetrate. Flip the panel over, square it, and nail through the front with 8d finishing nails. Trim the four edges to fit the opening, then scribe a center line and slice the panel in two with a portable saw. Clinch the 8d nails before hanging the doors

wieldy and space-wasting. So we used regular dropped-header framing: As shown on pages 1130 and 1131 (where the framing of the *outer* wall is indicated in color), 2 x 4 trimmers 80-in. long support doubled 2 x 10s; these are spaced apart with ⅜-in. shims to increase thickness, and spiked to a 2 x 4 for greater height. The board-and-batten doors, therefore, are a standard 6 ft. 8 in. in height. In the case of the two doors to the storage room and the garage entry, this permits installation of storage shelves above the doors, inside.

The other colored sketch (page 1131) shows

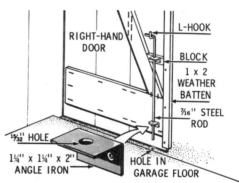

The double doors must have one panel anchored for latching the other one. Install a pair of angle brackets as above, hold the door shut and drop the rod sharply through the holes to mark the concrete. Drill 2-in.-deep holes with a carbide bit

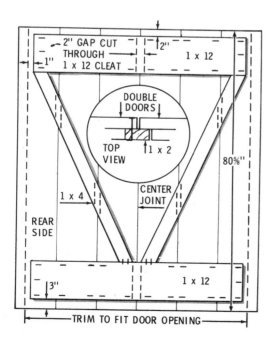

The sink alcove, seen from the patio (left), shows the faucet and duplex wall outlet left of
the pass-through. Back face of the same wall (right) is paneled, has 1 x 12 shelves

patio garage with a flair, continued

how, with careful planning, you can apply boards
and battens to the doors to carry through the
siding pattern. The lower-right section that's off
alignment is a short "return" of the patio privacy
fence. The wall siding starts just inside the fence,
where it joins the garage.

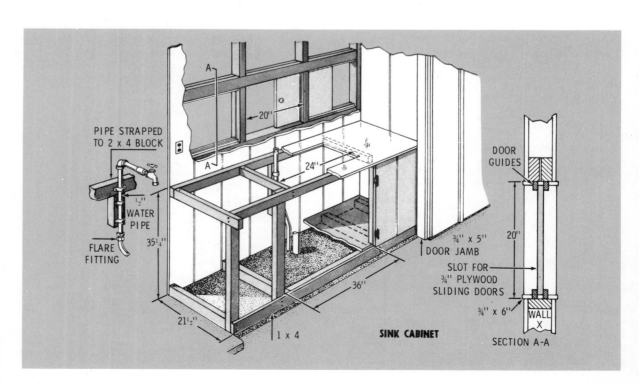

There are several ways to erect this wall. As with the other three, we chose to work flat on the garage floor to frame up the whole center section that involves soleplates, and includes two center door frames. The trimmers and header of the far-left (entry) door were installed *in place,* as was the right trimmer of the right-hand door. The center section has a single *full-width* (from front to back wall) top plate—in fact, the best way to space the studs is to lay out the door openings on this member as the first assembly step. When the framing is swung upright, this top plate should slide neatly beneath the 3-ft. crossties we left projecting inward from each eaves wall. Nail these ties, now, to the top plate, then measure the gap between them and cut a 2 x 4 to fill it, forming a full-width doubled top plate. Plumb the wall and spike the soleplates to the floor with 2-in. concrete nails. Finally, add the gable framing, as shown on page 1130.

But the exterior facade is only one plane of the patio wall. Unconventional construction calls for special solutions to framing problems and when it came to sway-bracing the main partition wall (behind the two righthand doors) I was grateful for the professional know-how of my contractor neighbor, Dick Chilson, since the door openings in the exterior wall prevent any angle-bracing. His solution is sketched at the top of page 1132. The partition brace is set against the

The finish work can go on in all weather if you move your radial-arm saw inside after the wiring is completed. This will be my new shop area

The optional deck on top of the ceiling joists greatly increases storage space. For access, leave an opening between two joists and frame as shown above

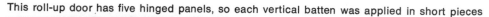

This roll-up door has five hinged panels, so each vertical batten was applied in short pieces

Wiring the post lamps is a simple matter of twisting and taping leads from the fixture and wires you previously ran up both posts

mud sill and soleplate of the rear wall, and extends up to tie into the joist and rafter on the far side.

After this partition is erected and plumbed, the other three partitions are set in place, to define the sink alcove and storage closet. The only extra bracing here is the 2 x 4 shown in white in the colored sketch on page 1132. This is spiked near the patio end of the center partition and to the collar tie that helps support the ridge beam. (This construction, incidentally, brought a whistle of approving surprise from the building inspector.)

If you don't feel a pass-through feature is of value to you, you can simplify the framing of divided wall X. Since my garage doubles as my shop, I thought it would be handy to have access to the sink tap without having to go out onto the patio. The pass-through doors are panels of exterior plywood that slide into wall-pockets at either side.

The double doors that grant access to the sink from the patio are easier to make as a single panel. You trim this panel for a good fit in the opening, stand it in place on ¾-in. shims laid on the concrete, tack it temporarily while you locate and drill for the hinges. After attaching the door-frame leaves of these hinges, knock the panel out of the opening, slice it down the middle, cut back both 1 x 12 cleats on each side of the cut, apply a weather batten and hang the doors on their hinges. They'll mate perfectly.

After I'd framed up the sink cabinet, as shown on page 1134, I applied the laminate-faced countertop, marked it for the sink opening and

WIRING PLAN

TO SERVICE ENTRANCE

GARAGE LIGHTS

GARAGE ENTRANCE BOX

CLOSET LIGHT

STORE-ROOM LIGHT

SW.

SINK LIGHT

GARAGE LIGHT SW.

SW.

SW.

JUNCTION BOX FOR PATIO POST LAMPS

POST-LAMP SW.

PATIO-WALL LIGHTS

OUTDOOR SW. FOR PATIO-WALL LIGHTS

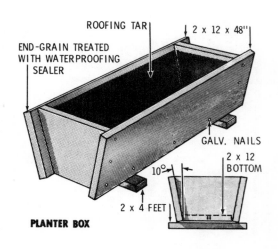

ROOFING TAR

2 x 12 x 48"

END-GRAIN TREATED WITH WATERPROOFING SEALER

GALV. NAILS

10°

2 x 12 BOTTOM

2 x 4 FEET

PLANTER BOX

cut it out with a saber saw. No matter how carefully you measured when you installed the sink drain pipe before pouring the slab, it'll be a miracle if it's exactly centered on the drain once the sink is installed (unless, of course, you don't mind shifting the sink off-center to compensate). Since my sink is serviced by a dry well—into which only clean water should drain—no trap is necessary. So I merely joined the neck of the sink drain to the pipe with a length of radiator hose and a couple of hose clamps. I installed a faucet with hose-threads, for convenience in watering nearby plants.

I did all the wiring myself, with a good "simplified" book on household wiring in one hand and the sound advice of local inspectors ringing in my ears. Even with these distractions, it only took me a week-end—and I got fairly elaborate—more so than my simplified diagram, below left, suggests. I included a 220-v. No. 10-wire circuit for a recessed wall heater, fused for 30 amps, plus a 220-v. crowfoot receptacle for my welder, fed by three No. 6 underground cables and fused for 40 amps.

Since my service entrance already had a 200-amp box, I could add as many circuits as I chose. But it's a good idea to consult your local power company about your entrance facilities beforehand.

I'd ordered enough roofing shiplap to deck in an "attic" with the leftovers. This floor, nailed to the top edge of the joists and provided with a hatchway, gives me vast additional space for storage of seasonal or unneeded items. It also helps insulate the garage until I get around to installing real insulation. Planning toward that, incidentally, I put fiberglass batts in all partition walls exposed to cold, before I paneled the inside.

already much-used

But after weeks of work, my only thought by this time was putting that patio to use. Already, it's been the scene of many social gatherings. Friends we'd not heard from for years began to turn up once the word was out that we had a new and very unusual addition. They all want to be entertained on the famous patio. In fact we considered renting out our house for the summer, it was getting so little use.

Once you take on a project like this, I discovered, it's pretty hard to stop thinking up ways to continue to improve it. I mentioned that I intend to insulate the new garage—and that's just the beginning of finishing the interior. I haven't yet decided what material I'll use, but the walls will be finished both for appearance and for practical reasons.

If you plan to use your garage for more than just car storage, you will enjoy having finished walls. There are several practical ways to complete the interior areas, including gypsum drywalls and wood or hardboard paneling. The cost can be pretty much what you want it to be—from relatively small for drywall to very expensive for some types of hardwood paneling.

The final wiring of your garage should reflect the uses to which you expect to put it. If you intend to have a workbench and power tools, make electrical provisions for them. You'll want to plan outlets in convenient places around the walls and handy wall switches near the doors—the number of these depending on your final use.

teens rumpus room

Some people I have known have used their garages as teen-age rumpus rooms, decorating them for parties on special occasions such as Halloween. Others seldom use theirs except for car storage and an occasional painting chore. It is likely that with this design, focused as it is on the entertainment patio, you may find yourself turning to more living uses. Plan for these uses now.

The floor of the garage, for example, can be painted with game layouts—a large-scale checker board, a shuffleboard (scaled down), a tic-tac-toe design, etc.—to turn it into a sheltered playing area for use on rainy days.

If you devote a portion of the new garage to a workbench area, you find that perforated hardboard makes an excellent wall finish for this part, and at the same time provides full-wall hanging space for tools.

In most climates, if you plan to use the garage through the winter, you'll need some heat—and in some localities you'll need a goodly amount. After you have insulated and finished the walls, heating the garage becomes practical with either a gas or electric wall unit. Both offer efficient heating, and the wall units have the additional advantage of having to be turned on only when you intend to be in the garage.

Whether you go all out on the interior—or just decide to settle on enjoying the new patio—you are going to get more than your money's worth out of this new addition to your living area.

We have already.

See also: garages, door openers; home additions; measurements; patios; remodeling ideas; shelters; weather stripping.

CARPORT VERSION
The carport version ha[s] contemporary flat roof: has separate entrance[s] to compartments for ga[rden] tools and large toys

A suburbanite's dream garage is the result of adding storage compartments to the rear of the existing structure. Garden-tool area is big enough for a riding tractor and has full doors

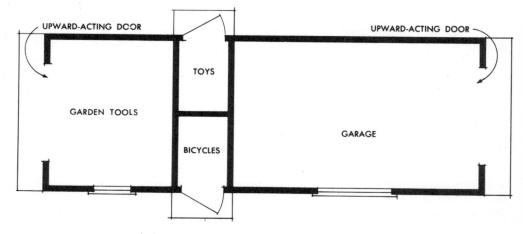

Build double duty into your garage or carport

■ TODAY'S GARAGE is more than just a place to keep the family chariot. It's a storage room for rakes, lawnmowers, bicycles, charcoal grills and dozens of other items. So if you'd like to design more *usable* space into your present garage, or build a new one that will serve you better, here are some ideas you can adapt—in whole or in part—to suit your needs.

You'll note on these pages that we show a number of ways you can combine both car protection and general storage, for both garages and

The two-car model has overhead doors in front (as in drawing, below) for cars, swinging doors on storage areas. Designing for a standard car and a compact increases size of one storage compartment to accept bulky garden tools, mowers. Smaller compartment is for toys and other small items. Optional but practical is the overhang on front, which can be added to any garage. It keeps you dry as you struggle with the garage-door lock

turn the page

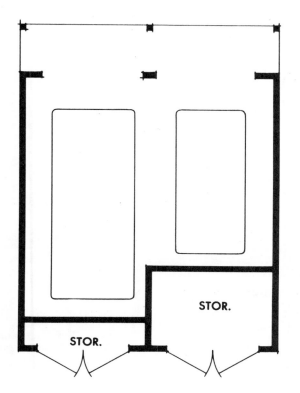

STOR.

STOR.

carports. What each plan tries to do, essentially, is to make it possible to reach the car, or cars, without climbing over, under or around the garden tools, or to reach the garden tools without squeezing around the car. Sounds trivial, but it can save you hours of time on a busy weekend, plus a lot of aggravation.

When studying the designs, incidentally, note how a few homey touches like a window or a cupola vent can make a garage look more like it belongs with the house.

DOORS TO STORAGE ABOVE AUTO HOODS

STOR.

STOR.

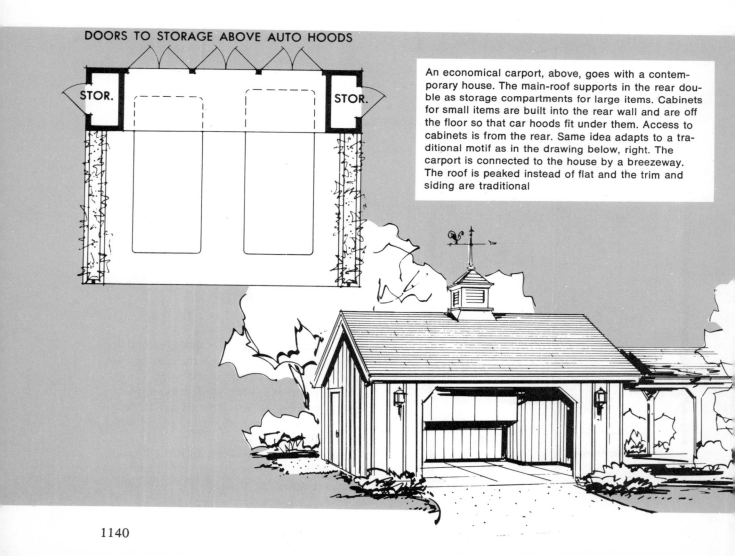

An economical carport, above, goes with a contemporary house. The main-roof supports in the rear double as storage compartments for large items. Cabinets for small items are built into the rear wall and are off the floor so that car hoods fit under them. Access to cabinets is from the rear. Same idea adapts to a traditional motif as in the drawing below, right. The carport is connected to the house by a breezeway. The roof is peaked instead of flat and the trim and siding are traditional

turn the page

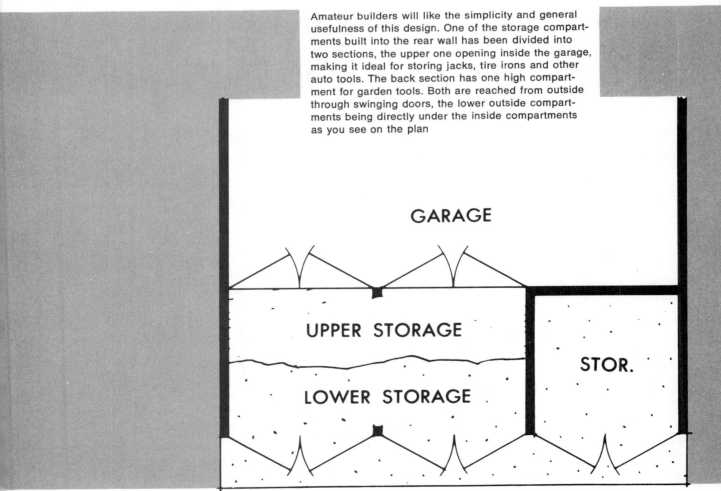

Amateur builders will like the simplicity and general usefulness of this design. One of the storage compartments built into the rear wall has been divided into two sections, the upper one opening inside the garage, making it ideal for storing jacks, tire irons and other auto tools. The back section has one high compartment for garden tools. Both are reached from outside through swinging doors, the lower outside compartments being directly under the inside compartments as you see on the plan

GARAGE

UPPER STORAGE

STOR.

LOWER STORAGE

Side walls of this modern single-car carport have four generous storage areas built right into the walls. Three of these open outward as you see, but one opens inward for storing car tools and other items, any one of which can be easily reached through the out-fold doors. Any shelf arrangements in this storage area are your choice; shelves can be rigid or adjustable. Notice that the overhang has been extended to the house to keep you dry in any weather

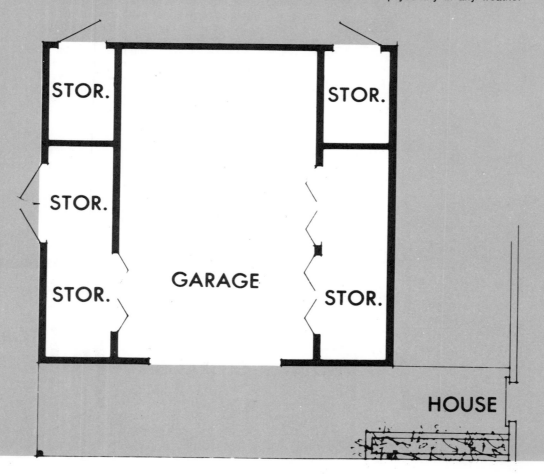

Flick your headlights to high beam and they activate the
photocell that opens the garage door and turns on yard light

When the high beams of your
headlights hit this unit's photocell,
garage doors open and yard lights
go on. When doors close, garage
lights go off, but others wait 'til
you're inside

Photocell door opener turns on yard lights

■ THERE'S A pounding rain outside. You pull the
car into the driveway, make a run for the garage
door and get soaked while you wrestle the door
open. Then, with the car safely inside the garage,
you dash for the house. Ooops! Didn't see the
kids' plastic pool in the dark, did you? Oh well,
you were wet anyway.

You can avoid such soakings if you install this
photocell garage-door opener. The photocell control kit costs $14.95 (Lafayette Radio, 19C0904)
and the garage-door opener motor, rails and
switches are available for $69.95 (Heathkit
#GDA-20-3). But some ingenious chaps have
even adapted old washing-machine motors to
open garage doors.

Your car's high-beam headlights trigger the
circuit which opens the garage door, then the

Black tube, made from a paper towel center tube, keeps out ambient light, restricting operation to times when your headlights are aimed directly at the aperture. Limit switches, shown below, are installed on the guide rails of the door and cut power when door has reached correct opening

door opener, continued

opening of the door turns on both garage and yard lights. The motor-rail control circuit kit also includes a delay circuit which shuts off garage light when door closes but keeps yard light on long enough for you to make it to the house without tripping over something in the dark.

Photocell door openers have an advantage over radio-controlled types, which can be activated inadvertently by nearby ham operators or other radio controlled garage door installations. The result? A garage left wide open to the weather or, should you happen to leave your convertible halfway in or out of the garage, a good start on a two-part car.

When mounting the photocell, place it at a level slightly higher than your car's low beams. Mark the area to be cut out in the garage with a pencil, and check it against your headlights at

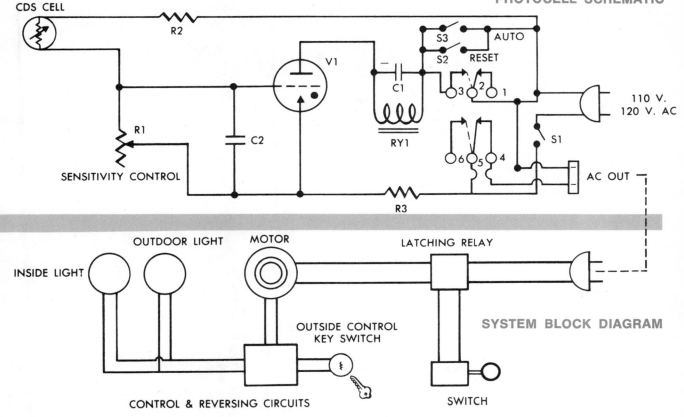

SYSTEM BLOCK DIAGRAM

PARTS LIST

V1—5823 tube
CDS—Clairex CL-3 photocell
R1—5 megohm potentiometer
R2—150K, ½ watt
R3—125 ohm, 5 watt
C1—8mfd, 250-volt electrolytic
C2—270 mmfd
RY1—DPDT 115-v.a.c. coil
S1—SPST slide switch
S2—SPST slide switch
S3—SPST slide switch, spring return

All above available as a unit (La-
fayette Radio Kit #19C0904) from
Lafayette Radio Co., 111 Jericho
Turnpike, Syosset, L.I., N.Y. 1179

night. When the placement is correct, cut the aperture and form a light shield to prevent ambient sunlight from operating the unit.

Place a cardboard tube between the photocell and the aperture to better direct the light, and use some screening to keep children from poking into the unit. Follow the diagram for the photocell circuit, or you can obtain this in kit form from the distributor. Instructions for installing the motor, rails and switches come with the kit of these parts.

A top-limit switch turns off the motor when the door is fully raised. By the use of a compound thermal-delay switch here, the garage light is turned off when the door closes, but the yard light stays on a few seconds longer.

See also: alarms, burglar; garages; weather stripping.

Build your own electric door opener

BY FRANK L. GREENWALD

Here's a safe and inexpensive garage door opener which is easy to make, and it can be done at a cost of $50 or less

■ You TURN INTO YOUR DRIVE and glide to a stop beside something resembling a plumber's periscope rising out of the shrubs on the left. You reach through the car window, insert a key, and the garage door at the far end of the drive rolls up to let you in.

This setup isn't new, of course, because you've seen many types of garage door openers. Most of them are regarded as a luxury, but the one shown here certainly isn't. You can make it yourself at a fraction of what commercial units cost.

Up to now, economy-minded homeowners have often been discouraged from building their own systems because construction called for a "bomb-bay door opener" or a "king-flap actuator" to serve as the reduction unit. This opener neatly sidesteps the need for *any* reduction unit. Using only standard hardware items, plus a few parts from an electronics supply house, you can make it for $20 or so if you already have a ¼ or ⅓-hp motor on hand.

One valuable feature not usually found on home-built openers is the safety trip located along the lower edge of the door. Should the door encounter any obstacle while it's closing, the trip wire automatically shuts off the mechanism. (Perhaps a child has wandered into its path, or you've neglected to drive the car into the garage far enough to clear.) And it won't start again until it's reactuated by the key switch or an interior push button.

First construction step is to weld up a 9-ft. length from three 3-ft. sections of threaded rod, as shown in photos on page 1151. When you

The mechanism can be operated at several convenient locations inside the garage with switches. The traveler attached to the door is drawn toward the control box (center) where it will break a contact, shutting off the motor. Door is then up and ready for a return to the down position

turn the two sections into a ½-in. nut for thread-alignment, leave ⅟₁₆-in. gap between the ends for weld penetration.

The task of running a ½-in. die over three feet of thread to reach the welds from each end can be speeded up by locking two nuts on one end and using a socket and speeder wrench.

Next, make up the track by bolting two 96-in. lengths of angle iron back-to-back to form an inverted T. You can find ⅛ x ⅞ x 1⅜-in. angle available at a local iron shop, but more-standard ⅛ x 1 x 1-in. angle works as well without altering any of the other measurements. If continuous lengths aren't available, you can make up a track from six 3-ft. lengths of 1 x 1 angle, available at most hardware stores. One length should be cut in half, with one of the halves bolted to a full length at the start. The resulting track, with staggered joints, will function satisfactorily if you carefully align the joints in the horizontal flanges.

The easiest way to bore the bearing blocks on the split line is to groove the mating faces down the center before clamping them together. The aligned grooves provide a pilot hole for the drill —which should be a full-size body (carpenter's) bit. Before assembly, soak the maple blocks thoroughly in light engine oil, then shim the split line as needed for running clearance for the bushings.

The two bushings for the rear bearing are forced onto the shaft over wire wound in the threads. A fillet of solder is placed at both ends to secure the wire and bushings to the shaft. This is not necessary with the front bushings.

The traveler—which rides both track and lead screw—is made of two pieces of angle iron with a window cut in each to house two ½-in.-square nuts. Run these nuts on the lead screw before you hang it in the bearings. Assemble the traveler

Just a flick of the switch mounted on a post at the head of the drive triggers the mechanism located inside the garage. A key activates the switch

electric door opener, continued

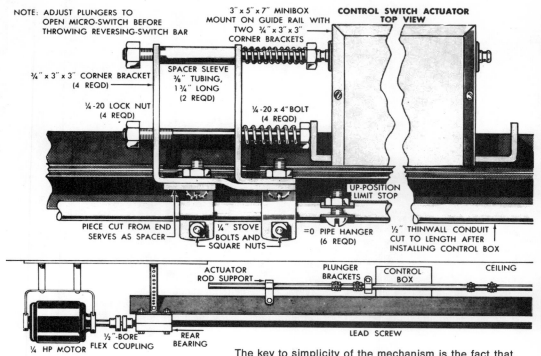

NOTE: ADJUST PLUNGERS TO
OPEN MICRO-SWITCH BEFORE
THROWING REVERSING-SWITCH BAR

3" x 5" x 7" MINIBOX
MOUNT ON GUIDE RAIL WITH
TWO ¾" x 3" x 3"
CORNER BRACKETS

**CONTROL SWITCH ACTUATOR
TOP VIEW**

¾" x 3" x 3" CORNER BRACKET
(4 REQD)

SPACER SLEEVE
⅜" TUBING,
1¾" LONG
(2 REQD)

¼-20 LOCK NUT
(4 REQD)

¼-20 x 4" BOLT
(4 REQD)

UP-POSITION
LIMIT STOP

PIECE CUT FROM END
SERVES AS SPACER

¼" STOVE
BOLTS AND
SQUARE NUTS

=0 PIPE HANGER
(6 REQD)

½" THINWALL CONDUIT
CUT TO LENGTH AFTER
INSTALLING CONTROL BOX

ACTUATOR
ROD SUPPORT

PLUNGER
BRACKETS

CONTROL
BOX

CEILING

¼ HP MOTOR

½"-BORE
FLEX COUPLING

REAR
BEARING

LEAD SCREW

The key to simplicity of the mechanism is the fact that a ½-in.-13 threaded rod, turning at 1725 r.p.m., will advance a nut about 2 in. per second—just right for opening or closing garage doors. The length of the spring-loaded bar of the door link (far right) must be sufficient to fully seat the door before reaching vertical position

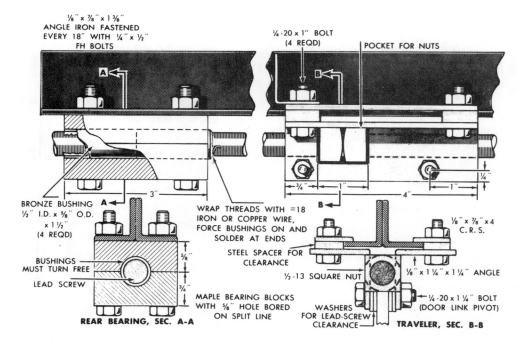

⅛" x ⅞" x 1⅜"
ANGLE IRON FASTENED
EVERY 18" WITH ¼" x ½"
FH BOLTS

¼-20 x 1" BOLT
(4 REQD)

POCKET FOR NUTS

A

B

BRONZE BUSHING
½" I.D. x ⅝" O.D.
x 1½"
(4 REQD)

WRAP THREADS WITH =18
IRON OR COPPER WIRE,
FORCE BUSHINGS ON AND
SOLDER AT ENDS

⅛" x ⅞" x 4
C. R. S.

BUSHINGS
MUST TURN FREE

STEEL SPACER FOR
CLEARANCE

LEAD SCREW

½-13 SQUARE NUT

⅛" x 1¼" x 1¼" ANGLE

MAPLE BEARING BLOCKS
WITH ⅝" HOLE BORED
ON SPLIT LINE

¼-20 x 1¼" BOLT
(DOOR LINK PIVOT)

REAR BEARING, SEC. A-A

WASHERS
FOR LEAD-SCREW
CLEARANCE

TRAVELER, SEC. B-B

3"

¾"

1"

4"

1"

¼"

⅝"

¾"

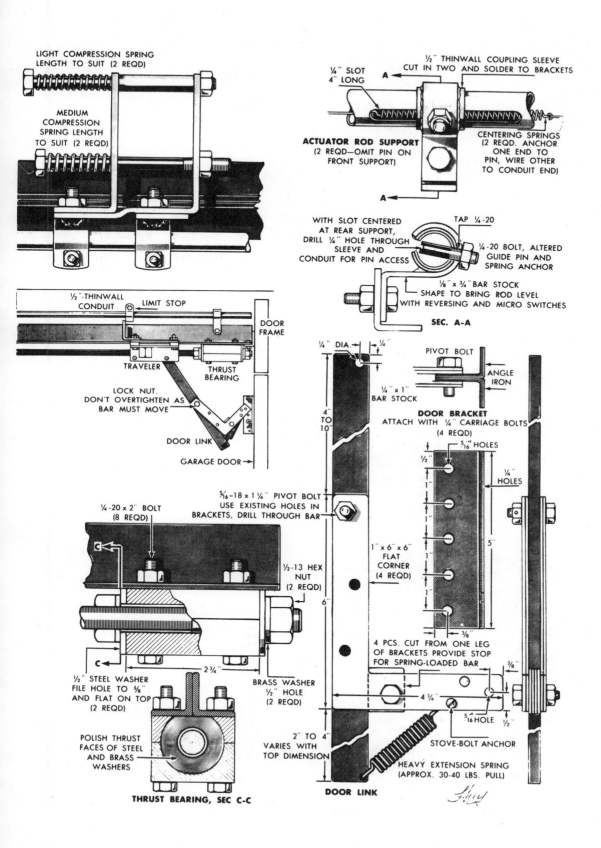

LIGHT COMPRESSION SPRING
LENGTH TO SUIT (2 REQD)

MEDIUM
COMPRESSION
SPRING LENGTH
TO SUIT (2 REQD)

½" THINWALL COUPLING SLEEVE
CUT IN TWO AND SOLDER TO BRACKETS

¼" SLOT
4" LONG

A

ACTUATOR ROD SUPPORT
(2 REQD—OMIT PIN ON
FRONT SUPPORT)

CENTERING SPRINGS
(2 REQD. ANCHOR
ONE END TO
PIN, WIRE OTHER
TO CONDUIT END)

A

WITH SLOT CENTERED
AT REAR SUPPORT,
DRILL ¼" HOLE THROUGH
SLEEVE AND
CONDUIT FOR PIN ACCESS

TAP ¼-20

¼-20 BOLT, ALTERED
GUIDE PIN AND
SPRING ANCHOR

⅛" x ¾" BAR STOCK
SHAPE TO BRING ROD LEVEL
WITH REVERSING AND MICRO SWITCHES

SEC. A-A

½"-THINWALL
CONDUIT

LIMIT STOP

DOOR
FRAME

TRAVELER

THRUST
BEARING

LOCK NUT.
DON'T OVERTIGHTEN AS
BAR MUST MOVE

DOOR LINK

GARAGE DOOR

¼" DIA.

¼"

¼" x 1"
BAR STOCK

PIVOT BOLT

ANGLE
IRON

DOOR BRACKET
ATTACH WITH ¼" CARRIAGE BOLTS
(4 REQD)

4"
TO
10"

5/16" HOLES

½"

1"

1"

1"

1"

¼"
HOLES

5"

¼-20 x 2" BOLT
(8 REQD)

5/16-18 x 1¼" PIVOT BOLT
USE EXISTING HOLES IN
BRACKETS, DRILL THROUGH BAR

½-13 HEX
NUT
(2 REQD)

1" x 6" x 6"
FLAT
CORNER
(4 REQD)

3/8"

6"

C

½" STEEL WASHER
FILE HOLE TO 5/8"
AND FLAT ON TOP
(2 REQD)

2¾"

BRASS WASHER
½" HOLE
(2 REQD)

4 PCS. CUT FROM ONE LEG
OF BRACKETS PROVIDE STOP
FOR SPRING-LOADED BAR

3/8"

½"

4¾"

5/16" HOLE

POLISH THRUST
FACES OF STEEL
AND BRASS
WASHERS

2" TO 4"
VARIES WITH
TOP DIMENSION

STOVE-BOLT ANCHOR

HEAVY EXTENSION SPRING
(APPROX. 30-40 LBS. PULL)

THRUST BEARING, SEC C-C

DOOR LINK

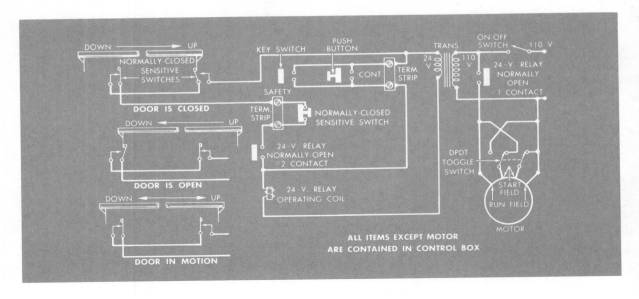

electric door opener, continued

CONTROL BOX ALTERATION

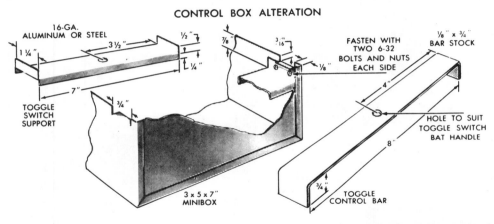

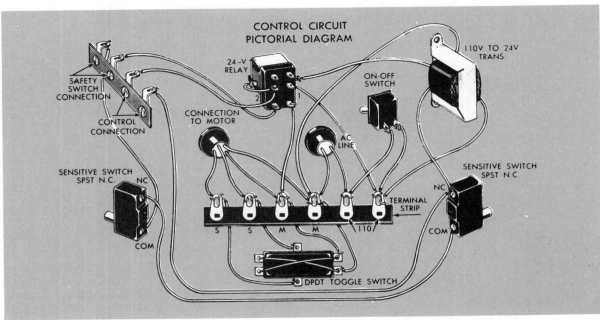

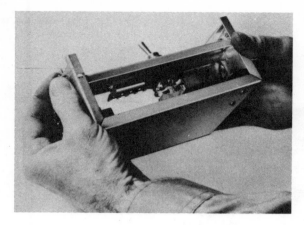

The control box is a modified Minibox. An ordinary toggle switch reverses motor connections. The switch is flicked by a sliding bar which has a hole to take the bat handle; mounting is shown, left

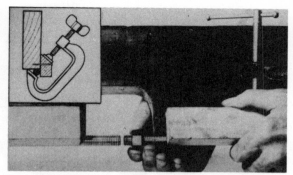

The positioning jig is a long plank with cleats nailed along one edge to create a shoulder for clamping rods as shown in the inset. The nut aligns the rods

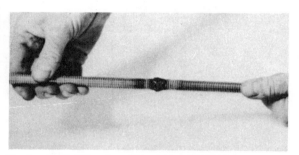

Back nut off after clamping, and weld the joint. The joint will have a bulge of excess metal which must be ground down to a diameter of ½ in.

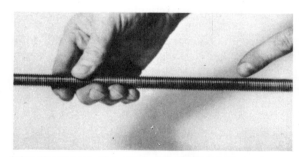

Joint disappears when ½-in.-13 die is run through the weld to produce a continuous thread. You weld three 3-ft. lengths to make a rod 9-ft. long

around the nuts, inserting steel spacers or square nuts between the angle and the 4-in.-long steel flange pieces, to provide running clearance on the track.

Hang the track at the lowest position that will permit the upswinging door to clear. The door end of the track rests on an angle-iron bracket fastened to the door header with ⅜ x 1½-in. lag-screws. The rear end is supported by ⅛ x 1-in. flat steel and braced by perforated hanger strap. To simplify the hanging from an unfinished garage ceiling, span three joists with a 4-ft.-long panel of ½-in. plywood, to create a mounting platform.

The electrical circuit is designed for reliable operation without use of fancy components. A 24-volt filament transformer and double-pole-double-throw relay provide a safe, low-voltage control circuit.

Any momentary connection across the control terminals completes the circuit to the relay operating coil. When the relay closes, the No. 1 contact closes and starts the motor. A holding circuit is completed through the "up" and "down" sensi-

tive switches, the normally-closed safety switch, and the No. 2 relay contact. The motor continues to operate until the "down" switch is opened at the end of the travel. The No. 1 relay contact opens, stopping the motor, and the No. 2 contact opens in the maintaining circuit to the relay. After the motor circuit has been opened but before the travel-action stops, the spring-loaded plunger throws the toggle switch, reversing the starting field leads.

After wiring, check out the circuit as follows: Separate the starting and running field leads, con-

1151

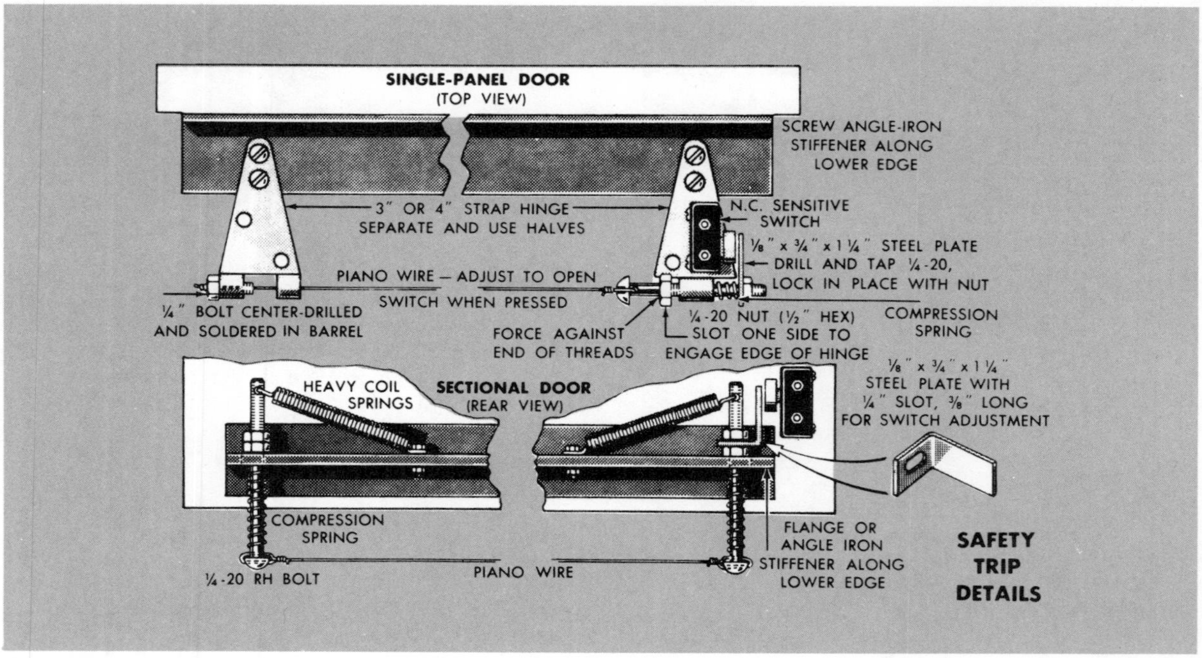
SINGLE-PANEL DOOR
(TOP VIEW)
SCREW ANGLE-IRON STIFFENER ALONG LOWER EDGE
3" OR 4" STRAP HINGE SEPARATE AND USE HALVES
N.C. SENSITIVE SWITCH
1/8" x 3/4" x 1 1/4" STEEL PLATE
DRILL AND TAP 1/4-20, LOCK IN PLACE WITH NUT
PIANO WIRE — ADJUST TO OPEN SWITCH WHEN PRESSED
1/4" BOLT CENTER-DRILLED AND SOLDERED IN BARREL
FORCE AGAINST END OF THREADS
1/4-20 NUT (1/2" HEX) SLOT ONE SIDE TO ENGAGE EDGE OF HINGE
COMPRESSION SPRING
HEAVY COIL SPRINGS
SECTIONAL DOOR
(REAR VIEW)
1/8" x 3/4" x 1 1/4" STEEL PLATE WITH 1/4" SLOT, 3/8" LONG FOR SWITCH ADJUSTMENT
COMPRESSION SPRING
1/4-20 RH BOLT
PIANO WIRE
FLANGE OR ANGLE IRON STIFFENER ALONG LOWER EDGE
SAFETY TRIP DETAILS

nect the power cord to a 115-volt supply and flick on the on-off switch. Connect the safety-switch terminals, then make momentary contact across the control terminals. The relay should pick up and stay in. Actuation of either sensitive switch should drop out the relay.

Mount the control box on top of the rail with corner brackets, as shown on page 1147. Form the two actuator rod supports so that the conduit moves on a level with the toggle control bar and sensitive-switch buttons. Attach the plunger assemblies to the conduit so that the pair on one side has about 2-in. clearance when the other pair is making contact. The actuator rod is moved back-and-forth by means of a right-angle bracket extending above the traveler to contact the two limit stops.

To install these stops, first position the traveler several inches from the front bearing, attach the "down" stop as shown in the sketch on pages 1148 and 1149 and connect the door link. Note that with the door fully-closed, the link should have a slight amount of spring load. Now, set the reversing switch to open the door, starting at full-open position. Stop the action by pressing either sensitive switch. Attach the "up" stop so that it is in contact with the traveler bracket. Now, close the door, making sure the "down" stop halts the door for smooth seating.

For my key switch, I drilled a 1/16-in. aluminum disk and wedged this assembly tight in the threads of a 1¼-in. pipe elbow. Plastic bell wire is run down inside the pipe and trenched back to the garage.

For the person who is tired of hopping out of the car in rain or sleet (and who isn't?) to tug on that exasperating door, here is the least expensive way to solve the problem.

Even though you may not be the most accomplished handyman in the world, you'll find this helpful device easy to build and even easier to enjoy, and it can all be done at relatively low cost, even if the price of a motor is included.

MATERIALS LIST

ELECTRICAL	
1	DPDT 24-V. Relay (Guardian 1205-2C-24DC)
1	DPDT Toggle Switch (Cutler-Hammer) 7564-K6
3	SPST Normally-Closed Sensitive Switch
1	24-V. Filament Transformer
1	3 x 5 x 7-in. Bud Minibox (CU-3008-A)
1	Key Switch, s.p.s.t. (Arrow-Hart 81715-L)
MECHANICAL	
3	½-in.-13 Threaded Rod (3-ft. lengths)
16 ft.	⅛ x ⅞ x 1⅜-in. angle iron
10 ft.	½-in. Thinwall Conduit
4	1 x 6 x 6-in. Flat Corner
6	¾ x 3 x 3-in. Corner Bracket
6	Pipe Support Clamp, Size 0
12	¼-in.-20 Nylon-Pellet Lock Nuts
4	½ I.D. x ⅝ O.D. x 1½-in. Bronze Bushing
1	½-in. Bore Flex Coupling
1	¼-HP. Motor, ½-in. Shaft (Sears)